AF531535

PLIGHT OF HIV INFECTED WOMEN

PLAN OF ACTION FOR PREVENTION AND CONTROL

PLIGHT OF HIV INFECTED WOMEN

PLAN OF ACTION FOR PREVENTION AND CONTROL

By

Dr. S. Sakthi

Reader

Deptt. of Sociology

Queen Mary's College (Autonomous)

Govt. of Tamil Nadu

Chennai–600 004

DISCOVERY PUBLISHING HOUSE PVT. LTD.

NEW DELHI-110 002

First Published-2010

ISBN 978-81-8356-635-3

Published by:

DISCOVERY PUBLISHING HOUSE PVT. LTD.
4831/24, Ansari Road, Prahlad Street
Darya Ganj, New Delhi-110002 (India)
Phone: 23279245, 43764432 • Fax: 91-11-23253475
E-mail: parul.wasan@gmail.com
info@discoverypublishinggroup.com
Website: www.discoverypublishinggroup.com

Printed at:

Sachin Printers
Delhi

PREFACE

Women were at the periphery of the AIDS epidemic in its earlier years. They are at the forefront today due to feminization of the dreaded disease which has no cure and vaccine. Women are able to exercise little or no control over the risk of acquiring HIV infection as a result of little or lack of access to appropriate reproductive health information and rights. Women's vulnerability resulted from an interplay among factors, both personal (individual and biological) and societal. Their vulnerability is magnified by societal factors such as marginalization or discrimination on grounds of sex, race, age and sexual orientation. Therefore, across the globe, women are considered as the most vulnerable groups to AIDS.

In India, women are the innocent victims of HIV infection. About 20 lakhs Indian women in monogamous relationship land up with HIV/AIDS and most of them contracted infection from their husbands, who refuse to use condom and exercise power over women's reproductive health. The Indian women have been socialized to accept socio-economic subordination and to be ignorant about sex and sex-related issues. Indian culture plays a dominant role in the discussion of sex and safe sex. In India, sex is not a topic to be discussed openly even with husbands. The taboo associated with sex made women more vulnerable to AIDS.

This research endeavour has been undertaken among women living with HIV positive in Chennai city of Tamil Nadu, with the objectives of investigating the socio-economic background, marital status, circumstances leading to HIV infection, sexual behaviour after infection, impact of HIV/AIDS in social relationships and their attitude towards pregnancy and child birth after infection. Since the prevalence of HIV is an estimated figure based on sentinel surveillance data on the selected sites according to UNAIDS/WHO criteria, the universe is not taken into consideration for this study. Therefore, purposive sampling technique is adopted to contact the respondents by resorting to snowballing procedure. Accordingly, 200 women living with HIV positive in Chennai city were interviewed with the structured interview schedule to collect required information on the line of objectives formulated for the study. Apart from interview with the respondents, discussion was also held with Government officials and NGOs working in AIDS intervention programmes. Available data had been subjected to process statistically leading to analysis and interpretation. Based upon the analysis and findings, a specific action plan has been evolved to provide care and support for the women infected with HIV and to create AIDS free society.

The present study is comprised of seven chapters. The First chapter presents an introduction to women infected with HIV with brief account of causes and consequences of HIV on women and the theoretical frame work. The Second chapter presents a review of literature related to the study in order to establish research gap. The Third chapter deals with the methodology adopted which includes objectives, operational definition of concepts, sampling procedure and sample size, tools of data collection and method of analysis. A comprehensive view on the global scenario of HIV/AIDS is presented in Fourth chapter. The Fifth chapter deals with analysis and discussion of primary data with a view of derive findings based on the objectives designed for the study. The Sixth chapter contains the major findings, suggestion and conclusion. The implication of research in the form of Action Plan towards prevention and control of HIV/AIDS and care and support and relief and rehabilitation of infected people with the goal of creating AIDS free society is presented in the Seventh chapter.

"Let's arm our children with opportunity and hope.
Our slogan is 'parents to work and children to school' "

Aditya Kumar Patra

Sakthi S.

Acknowledgements

I express my profound gratitude to my guide Dr. S. Gurusamy, Professor and Head, Department of Sociology, Gandhigram Rural Institute for providing me guidance and encouragement to complete the research work in time. I am deeply indebted to his family members for showing concern towards me.

My sincere thanks are due to Dr. T. Karunakaran, Vice-Chancellor, Dr. Sundaravadivelu, Registrar, Dr. Susila Kirubaharan, Deputy Resistrar, Gandhigram Rural Institute for permitting me to pursue my research work in the Department of Sociology under Faculty Improvement Programme. At this juncture, the help extended by Dr. Dwaraki, the former Professor and Head, Department of Sociology is deeply remembered.

I am thankful to Dr. Kubendaran, Professor and Head, Department of English for editing my work. I am also indebted to Dr. Ramachandran, Professor and Head, Department of Economics and Dr. Sumangala, Professor, Department of Economics, Gandhigram Rural Institute for providing valuable suggestions to strengthen my Action Plan.

I express my deep sense of gratitude to Malini Subramani, former Principal of Queen Mary's College, Mrs. Saraswathi Govingdaraj, Dr. Ananthi, Dr. Prema Gopinath, Mrs. Anusuya, Mrs. Rajalakshmi, Mrs. Prabha and Mrs. Kalavathi, my beloved professors and friends, Department of Sociology, Queen Mary's College for their encouragement and help throughout my study and permitting me to avail F.I.P. to pursue my research work.

I am deeply indebted to my friends Mrs. Uma, Lecturer, Department of Physical Education, Ms Kala Devi, Lecturer, Department of Geography, Mrs. Sumathi Lecturer, Department of English and Mrs. Asha, Lecturer, Department of Commerce, Queen Mary's College, Dr. Lakshmana Singh, Professor and Head, Department of Sociology, Bharathiar University, Coimbatore, Dr. Karupaiah, Reader in Sociology, Madras University and Dr. Alphonse Raj, Reader in Sociology, Loyola College, Chennai for their valuable guidance and support throughout my study.

I express my due gratitude to Dr. Kannan, Reader in Sociology, Manonmaniam Sundaranar University, Tirunelveli and Dr. Ani, Professor and Head, Department of Sociology, Mother Theresa University, Kodikanal for helping me by providing literature related to women and HIV/AIDS.

My heartfelt thanks are due to Mr. Christudas Gandhi, I.A.S, Dr. Gobal, I.A.S and Mr. Viajakumar, I.A.S, the Directors of Tamil Nadu State AIDS Control Society for helping me to collect statistics and the list of NGOs working in AIDS Intervention Programmes in Chennai.

I also deeply indebted to Dr. Krishnamurthy, Director of AIDS Prevention and Control Project (APAC), Dr. Manorama, Director of CHESS, Dr. Hariharan, Director of Indian Community welfare Association, Dr. Dhanikachalam, former NGO Advisor of Tamil Nadu State AIDS Control Society and the members of World Vision, Chennai for supporting me to collect primary Data and to shape Action Plan, the part of research work.

I am happy to extend my profound thanks to Mr. Arulmoni, Madurai Meenakchi Mission Hospital, Mrs. Sasikala, Family Planning Association of India, Madurai, Mr. Raja and Prassana Raja, the Director and Secretary of Mother Saratha Devi Social Service Society, Ottenchatram for extending their support during my pilot study.

I sincerely acknowledge the support of Ms. Kausalya, President, Indian Positive Net Work, Chennai, Mrs. Varalakshmi, Mrs. Seethalakshmi, staff of Tamil Nadu State AIDS Control Society, Mr. Pitchamani, President, Positive Net Work, Theni. I am also deeply indebted to all my respondents for providing valuable information and suggestions.

I am extremely thankful to my friends Mr. Mani, Mr. Jayaseelan, Ms. Thirukani and Ms. Shilpa, the Research Scholars, Department of Sociology, and Mr.Sabesh Manikandan, Kubendran Gandhigram Rural Institute for their encouragement and assistance in computerizing thesis.

I am always remembering my father Mr. G. Shanmugam Pillai, who is blessing me from the heaven for all my success in life.

I place on record my deepest appreciation to my mother Mrs. Ponnammal Shanmugam, brothers S. Govindaraj, S. Guru and S. Mohan and my beloved G. Karthiha and G. Dinesh Kumar and G. Iswarya and Mrs. Anitha Guru. I am highly indebted to my mother-in-law Mrs. Gomathi Alwar, sister in-law

Dr. Lalitha, Mrs. Rani Alwar Ramanujam, and my borther Dr. Alwar Ramanujam for their affectionate interest in my health and studies which helped me to provide deep concentration on research. I am extremely thankful to my sister Mrs. Raji Muth, my brother-in-law Lr. Muthu, Mr. Mani and all my family members and my friends Mrs. Padma Vasu and Mr. Vasu for providing moral and psychological support during my critical period which helped me to recover my physical strength to speed up my research work.

I am highly proud of my husband Mr. A.V Ravi Prakash, Asst. Professor, Pondicherry Engineering College, Pondicherry. Without his moral and psychological support it is very difficult for me to complete this research work. I am also highly indebted to my son Goutham R Prakash for tolerating my absence in home. I am very grateful to my son Mr. Prabu for heart warming encouragement throughout my study period.

Finally, I extend my thanks to each and everyone who have helped me in some way or other in this endeavour.

Sakthi, S.

Contents

Contents

LIST OF ABBREVIATIONS

AIDS - Acquired Immuno Deficiency Syndrome

APAC - AIDS Prevention and Control Project

ART - Anti Retroviral Therapy

ARV - Antiretroviral Drug

CAPACS - Chennai Corporation of AIDS Prevention and Control Society

CSW - Commercial Sex Worker

ESI - Employees State Insurance

FHAC - Family Health Awareness Campaign

FSW - Female Sex worker

GIPA - Greater Involvement of People living with HIV/AIDS

GOs - Government

Govt. - Government

HIV - Human Immuno Virus

IDU - Injecting Drug User

IUD - Intra Uterus Device

MSM - Men Seeking Men

NACO - National AIDS Control Organisation

N.G.Os - Non-Governmental Organisations

PFA - Parliamentary Forum on AIDS

PHC	-	Primary Health Centre
PLWHA	-	People Living with HIV/AIDS
PPTCT	-	Prevention of Parent to Child Transmission
PTCT	-	Parent to Child Transmission
RTI	-	Reproductive Tract Infection
STD	-	Sexually Transmitted Disease
SHG	-	Self Help Group
TNSACS	-	Tamil Nadu State AIDS Control Society
UNAIDS	-	United Nations Programme on HIV/AIDS
UNDP	-	United Nations Development Programme
UNFPA	-	United Nations Fund for Population Activities
UNIFEM	-	United Nations Development Fund for Women
VCCTC	-	Voluntary Confidential Counseling and Testing Center
WHO	-	World Health Organisation

1

Introduction

"Every human being is the author of his own health or disease."

—*Buddha*

Human beings are affected by a number of diseases caused by germs, bacteria, viruses, fungi and parasites. But epidemic produced by bacteria and other viruses are controllable and preventable and we have controllable vaccines and medicines to safeguard the population from these epidemics. There is no discrimination or stigma with the diseases caused by bacteria, germs, virus and parasites. But as far as Human Immuno-Deficiency Virus (HIV) and Acquired Immuno Deficiency Syndrome (AIDS) are concerned, it is entirely different from other diseases which society is faced today.

The first documented case of AIDS in the United States was identified in 1980s by a young immunologist, Dr. Michael S. Gottlieb at the University of California, Los Angeles. HIV-1 was identified in 1983 by Dr. Robert Gallo and other medical scientists at the National Cancer Institute in Bethesda, Maryland. At about the same time, Dr. Luc Montagnier of the Pasteur Institute in Paris isolated HIV-2 from AIDS patients (Singhal *et al.*, 2003: 46-49).

HIV/AIDS have a peculiar character of affecting the immune system of the body and make body susceptible to a number of infections leading to AIDS – a fatal stage of the body. Unlike other epidemics there is no vaccine for prevention and no medicine for the cure of the diseases. It affects the entire demographic and economic structure of the society by increasing mortality rate among the youth and children who are considered as the back bone of the development of any nation.

For AIDS, the transmission routes are clear and it is closely associated with individual behaviour. Therefore, it is hundred per cent preventable if the behaviour of individual is very much in line with societal expectations.

Certain behaviours such as sex outside matrimonial life, homosexuality, drug addiction, prostitution are unapproved behaviours and these are stigmatized in the society. The spread of HIV has its route in these stigmatized behaviours. Therefore, those who got AIDS/HIV are socially neglected, economically isolated and psychologically deprived by the society in general and by their family members in particular. As a result of social discrimination many infected people are generally out of the mainstream of social life. The social stigma makes them to develop mental strain and stress and unbearable fear about their future

In the beginning of the epidemic it was said that it is the disease of gay men or homosexuals and confined only to the western countries where these behaviours are not considered as abnormal behaviours. But now the disease is more and more identified with general population and it made us to feel that every one is under risk. The epidemic encircled the whole globe with out leaving any country with AIDS free status. The disease has no compromise with the people based on their caste, class, religion sex, age, power etc.

If there is no control on the rapid spread of the disease, it will threaten the entire survival of the society. Therefore, HIV/AIDS should be treated not only as major public health problem but also a social problem. Because, it has all the characteristics of social problems which affect larger sections of population to produce adverse impact on the society (Horton and Leslie 1970: 4).

Immune System

The immune system is a complex assembly of organs, cells, and proteins that defend the body against potentially harmful foreign substances. The co-ordinate action of these components against such substances is called immune responses. The immune system is involved in various major activities within the body. It defends the body against invasion by pathogens, which are disease-causing micro organisms such as viruses, bacteria, fungi and parasites. It identifies and destroys abnormal or mutant cells and thus defends the body against the growth of cancerous tumor cells. It also eliminates worn out dead and damaged cells and rejects cells from other organisms.

The immune system accomplishes many of its activities by the action of white cells, which are technically called leukocytes. The leukocytes are divided into three sub groups called 'T' cells, 'B' cells and natural killer cells. Specific immunity is carried out by 'T' cells and 'B' cells. The 'T' cells also called CD4+ cells.

When HIV entered into the body it not only replicates at enormous speed but also cause the death of the host cells by selectively targeting CD4+ cells. The CD4+ cells become its virus factory. Although the body wages a battle against HIV from the first day of infection–replacing upto 1 billion 'T' cells killed by HIV very day. But over a period of years the immune system gradually wears out and loses its ability to regenerate immune system cells killed during battle. This leads to a steadily widening gab between the number of cells killed each day and the number replaced. Once the gap widens the point that immune function is compromised, an individual with HIV is open to the opportunistic infections and cancers characteristics of AIDS (Kimberly *et al.* 1998: 13).

HIV – A Description

Acquired immunodeficiency syndrome (AIDS) is a disorder caused by the human immunodeficiency virus (HIV), which like all viruses is a submicroscopic parasite that can only survive and reproduce inside the cells of a host organism. HIV is a particular type of virus, a retrovirus, and more specifically, a lentivirus. HIV is able to infect CD4+ cells, a component of the immune system. The losses of CD4+ cells largely devastate the immune system in individuals with AIDS. HIV's sole activity is the production of new copies of itself. HIV infection persists for many years and attrition of the immune cells needed to fight infection gradually leads to an inability to generate new immune responses required to suppress HIV, and the replication rate of the virus increases to very high levels. The loss of CD4+ cells and a rise in the amount of HIV circulating in the blood stream (called the viral load) are the hall mark of AIDS (Harry W. Kestler *et al.*, 1998: 5).

Definition of AIDS

AIDS case definitions are established by the Centers for Disease Control and Prevention (CDC) in the United States. In 1981, after reports of Pneumocystis carinii pneumonia, Kaposi's sarcoma and other opportunistic infections in young gay men in San Francisco, New York and Los Angeles, the CDC began surveillance for a newly recognized disease to be called AIDS. In 1982, CDC developed a surveillance case definition for this syndrome focusing on the presence of opportunistic infections. AIDS case definition was expanded in 1985 by including the total of 20 conditions. Four of these conditions were cancers, kaposi's sarcoma and three distinct types of lymphoma. The remaining conditions were opportunistic infections – those caused by bacteria, fungi, protozoans and other infectious agents. The CDC has made another revision in 1987 by including three additional conditions. One of the new conditions was an opportunistic infection called tuberculosis (TB), but only the extra pulmonary (outside the lungs) type. The other conditions were nct opportunistic infections, but rather conditions resulting from the direct effects of infection by HIV in the digestive system (wasting syndrome) and the central nervous system. These conditions were found among heterosexual African American and Latino individuals. These new cases also included high number of injecting drug users. In 1992, the CDC has again taken steps to expand the surveillance definition to address certain populations, namely women, injecting drug users and communities of color. In November 1994, the CDC announced that it was expanding the surveillance definition with effect from January 1, 1993.

According to this definition any HIV-positive individual with a CD4+ cell count of 200 or less or whose CD4+ cells represented less than 14 per cent of all lymphocytes are called AIDS patients. Two additional illnesses are also included in the case definition that is AIDS – defining in children but not in adults. (*Theresa et al.*, 1998: 11).

Historicity of HIV/AIDS

The sudden appearance of AIDS in early 1980s prompted studies of the origin of this apparently new, fatal human disease. Sabatier (1988: 34-35) has given three explanation of the origin of the HIV virus. The first explanation is that it may originate from an old human disease unknown to science for the long time. The second assumption is that it has originated from species other than human beings like apes, monkeys. The third explanation is that it may accidentally originated in labouratories while conducting experiments.

The early theory believes that the virus has spread through homosexual contact of men. This syndrome therefore was initially called guy-related immunodeficiency or GRID (Parvi, 1992: 2). The spread of the syndrome soon identified as contagious agent which transmitted through sexual contact, transfusions of contaminated blood, and use of contaminated hypodermic needles. A new retrovirus was identified in 1983 and was subsequently demonstrated to be the cause of AIDS. This virus was named human immuno deficiency virus, or HIV.

The cross species theory reveals that the virus was already existed in animals and transmitted to human beings (Sahmi 1993: 2). The first evidence to support the cross over theory for HIV came in 1985, when an HIV-like virus was discovered in rhesus monkeys (macaques) that had developed Simian Acquired Immuno Deficiency Syndrome (SAIDS). The virus was named Simian Immunodeficiency Virus of macaques, or SIV mac. SIV mac was shown to be related to both HIV-1 and HIV-2 but was more closely related to HIV-2. Since those first studies, the SIV family tree has expanded to five branches representing five different simian species, all from Africa. The SIVs have been detected in sooty mongabeys in West Africa; in African green monkeys in East, Central and West Africa; in the Sykes monkey in Kenya; in a mandrill colony in Gabon; and finally in chimpanzees, also from Gabon.

The sooty mongabeys were kept as household pets in West Africa and the Africans may be infected with SIV in the past through the contact with house hold pets or monkeys hunted for food. Inadequately sterilized needles or contaminated blood products may have played a role in spreading SIV among humans. Needles that could be reused were widely introduced into rural African clinics after world war second and this widespread needles use coincides with the emergence of HIV. Needle reuse may have resulted in SIV being rapidly transmitted from person to person, allowing SIV to adopt humans through mutation. SIV became HIV when it was able to cause disease in human beings and be sexually transmitted. Once SIV had adapted to humans and was capable of being spread by sexual contact, the virus spread worldwide through international travellers (Mark 1998: 17).

The virus HIV-1 and HIV-2 are believed to have had a common ancestor in Africa. Very recently new HIV, which is more dangerous than HIV-1 and HIV-2 is detected in New York in America among homosexual men. This new HIV is more susceptible to opportunistic infection very quickly than other two HIVs. Researches are going on to study further details about the virus (*Sun News*, 1.30 PM on 17-2-05).

The medical condition, which was later to be called AIDS, began to be noticed in the late 1970s and early 1980s in several widely spreaded locations, including Belgium, France, Haiti, the United States, Zaire and Zambia (Tinker, 1988: 33-35). The first medical reports of the syndrome were published in the United States in June 1981 (US Centre for Disease Control, 1981: 250-252). For few years preceding these reports, a small but growing number of homo sexual men and their physicians in New York city, Los Angeles and San Francisco were noticing rare or unusual disease symptom –pneumocystis pneumonia, kaposi's sarcoma in young men. These ailments seemed to be related to inexplicable deterioration in the men's immune systems (Randy Shills, 1987: 630). Doctors began to suspect the existence of a new, sexually transmitted infection. Doctors at the US Centre for Disease Control (CDC) in Atlanta, Georgia, began to suspect that blood transmission could be a factor and similar symptoms were also recorded among intravenous drug users. By the end of 1981, doctors in Zaircan capital of Kinshasa had also begun to documents dozens of cases where their patients multiple infections seemed to relate to a collapse of the body's immune infection (Lamey and Malemeka, 1982: 507-11). It prompted the physicians to observe the similarity between the symptoms of Zambian patients and those which had broken out among American homosexual (Bayley, 1983: 1318-1320).

During 1970s cases of AIDS had been seen by Belgian doctors in Africans. The first seems to have been a 34 year old *Zairian airline* secretary (Vandepitte. *et al.*, 1983: 925-926). Late 1980s and early 1981 doctors at a Parisian clinic identified a case of pneumocystis pneumonia in a Portuguese man, in a Zairian women and in a French woman who came from Zaire (Offenstadl. *et al.*, 1983: 775). Of the two hundred patients affected by the new disease in Europe, fifty two were Africans (Biggar, *et al.*, 1984: 157-173). In Haiti, the combination of kaposis sarcoma and uncontrollable opportunistic infections has appeared in 1978-79 (Pape, *et al.*, 1983: 945-950). Haitian refugees with immunodeficiency disease were seen in increasing numbers in New York City and Miami during 1980-81. By mid 1982, the CDC had documented thirty four such cases. By October 1982, researchers in Haiti had diagnosed sixty one cases (*Morbidity and Mortality Weekly Report*, 1982: 353-361). Since 1982 the similar symptoms of cases were reported from various parts of the world and HIV/AIDS became the global problem.

The Unique Feature of HIV/AIDS

AIDS epidemic is vastly different from epidemics of yesteryears for the following reasons:

- Primarily it is a sexually transmitted disease. Sexual activity is not something that can be banned morally, socially or legally.
- The new infection is rapidly increasing in every country. The moment the AIDS virus HIV enters a person's blood stream he/she is capable of infecting the next person he/she has sex with.

- Social stigma is attached with the AIDS since it has its roots with sexual behaviours. Therefore infected people have lack of courage to face the reactions of the society.
- Majority of the people are ignorant about the spread of HIV and its preventive mechanism.
- Limited facilities for testing and lack of affordability increases the spread of HIV/AIDS even without the knowledge of the infected people.
- The causative organism of AIDS is a virus and these viruses are not affected by antibiotics at all. It is not easy to find a curative agent for AIDS. Vaccines are not yet available, treatments are limited and a cure is still a vision for the future.

Therefore AIDS will create severe damage to our society. The increasing trends of HIV infection and deaths due to AIDS would not only produce adverse impact on individual, households and communities but also on the benchmarks of human development like infant survival, life expectancy, per capita income, school enrolments, health, and loss of trained human resources and so on.

Routes of HIV Transmission

HIV may be found in the cells, bodily fluids and secretions of infected persons and the presence of virus in the bodily fluids and secretions have different degrees of transmission risk. HIV can be easily isolated in semen, vaginal secretions and blood and breast milk. It is not easy to isolate the virus from tears, saliva, perspiration and urine. Therefore, it is currently accepted that the virus is transmitted to others only through blood, semen, vaginal secretions and breast milk (Digumarti Baskara Rao, 2000: 6).

According to Thomas *et al.* (1997: 26) the HIV can pass on to an individual mainly through the following three routes:

1. *Sexual exposure*: It is most commonly transmitted through sexual contact: from women to men, from men to women, between men seeking men.

2. *Contact with contaminated blood and blood products*: HIV is also transmitted through infected blood. People have become infected by blood transfusion, infected blood products including donated organs and by sharing of syringes and hypodermic needles. In many parts of the world, donated blood is now screened for antibodies to HIV, making this form of transmission is rare. However, in places where blood is not systematically tested and where many people are infected with the virus, transmission in this way may still be common. The virus has been also transmitted by recycling needles that have not been properly sterilized.
3. *From parent to child through pregnancy and birth*: This is known as pre-natal transmission. Before, birth it may be transmitted across the placenta to the developing foetus. During birth, the virus may be transmitted via the mother's blood or bodily secretions. A small number of cases of transmission through breast milk have been recorded in some regions.

HIV can also be transmitted through some innocuous routes like ritual tonsuring of the head at religious places where mass ritual tonsuring is taking place, common razor used in hair-cutting saloons and by village barbers who shave customers without changing disinfecting blades and piercing the ears, tattooing and ritual circumcision, if done in group (Sahami, 1993: 19).

The Groups Vulnerable to HIV Infection

Though every one is under the risk of acquiring HIV infection, certain groups are more vulnerable to HIV based on their life on high risk situation. These groups are called high risk groups. The high risk groups identified by the UNAIDS are past and present intravenous drug users, prostitutes, devadasis and their sexual partners, homosexual and bisexual men, Eunuchs involved in sexual activities particularly with homosexual men, prison inmates involved in homosexuality, multi-sexual partners, drug addicts, street children involved in sex and drug abuse, truck drivers who involved in sexual activity in the highway. Defense personnel who are engaged in sex with prostitutes, children of HIV positive women, sexual partners of HIV infected people, thalassemia patients who often receive blood from the donors, migrants who are away from their home for a long time and are involved in extra marital sex, construction workers etc. (Thomas *et al.*, 1997: 29).

Implications of HIV/Aids

The dreaded disease caused by HIV not only produces adverse impact on the individual but it also threatens existence of the basic social institutions of family and community and nation at larger level. HIV/AIDS is not only a health problem, but it is also a societal problem with important social, cultural and economic dimensions (Ahuja, 1999: 415).

Implication on the individuals

If the person is infected by HIV, immediately his/her character is assassinated by the public even without considering the mode of infection. The individual with HIV is subjected to criticism, boycott, segregation and dissociation, by their family members, friends, neighbours and fellowmen in the community.

Still the people have the fear that the virus can be transmitted even by touching or sharing of articles with the infected persons. The fear of death and the socially unapproved behaviours linked with the transmission of HIV resulted in stigmatization and discrimination towards the people infected with HIV positive.

The HIV positive people are looked down and they are isolated and rejected by the members of the society from the normal day to day life. In majority of the cases the individuals are blamed for their infection and they are treated like strangers who are involved in spreading HIV into general population. As a result they are denied proper care and support to lead a positive life with HIV positive status. The societal isolation creates psychological depression and mental stress and strain which affect the health of the people infected with HIV positive and invite the opportunistic infection without giving opportunity to prolong their life span. Loss of courage to face the society leads them to feel themselves as inefficient persons to continue or to take up work. Besides, the people with HIV positive also face lot of discrimination in their work places. In many cases they are thrown out of employment due to fear of contracting infection. Loss of hope on peaceful and dignified future questioned them about the meaning of life and resulted in alienation which forces them to end their life by committing suicide. The discrimination and stigmatization forced many people infected with HIV positive to get away from their own location to far away places where their infected identity can be hidden. And also the individuals who cannot cope up with their positive result normally get scared to face the friends and family members. These persons will try to hide their HIV status from the society in general and family members in particular.

Implication on the family

The whole family will get affected if any of its members is infected by HIV. The stigma associated with HIV not only affects the individual but also the entire family. If the infection is known to the public, the total family will be criticized and they may be excluded from the social activities of the society/community. In many cases the education, employment and marriage of the sibling is affected to a larger extent and force them to change their residence from their original place. The burden is heavy on the women. Because she has to bear the economical responsibility due to loss of employment and income of the infected persons. The early death of the economically productive youth leads to loss of income to the family. The expenditure incurred to treat the opportunistic infection forces them to lose all their resources and lead them towards indebtedness. The children are also affected for none of their faults. Significant per centage of children have been orphaned due to the loss of their parents.

Implication on Community

High prevalence of HIV infection in the community will leads to shortage of labour force which is highly essential for the development of any community. The increasing rate of women infection will definitely question the morality and ethics of particular community/society and it will strengthen the stigma associated with HIV/AIDS.

Implication at National level

The impact of the epidemic is visible in the demographic structure of the society. The morbidity and mortality rate is high among the youth–the most productive age groups. As a result children and old population will be found more in the region where the HIV and AIDS prevalence is high. South Africa is adversely affected by the increasing proportion of mortality and morbidity (Carael *et al.*, 1998: S1). The large increase in adult mortality and moderate increase in child mortality lead to dramatic falls in life expectancy (Boerma *et al.*, 1998: S3). The infection is high among the women. Around 25% of the women infected with HIV positive in the world are at their reproductive age. The higher infection rate among the women of reproductive age will affect the fertility rate of country (Stover and Way, 1998: S29). Since there is no cure for AIDS, the epidemic produces adverse impact on the economic structure of the country. The loss of human resource and loss of labour forces due to sickness also create adverse impact on the growth of national income. The growth of per capita income depends on the growth rate of healthy labour and capital that can be invested by the country towards the development activities. Sub-Saharan Africa has the lowest levels of per capita income of any developing region and it has faced lot of economic problems since 1980 due to AIDS (Ainsworth and Over, 1994: 232-233). The treatment for HIV/AIDS is very costly and the Government has to divert a major portion of its resources to distribute medicines either at subsidiary cost or free of cost like India. At national level the costs are incurred primarily through testing blood and blood products, improving treatment for sexually transmitted diseases, implementing precautions in health care settings, tracking the diseases and educating the public about the risk of the diseases. Besides, the medical researches require huge money to develop vaccine to prevent HIV/AIDS and drugs for the treatment of people infected with HIV/AIDS. At present the developed drugs are very expensive and beyond the reach of an average man (Ramamurthy, 2000: 1-21.

Women's Vulnerability To HIV/AIDS

HIV/AIDS is projected as women's epidemic. There is a common belief that the women in sex work are the major cause for spreading the virus in the society. The tendency of feminizing the disease is found among the general population in almost all countries without considering the real risk of women to acquire infection through their sexual partners. The disease becomes women specific by blaming the sex workers and women are perceived as virus carriers in many developing countries.

According to UNAIDS Global Epidemic 2004, majority of the women were infected through their single sexual partners especially in their marital life. Women usually have a faith that they will not get infection since they have sex with their single sexual partner/husband. Therefore, majority of the women will not be aware of their infection till their pregnancy or the death of her faithful partner. The negative attitudes towards HIV/AIDS by the society make her sexual partner to hide his HIV status with his family members. As a result, when men's infection is known to their family members, they blame their innocent wives/sexual partners for transmitting infection. The women's behaviours and character are questioned rather than analyzing real fact for men's infection. Many infected women have been abandoned by their family members as a result of such baseless blame.

In reality women are particularly vulnerable to infection and increasing numbers of women are becoming infected. Among the people infected with HIV/AIDS 57% are women and in many countries women outnumbered men as in the case of Africa.

Women's vulnerability to HIV/AIDS has different dimensions due to the following factors:

Social status of women in the society

Throughout the world irrespective of the development of the nations the women enjoy only secondary social status in the society. Globally around 60 per cent of women live below poverty line with illiterate status. They have inadequate access to property and other infrastructural facilities related to health care services (Usha, 2000: 12). The lower status of women within the family and society is heightening by their economical dependence on males. This makes women to feel less power to control their reproductive health. The feeling of powerlessness both in the personal relationship and in the society has resulted in keeping silent in sexual interaction and changing their traditional role by demanding the use of condom for safe sex. If a woman demands these she will be treated as of bad woman or thought to be inferring the infidelity of her husband and in the case of sex worker she has to face the risk of violence or lose clients and income if she advocates the use of condom (United Nations Commission on the Status of Women, 1998: 3). Therefore the powerlessness as a result of lower social status increases the risk of getting HIV infections.

Economic Subordination

Economic factors, such as poverty increases the risk of HIV for poor women mainly in two ways: 1. Poverty and lack of better resources lead many unmarried women to exchange sexual favors for economic survival. 2. Struggle for economic survival coupled with personal autonomy may lead many to form relationships with many partners and consequently increase the risk of HIV infection. Significant proportions of unmarried women are driven to become sex-workers due to destitution. There is a growing trend among poor married women living along the busy inter-State routes on national highways to take up prostitution as a means of coping with poverty. They mainly have truck drivers as their clients who now have emerged as the major high risk group. In the cross-border areas of the nations, the poor women have engaged in sex work with professional groups like armymen and other security personnel who have very high incidence of HIV. (Usha, 2001). They will be less successful in negotiating protection, and it is less likely that they will leave a relationship where they perceive more risk. Malnutrition, uncontrolled fertility, complications of childbirth, poorly performed abortion, predisposes women to intrapartal hemorrhages. This directly increases the risk of HIV through unmonitored transfusion of blood). The groups of young women most vulnerable to HIV infection are those who are homeless or living in poverty. UNICEF estimates that over 40 million young people in the world are living on the streets. Many of those have left home because of sexual abuse or poverty (Digumarti Bhaskara Rao, 2000: 122).

Cultural and Traditional Factors

Power imbalance is found in all societies and it is supported by socio-cultural system and controlled by men. As a result culture of silence is found around sex. It prevents the open discussion of sexual matters not only with men but also with women. The culture of silence dictates that the women should be ignorant about sex and passive in sexual interactions. Therefore, it is very difficult to reach the women with the message of safe sex practices. Even when the women are informed about safe sex, it is very difficult for them to negotiate its practices with their sexual partners. (Carovano, 1992: 131-142). The traditional norm of virginity for women that exists in many societies increases the risk of infection for young women. Because, it creates fear and it restricts their ability to ask for information about sex. The concept of virginity also puts young girls at risk of rape and sexual coercion in high prevalence countries because of the erroneous belief that sex with a virgin can cleanse man's infection. In addition, in cultures where virginity is highly valued, some young women practice alternative sexual behaviours, such as anal sex, in order to preserve their virginity, although these behaviours may place them at increased risk of HIV. (Weiss *et al.* 2000: 233-245). The strong norms of virginity and the culture of silence that surrounds sex prevent women to take treatment for sexually transmitted diseases which is highly stigmatized in the society (Weiss *et al.*, 2000).

In the Indian context, sex is highly sensitive, confidential and purely related to the private life of the individual and it forces people not to discuss any aspects of sex in the public sphere. Therefore, culture itself acts as a stumbling block to access knowledge about sex and sexuality and its related issues including STD, HIV/AIDS etc.

Cultural practices

In many societies sex is considered as taboo, not for discussion. Women are ill-informed on sexual matters and their sexual desire and decision on sex is controlled by men. Women have no negotiating powers and the societies have double standards on the sexual behaviour of its members. It imposes **rule of chastity** on women but accept men's multiple sexual partners. The use of contraceptive measures depend on the willingness of the male partners and women's social status depends on bearing children and the uses of condom is opposed to the cultural tradition of having children. Males are expected to initiate relationships, and sexual assertiveness in women is often stigmatized or even punished. **Age differences for sex** is strictly maintained by culture of many societies like India. In such countries women usually have sex with older men who have been sexually active for longer period and have had more chances for sexually transmitted infection. Certain cultural practices of the regions increase the risk of HIV infection for women. In some parts of the world, women use herbal and other agents in the vagina to cause dryness, heat and tightness. This practice is referred to as **"dry sex"** in which women feel like virgins and because they think that female secretions are unclean. The material used by women may include pieces of cloth, leaves, ground stone, herbs or western medications and their use has been reported in Nigeria, Zaire, Zamba, Malawi, Zimbabwe and South Africa (Sandala *et al.*, 1995: S61-S68). The substances used can cause inflammation and erosion of the vaginal mucosa, making it easier for HIV to enter. **Female genital mutilation (circumcision)** is practised in various African countries (Jones *et al.*, 1999: 219). Infibulations leads to extensive tearing and bleeding when sexual intercourse is attempted. It may also cause couples to practice riskier anal sex. The procedure itself could be risk if unsterilized instruments are used for several patients in succession (UNAIDS 1998: 11).

Early marriage of women is another important cultural practice which increases the risk of sexually transmitted infections for women. Most of developing countries like India, Pakistan, Sri Lanka, Bangladesh, etc. are practising both child marriage and early marriage. In these countries women are withdrawn from the school soon after they attained puberty. The girls are forced into marriage with men who are elder than her age. Most of these girls are entering into marriage without knowing anything about sex and sexuality and reproductive health. Along with other social norms their age at marriage becomes a barrier for them to discuss or to learn the matters related to sex. In this context, they accept the domination of their husbands on their body as well as on their day to day life. Poor knowledge on reproductive health increases the risk of HIV infection. The knowledge on reproductive health is either poor or lacking among the age groups of 15-40 years. At these ages both men and women are sexually active and many a times their unsafe sexual activity increases the chances of infection. There are lots of discussions throughout the world about reproductive health, but the message has not reached the vulnerable group of 15-40 years and the women become innocent victims in the context of HIV/AIDS.

In recent years, in various parts of the globe **male circumcision** is getting more popular since the people believe that circumcision may reduce the risk of HIV infection (Kim Best, 2001). There is evidence that male circumcision protects against HIV infection in Africa and the uncircumcised men in Africa are twice as likely to be infected as circumcised men (Singhal, 2003: 48).

Male circumcision is considered as a ritual practice by many communities especially Muslims. It is also a traditional ritual practice for the Christians in the continent of Africa. Similarly, circumcision is the common cultural and traditional practice in North America. The rate of infection identified here is only less than one per cent. But in South Africa, the rate of infection ranges from 15 to 25% where less per centage of men have undergone circumcision (Halperin, 1999). Male circumcision provides significant protection against HIV infection and other sexually transmitted diseases such as syphilis and gonorrhea. The circumcised males are two to eight times less likely to become infected with HIV (*AIDS Update*, 2000). The specific cell called 'Langerhans cells' are found in the foreskin of the male. These cells are the major receptors of HIV primary infection (Best, 2001). Therefore, the removal of specialized cells in the penis reduces the risk of HIV infection (Szobo, 2000). But if it performed in an unsterilized situation it will increases the risk of all HIV. **Lack of male circumcision** is found in many countries such as India. Many women are getting infected through their faithful male partners. If men had undergone circumcision, they may not get infected with HIV and in turn the women may not get infected with the dreaded diseases.

In many developing countries including India, sons are preferred over daughters. The concept of **son preference** is the principal determinant of high fertility in most regions. In the regions where son is given more importance, the women never come forward to use condom as safe sex to prevent them the STDs. Their attitude towards giving birth to male child may increase the risk of HIV infection in their marital life.

Female Biological Vulnerability to HIV

Women are biologically more vulnerable than men to HIV infection and other sexually transmitted diseases. The major factors responsible for differential transmission are the larger mucosal surface areas exposed to virus in women and the semen having high concentration of virus compared with vaginal secretions. Young girls are particularly vulnerable. Their immature cervix and relatively low vaginal mucus production presents less of barrier to HIV, making them biologically more vulnerable to infection than older pre-menopausal women (Digumarti Bhaskara Rao, 2000: 281).

Many women get HIV infections by a single sexual contact. The chances of a woman being infected by one act of sexual intercourse with an HIV positive man are about one in 100. The chance of a man being infected by one act of sexual intercourse with an HIV positive woman are about one in 1000, but this probability may increase considerably if one of them has STD (Moses *et al.*, 1991: 407-11)

Women are disproportionately the recipients of blood transfusions and other blood products (e.g. for anemia or child birth complications). In the absence of adequate blood screening, women's vulnerability to blood-borne HIV transmission increases.

Marriage increases the women's vulnerability to HIV

Marriage may be viewed as a social and economic commitment between individuals and families. Sexual access, procreation, child rearing and other services are universal to social expectation of marriage. Because of this and as well as lower social status and economic dependence, married women may be unable to challenge their husband's extra-marital affairs or insist on condom use for themselves. The magnitude of HIV transmission in stable/monogamy relationship in the event of disloyalty is high inspite of vigorous and purposive intervention programmes. The infection among women in monogamy relationships are current problem in all regions of the world in general and India and Thailand in particular. In these regions the men who visit sex workers also have wives or other stable partners (Isabella de Zoysa *et al.*, 1996: S197-S203). Marriage provides no protection against HIV. Across the world millions of women infected through heterosexual sex were infected by their husbands. Double standard of culture with regard to virginity keeps silence when men have multi sexual partners or engage sex with sex workers. If the men are infected through their behaviours of multisexual contact, they will pass the infection to their wives or stable partners. The women in monogamy relationship never emphasized the need of using condom with the faith that they will not get infected through their husbands or stable partners. The married women have higher rate of infection than their unmarried, sexually active peer (Isabella de Zoysa *et al.*, 1996: S197-S203).

Most of the men who got infections are highly ignorant about their infections. Because they never relalised the need for taking HIV test before getting married or whenever they had sex with sex workers. Some men will get married with the ignorance of their own infections and they will pass the infections to their wives. On the other hand some men are hiding their infections from others and transmit the virus to their wives. Therefore, many women are not aware of the risk of getting infection from their male partners. They are also not aware that their husbands have HIV/AIDS (Baingana *et al.,* 1995: S21-S30).

It is very difficult to implement HIV prevention among the married women. The factors which act as barriers to the prevention of HIV transmission in the stable relationships are: First, there is a widespread belief that sex with a stable partner carries few risks. Second, communication between stable partners about protective behaviours is compromised by prevailing norms about partner and gender relations. Third, condom use and other risk-reducing behaviours are problematic in long-term unions, because it prevents procreation. Many seem unable or unwilling to recognize that they may be exposed to HIV infection in their stable relationship, even when they are aware of their partner's past or current risk behaviours. Most people believe that the "normal" sex with a stable partner is safe and sex "outside" the marriage and with "promiscuous" partners is risky. Many preventive messages, such as "stick to your partner", "love faithfully", or "love carefully" reinforce the notion that HIV infection only strikes "others" who deviate from the norm of loving, being faithful and having trusting relationships. Thus, monogamy is somehow constructed as a protection against HIV (Isabelle de Zoysa *et al.*, 1996, S197-S203).

Sexually transmitted diseases and HIV/AIDS to women

Sexually transmitted diseases have challenged the control measures even in the most developed countries. It acts as a co-factor in HIV transmission by increasing susceptibility to HIV. The diseases are multi dimensional and their prevalence in any community depends on various socio-economic factors (Nair *et al.,* 1973: 1967). The presence of sexually transmitted diseases (STDs), particularly ulcerative conditions, increases the likelihood of infection in both men and women. STDs are common amongst young women, particularly in Africa, the Caribbean and Latin America and Asia. They are not easy to detect in women and so most women remain unaware of their presence. World Health Organisation estimates that about 330 million cases of treatable STDs exist worldwide at any time and 50-80% of STDs in women are asymptomatic or go unnoticed because they are internal (UNAIDS, 2000: 11).

STDs—especially those, such as chancroid and syphilis, which cause ulcerative lesions—greatly facilitate both the acquisition and transmission of HIV. However, women with STDs are often asymptomatic and fail to recognize any infections. As a result, women are more vulnerable to HIV infection because they are more likely to have untreated STDs. Often their vulnerability to STDs is the result of their partners' behaviour rather than their own.

Preventing and curing the STDs may reduce the incidence of HIV infection. But the women, who know their infection, tend to avoid STD clinics for fear of being recognized and stigmatized. Women normally used to visit primary health centers and family planning and maternal and child health clinics to seek medical services. But unfortunately, the facilities to treat STD are often less equipped to diagnose and treat STDs. Further, women's inaccessibility to STD clinics, economic dependency and house hold responsibilities, negative attitudes of health workers towards the women with STD prevent them from getting treatment. Lack of sex education also increases the risk of STD among youth. Biological and psychological changes associated with marked desire for sexual adventures during adolescence have put the teenagers in the "high risk" group. Urbanization and industrialization have not only broken down the established class structure but also shattered the social and religious constraints which prevented promiscuous sexual behaviour (Dutta, 1998: 16). The prevalence of STD is higher among the women involved in prostitution.

Innocent women never discuss any STD due to cultural constrains and the infection is tolerated by the women.

Female sterilization increases the risk of women's infection on HIV/AIDS

In many countries young women and adolescent girls were very much conscious about preventing pregnancy rather than getting infected from sexually transmitted infections. The women who involved in pre marital sex are often familiar with oral pills rather than condoms (Blanc and Way, 1998: 114). The magnitude of condom use is found to be less among the women at younger age. In a thickly populated country like India, Family Planning is an official policy. In these countries both men and women are motivated to undergo terminal methods of male and female sterilizations. Once any one of the spouses has undergone sterilization they never think about safe sex to avoid sexually transmitted infections (Biddlecom *et al.*, 1997: 108). In a country like India more and more women are enthusiastic about female sterilizations and their number is increasing by leaps and bounds. As a result of permanent method of birth control, these women were liberalized from procreation rather than sexually transmitted infection through their male sexual partners. The permanent family planning methods act as a barrier for both men and women to use condom for safe sex and increases the risk towards HIV and other sexually transmitted infections.

Lack of awareness on reproductive health enhances the vulnerability to HIV/AIDS

Many women have poor understanding over their own bodies, mechanisms of HIV/STD transmission and their level of risk in unprotected sex. Many men also have inadequate information about their own bodies and women's reproductive health. A time of growing sexuality and identity consolidation, adolescence is also at greatest risk of contracting sexually transmitted diseases (STDs) and the HIV virus. The women in general and adolescent girls in particular are ignorant about their reproductive health. The culture of silence prevents them from gaining information with regard to the problems associated with their reproductive health. In many developing countries women's education is compromised with the tradition and culture. Therefore, the illiteracy or poor education has not allowed them to acquire knowledge on their reproductive health and the information related to their own risk of getting sexually transmitted infection and HIV/AIDS. The women's inaccessibility to the reproductive health education has resulted in adolescent childbearing in developing countries. The proportion of birth to unmarried adolescents is increasing in the countries of North Africa, Asia, Latin America and Sub-Saharan Africa (Singh, 1998: 117). The increasing pattern of high pre marital pregnancy appears to reflect a low incidence of contraceptive use, especially condom (Garenne *et al.*, 2000: 47). The exposure to media and the influence of modernization and peer pressure has made many girls from the educated community to get involved in non-marital sexual activity without insisting on condom use for intercourse. Their involvement in unprotected sex is based on their insufficient knowledge and distorted judgments of the risks of becoming pregnant and acquiring sexually transmitted infections (Gage, 1998: 154).

Ineffective health programmes implemented by the government on the reproductive health is one of the major causes in Sub-Saharan Africa for the exposure of young girls into risky sexual behaviours (Zabin and Kiragu, 1998: 210). The regions of Ghana and the regions of Western Countries have open social environment. Such free social environment influences boys and girls to experiment with sex without giving much importance to the implication of reproductive health and the diseases associated with the risky behaviours (Mensch *et al.*, 1999: 95). The adolescent unproductive sexual behaviours increase the vulnerability to HIV infections both in rural and urban areas.

Attitude towards parenthood increases women's vulnerability to HIV infection

In most societies, women's primary role is to bear and nurture children. The status of women in the society is directly related to her capacity to become a mother. The childless women are looked down by the society and they are sidelined in all social and cultural ceremonial celebrations. Number of children given birth by the women is the rating scale to perceive the women's position is the family as well as in the society. The norms related to parenthood have two broad implications on women in relation to HIV/AIDS and STDs. One is that women are expected to concentrate more on their reproductive role rather than productive role as earning members to the family. The second consequence is that the childless woman used to try to become pregnant with unprotected sex without getting treatment for her/his infertility. In such cases if men are infected, the woman will also get infection without her knowledge.

Violence against women and HIV infection

Violence against women is an important factor which increases the risk of women's vulnerability to HIV infection. Rape is high risk factor which is inadequately recognized or addressed. In developing countries many poor and underprivileged women are subjected to sexual harassment like rape, molestation, and kidnapping and abduction either by the members known to their family or by the members of affluent community in work place. Drunken behaviour of the youth is reported as a major cause for the sexual harassment of women in the developing countries India (Sangmeswaran, 2004). Sexual harassment is a crime against women which increases the risk of HIV infection. Marital violence is more tolerated by the society than the violence outside the marriage. The rape within the marriage is not recognized as offence in many parts of the world and it is the privilege given to the men in the male dominated patriarchal society. Physical and sexual violence against women are intensified during wars and armed conflicts. Sexual violence can also occur against children, homosexuals, and transgendered people. The myth prevailing everywhere among the men in the society is that the sex with the children or young girls may cure or prevent all sexually transmitted infection including HIV/AIDS. As a result of this myth many girl children are trafficked and forced into prostitution. The sex under the condition of force or violence never think to use condom and it increases the risk of HIV and STDs infection to women.

Migration of male increases women's vulnerability to HIV infection

Male migrants are away from their home for a longer period. For example, transport workers, military and armed force workers, traders, seasonal agricultural labourers, are highly mobile and they have to leave their spouses and families for longer periods. Sex impulsion, separation from spouses, and stress and strain owing to their work influence male migrants to seek sex with sex workers and to use drugs with their peer groups in order to get relief from their personal problems. Thus, poor migrants are not in a position to value one's own life or to take steps to protect one's own health. Generally, the migrants are not much aware of the use of condom. The lack of or poor usage of condom increases the risk of HIV infection. These migrants were not coming forward to test their HIV status though they know their risk behaviours. As a result, they were unaware of their infection. If the men are infected due their risky behaviours, they well pass the infection to their wives or other sexual partners when they returned home. The impact of prevailing power imbalance and its associated gender inequality and women's faith on their male sexual partners do not permit the women even to suggest safe sex. The risky behaviour of men and their ignorance of their HIV infection increases women's vulnerability to HIV infection.

Migration of women increases their vulnerability to HIV

Generally the migrant women have least power to protect themselves from sexual exploitation. Many women migrants have ended up in prostitution to earn more money to improve the standard of living of their family members. Geographic mobility to young girls would lead to increased risk. Migration among the young girls under the age of 15 is predominant in rural areas in many Latin American Countries, in some African countries such as Ghana and Morocco and in Asian countries such as Bangladesh, India, Indonesia and the Philippines. They migrate to urban areas for seeking schooling and employment. A large proportion of the young women migrating to European countries from Asia and Africa end up in prostitution. Many sex workers move from place to place either voluntarily or involuntarily. For example, women from Cambodia, Laos, Myanmar and Vietnam work in brothels in Thailand. Sex workers from Thailand and Philippines work in Japan. Thai women became sex workers in Singapore and Nepalese women work in India. Sex workers may spread HIV from cities to rural areas when they returned home (UNDP, 2004: 1).

The process of increasing feminization of migration is found through out the world. It is estimated that roughly 48% of all migrants in the world are women (UNDP, 2004: 5). Women migrants from Asia constituted the largest number of unskilled workers in labour receiving countries. Rampant gender inequalities, low social status and lack of understanding of their sexuality and reproductive health and lack of access to information and service make migrant women especially vulnerable to HIV/AIDS. Large number of migrants face an acute risk of exploitation, physical violence, sexual abuse and socio-political marginalization. Sexual abuse and sexual exploitation will also increase women migrant's vulnerability to HIV infections (UNDP, 2004: 6).

Parent to Child Transmission of HIV

Parent-to-child transmission (also called PTCT, or "vertical transmission") is common today, resulting in millions of pediatric AIDS cases. The chances of a baby born to an HIV positive mother being infected are 40 per cent (Singhal *et al.*, 2003: 49).

Throughout the world hundreds of babies are born with HIV positive every day and there is no sign of decreasing trend in the world. Such increasing trend is mainly because of the failure of recognizing child's rights which is guaranteed under the United Nations Conventions of the Child Rights.

The HIV-infected mother can pass virus to her baby in the womb itself or during pregnancy, labour, delivery or after birth through breast feeding. The vertical or prenatal transmission is the major cause for the infant to get infection. The risk of transmission from mother to child is around 15-30% if the mother does not breast feed the child. But it can rise as high as 30-45% with prolonged breast feeding (Khurana, 1998: 103). Therefore, WHO has recommended bottle feeding for the children of HIV infected mothers (Thomas *et al.*, 1997: 42). In developing countries, the infection rate is increasing among the women at child bearing age. The increasing rate of infection among the women will increases the infection rate in infants (UNAIDS Briefing paper, 1997). The viral load of the mother is an important factor which influences the prenatal transmission. If the viral load is high, the risk of infection is also high (UNAIDS, July, 2004).

In 2004, around 640,000 children under 15 became infected with HIV mainly through mother to child transmission and 90% of these children are living in developing countries (UNAIDS, 2004). It is estimated that by the year 2010, if the spread of HIV is not controlled, around 75% of the infant mortality and under-five child mortality in the world will be due to AIDS (UNAIDS Briefing paper, 1997).

Since the beginning of the pandemic, over 5 million infants have been infected with HIV. Among them 90% were born in Africa and the worst affected region is Sub-Saharan Africa. In this region, the HIV infection rates of 10-30% are common among the pregnant women. At the same time the number of cases also increasing in Eastern Europe, India, and South East Asia (UNAIDS, 2002: 1-8). In these regions the infection rate among pregnant women ranges from 1% to 5% and it increases the vulnerability to infant infection (Gangakhedkar, 1999: 125-136).

HIV infection is a major contributing factor to childhood diseases and mortality in developing countries. It will threaten the survival of the child. The risk of transmission can be reduced up to 50% with the administration of anti retroviral drugs to mother and baby at the time of delivery, in conjunction with replacement of breast feeding (UNAIDS, 2002: 1).

In 1994, French and American researchers found that a two-month course of the antiviral drug AZT (Zidovudine) administered to HIV positive women in pregnancy during labour and delivery and after birth to their newborns reduced the rate of mother-to-child transmission by two-thirds in the absence of breast feeding. This preventive regimen is impossible to apply in many developing countries. Because, AZT is a very expensive drug and it is only available for the wealthy (UNAIDS Briefing Paper 1997). In Western countries the mother to child infection is found to be less due to effective voluntary testing and counseling, access to anti retroviral therapy, safe delivery practices and the widespread availability and safe use of breast milk substitutes (UNAIDS, August, 2001).

Poverty is the key reason for increasing pediatric transmission in developing countries. The women who are infected by HIV in developing countries are identified as poor and they are not in a position to avail anti retro viral drugs to prevent mother-to-child transmission. Besides, breast feeding is the common norm in most of the developing countries. Lack of awareness on supplementary feedings and lack of financial sources to avail such supplementary feeding force the women to depend only on breast feeding to their child. Therefore, the nursing mother has an increased risk of transmitting the virus to her infants.

The important factor which is responsible for mother to child transmission is lack of awareness and ignorance about the status of HIV infection. Most of the people are not interested to take up voluntary testing to know their HIV status owing to their risk behaviour. Therefore, many pregnant women are ignorant about their own infection and the need of taking anti-retroviral drug to prevent their babies from infection.

Stigma and Discrimination Associated with HIV/AIDS

Goffman (1963: 3) described stigma as "an attribute that is deeply discrediting within a particular social interaction". His explanation on stigma focuses on the public attitude toward a person who possesses an attribute that falls short of social expectations.

"Stigma" is a powerful tool of social control used to marginalize people. It can exclude people and can have great power over their lives with regard to social interaction. Generally, the public have a belief that they can get HIV by any kind of physical contact with the people infected with HIV positive. They also have a belief that the promiscuous individual alone can get HIV. The negative conception on HIV forces the public to treat the people infected with HIV very badly and indifferently. This problem of stigmatization is found all over the world. When people with HIV are treated as outcasts or as morally bad people, it is discrimination (PFA, 2004: 1).

HIV related stigma refers to all unfavorable attitudes, beliefs, and policies directed towards people perceived to have HIV/AIDS as well as towards their significant others and loved ones, close associates, social groups and communities. Patterns of prejudice, which include devaluing, discounting, discrediting and discriminating against these groups of people will strengthen the existing inequalities related to gender, sexuality and race.

Causes for HIV Related Stigma

According to Goffman (1963), diseases associated with the highest degree of stigma share following common attributes:

1. The person with the disease is seen as responsible for having the illness.

2. The disease is progressive and incurable
3. The disease is not well understood among the public
4. The symptoms cannot be concealed.

HIV infection has all these common attributes and attracts high level of stigmatization. First, people infected with HIV are often blamed for their life style and many people believe that HIV could be avoided if individuals made better moral decisions. The behaviours associated with HIV, for example, sex outside the marriage, sex between men, injecting drug use, and prostitution are already stigmatized in the society. Therefore, people infected with HIV positive are often thought of as responsible for infection. Second, although HIV is treatable, it is a progressive and incurable and life threatening disease. Third, HIV transmission is poorly understood by some people in general population. As a result of the poor knowledge and misconception, they scared of contracting HIV by accepting the presence of the people infected with HIV positive. Finally, although asymptomatic HIV infection can often be concealed, the symptoms of HIV related illness cannot be concealed. HIV related symptoms may be considered by the people as repulsive, ugly and disruptive to social interaction (Herek, 1999).

Impact of Stigma on the People Infected with HIV Positive

The stigma associated with HIV/AIDS prevents the high risk groups from taking up HIV test voluntarily. The delay in testing further increases the transmission of HIV. The discrimination and social stigma has made many people to be ignorant about their disease. The ignorance on the status of HIV leads to the spread of virus into the general population. Early detection of HIV infection is important. Knowledge of one's own HIV seropositivity can lead to earlier treatment and improved outcomes. Knowledge of seropositivity can also lead to changes in risk behaviours that can reduce or eliminate the risk of HIV transmission.

The nature of stigma also prevents the infected people by disclosing their HIV status in the society. Even after testing

HIV positive, many people have denied their seropositivity and many have not accepted their seropositivity status. The denial and hiding of the disease from others again aggravates the situations by spreading the disease to their sexual and needle injecting partners.

Delay in testing, denial and non-disclosure of the infection are major causes for the increasing rate of infection in the general populations.

Impact of Stigma on Women

Women's social and economic vulnerability and gender inequality make women to find difficulties in coping with the stigma and discrimination associated with HIV infection. HIV positive women bear a double burden: they are infected and they are women. HIV testing is a critical ingredient for receiving treatment or for accessing drugs to prevent the transmission of HIV from a woman to her child. But the woman is ostracized, marginalized and even killed as consequences of exposing her HIV status (*Hindu*, July 18, 2003). Since women are sexually, economically and biologically vulnerable to HIV/AIDS and other STDs, they are often stigmatized and blamed for "causing" HIV/AIDS and other STDs. Women are frequently identified as "reservoirs of infection" or as "vectors for transmission" to their male partners and their offspring. This inaccurate view on women by the public will neglect the focus on men's equal responsibility in preventing HIV/AIDS. It will also prevent the development of programmes to meet the needs of women to protect themselves from all sexually transmitted diseases including HIV/AIDS.

Generally, the people assume that if a woman has HIV infection, she has engaged with multiple sexual partners or engaged in prostitution. As a result, the infected woman's character is under the threat of assassination and such women are treated as "bad women". Many of such infected women have been dismissed from their jobs or not hired for jobs, evicted from their homes, abandoned by their husbands or other long-term partners, and denied the custody of their children, denied shelter and share of household property, refused access to treatment and care and often blamed for their husbands' HIV diagnosis. In addition, women perceived to be at risk of HIV infection have been denied health insurance.

Some countries have implemented mandatory testing schemes targeting women. Women who test positive or who are suspected of being infected suffer from increased discrimination, random and institutional violence, arrest, incarceration and deportation. Most often such testing is without the woman's informed consent, and without appropriate pretest and post test counseling (Digumarti Bhaskara Rao, 2000: 284).

In all regions women are expected to assume care giving responsibilities to the children and other family members who are sick. In the case of HIV/AIDS also women are expected to take care of their infected partners and it gives more stress and strain. Owing to sickness, loss of employment of the male partner forces her to take up employment outside the home to cope with loss of income of the male partners. When she becomes ill she will not get any one support to take care of herself.

Often women are blamed for husbands' HIV status. If the man is diagnosed HIV first, automatically the woman's fidelity is questioned by the husband and by her in-laws (Bharat, 2001). In case where the man has admitted his relationship with the sex workers, the burden of blame still falls on the wife for failing to "satisfy" her husband's sexual impulsions. These women were often isolated, shunned by family and friends, and become the target of abuse or gossip. Therefore, women infected with HIV positive tend to be more stigmatized than men due to social expectations of moral integrity. As a result, many women infected with HIV positive are experiencing violence in the homes (Sathiamoorthy and Suniti Solomon, 1997).

THEORETICAL FRAME FOR THE STUDY

Structural Functional Theory

Social structure refers to the recurrent and patterned relationship that exists among the components of social system. The social structures have interrelated and inter dependent parts in the form of institutions. Each institution or parts serves the function to maintain stability and equilibrium in the society at larger level for the existence of society and its members. The consequences which permit the adoption or adjustment of a system is called functions (Zanden, 1990: 29).

The social structure consists of invisible rules and institutional arrangements like family, religion, education, etc, to guide the behaviours of the individuals. The major assumption behind structural functionalism is to maintain stability, harmony in the society and to adopt changes according to new needs and demands through evolution. If any institution or parts of structure fails to perform its function, it will result in imbalance or disequilibrium in the society.

The social structure has two basic components – status and roles. Status refers to the individual's position and power in the society. It may be achieved or ascribed status. A status carries with it a set of culturally defined rights and duties. It is called roles. The norms of the structure specify the appropriate and inappropriate behaviour for the occupant of particular status.

According to functionalist perspectives, unequal distribution of social rewards is necessary to get the essential task of the society from its member to maintain harmony and equilibrium. Kingsley Davis and Wilbert Moore argued that social stratification is both universal and necessary, and hence no society is ever totally classless. In their view, all societies require stratification to fill all the statuses composing the social structure and motivate people to perform the duties associated with these positions (Zanden, 1990: 242).

For a functionalist, society is system, a combination of things or part that forms a larger whole. All the parts of the society are related to one another. Institutions such as family, religion, the economy, the state, education are among the crucial parts of any society. Changes in one institution have implication for other institution and for the society as a whole.

Robert K. Merton argues that the institutions and other parts of the society can contribute to the maintenance of the social system. But at the same time they can also do the opposite to other parts of the social system. The consequences that lessen the adoption or adjustment of the system are termed by him as dysfunctions. Merton also distinguishes between manifest and latent functions. Manifest functions are consequences that are intended and usually recognized by the participants in a system. Latent functions are consequences that are unintended and often not recognized (Turner, 2002: 87-97).

Durkheim argues that the social structure is made up of norms and values. It regulate the behaviour of the people which is considered as appropriate and worthy in different settings. According to him the individual can learn the normative behaviours through socialization. Socialization is a process which makes individuals become the members of society and makes social life possible. For Durkheim social solidarity is ensured by socialization. Durkheim's conceptualization of social systems in terms of "normal" and "pathological" states exclusively depends on the adoption and practices of culturally expected norms and values (functional needs) by the individual in the society (Jones, 2005: 37-40).

Talcott Parsons defined "social structure as a stable system of social interaction". Parsons takes "action" as the building block of the system. The term action refers to the behaviour of the individual. For Parsons, the cultural institutions of the society consist of cognitive beliefs, systems of expressive symbols and private moral obligations. The main function of the cultural system is the legitimation of the society's normative order. Cultural value patterns provide the most direct link between the social and cultural systems in legitimizing the normative order of society. They define what is appropriate and what is not, not necessarily in a moral sense but in accordance with the institutionalized order (Francis Abraham. M. 1982: 63). According to him the social system has the following characteristics (Turner, 2002: 58-65):

1. It involves a process of interaction between two or more individual
2. Each one of the individuals influences the another individual

3. Their interaction is mainly based on collective goal orientation or common value and of a consensus of normative and cognitive expectations.
4. The actor is confronted with a variety of situational conditions as societal environment t and ecological constrains
5. The actors' orientation to the situation is both motivational and value oriented.

It is evident from the structural functionalist perspectives, that members of society are expected to do their duties according to the norms and cultural values of the society.

For Weber, the society is existed because of social action. People do things because they decide to do so in order to achieve ends they desire. Having selected their goals, and taken account of the circumstances they find themselves in, they choose to act. Social structure is the outcome of such action; ways of living are the product of motivated choice. Existing action created social circumstances exercise constraint as structural forces but action is nonetheless still mental in origin – chosen in the light of the actor's perception of these structural constraints (Jones, 2003: 82)

Application of Structural functionalist theory to the present study

The individual has to act according to the norms and rules of the various institutions of the society. To fit in as a member of the society, the individual is learning all the culturally expected norms, values and rules from the childhood through various institutions like family, school, religious institutions, government etc. The individual is socialized in such a way as to act according to the norms and values of the society. The individual should not think of deviating from the laid norms and values of the society.

Indian society is highly a culture-bound society. The individual behaviours are encircled by the rigid norms, values, rules, moral codes, mores and traditions of the society. The Indian culture and traditions have a belief that the adoption of culturally expected norms and values alone help to maintain harmony and equilibrium in the society. It also has a fear that if the individual is allowed to act according to his own choice without giving importance to values of the culture, the Indian society will lose is credibility, reliability and integrity.

Family, marriage, religion and community are the important institutions which serve to socialize the individual in accordance with the cultural expectations of the society. Gender-related behaviours status and roles and sex and sexuality are learned by the individual due to the influence of these institutions. The society's norms regulate sexual behaviour by specifying who may engage in sexual behaviour with whom and under what circumstances. The Indian society is very rigid in regulating the sexual activities of the individual with the cover of silence around the sex. Discussing sexual matter is considered as taboo in India. The people are not allowed to discuss sex and sexuality with any one including spouse. As a result, fear is created among the people to learn or collect information related to sex and sexuality.

In India, family and marriage are highly valued. The individuals are expected to engage in sex only after marriage. Sex outside wedlock is highly devalued in the society. The pre marital and the extra marital sexual relationship will entirely damage the life of the people who engage in such activities. If such relationship is known to others, the particular individual has to face stigma and discrimination in the society. Murders due to extra or pre marital relationship are frequently reported in the local newspapers and magazines of India.

Indian society is patriarchal. Men are the dominant figures in the family. The women are expected to have the character of ideal wifehood. It means the husband must be considered as God and the wife should be faithful to him even if the husband has deviant behaviour and seek pleasure outside the marriage. The good wife must never do anything that would displease her husband. According to Manu – the Hindu code maker–"Women must particularly be guarded against evil inclinations. If they are not guarded, 3they will bring sorrow on both the families" (Kapadia, 1966: 254). Manu therefore wants woman to be under the surveillance of her father in her childhood, her husband in her youth and her sons on the death of her husband. "A woman should never think of independence from the father, the husband or the sons because by so doing she will make both the families contemptible." Her status is determined only through her reproductive capacity. She is expected to bear children, that too male children. As per social norms male has to take decision with regard to family matters. The male has to decide the contraception to control the birth.

But normally, the safe sex is not a rule in family among the spouses. Therefore, in the era of HIV/AIDS infection, women are subjected to the infection as a result of unsafe sexual behaviour.

With regard to marriage, age difference between bride and bridegroom is strictly maintained in the society. The bride must be younger than the bridegroom. This age gap further strengthens the inequality and low status of women. As a result of younger age, the woman can not raise her voice against her husband's sexual domination on her body. The hidden aspect of sex and sexuality which is deep rooted in the culture prevents the woman to gain knowledge on her reproductive health. According to the traditional norms of good woman, she cannot practice it in her life if she knows little knowledge about reproductive health.

Even the friendship between male and female is not encouraged in the society. The girl must be away from the boy. As far as sex is concerned, men are also not encouraged to involve or experience sex outside wedlock. As per religion and culture it is immoral. Sex is related to morality in India. If any one deviates from this norm he will be treated as an immoral person. Therefore, the secret behind sex influence the weak minded men as a result of poor socialization to experience it with the sex workers. The same secrecy prevents men to use condom to safeguard from sexually transmitted diseases. Once he is infected he will take the virus to his innocent wife and children through his wife.

In Indian society irrespective of regions, cultural taboo is associated with sex and it is not a open topic for discussion in the family and society. Religion also promotes the culture of silence around sex and it imposes virginity on women rather than men. Such kind of cultural notion and peer pressure encourages men to have an experience with sex outside their marital bond. Besides in every society the individual have certain status and accordingly roles. The society is expected value-oriented action or use of value rationality to satisfy their sexual urge. The individuals' irrational action is responsible for acquiring HIV infection for both men and women who have sex outside marriage. The infection among the spouse and children affect the institution of the family. It will question the socialization of the individual in the family with regard to morality and moral values of the stability of the family. If the institution of family is affected it will bring adverse changes in the institution of economy, government, politics, education etc. In turn it affects the social health and social fabric of whole society by bringing imbalance and disequilibrium among the different parts of the social structure.

Therefore, the structural functional aspects of society are responsible for acquiring as well as spread of HIV infection in India.

Theories of anomie and alienation

According to Durkheim, the mechanical solidarity is achieved in the traditional society where the simple division of labour and the feeling of togetherness exist. But in modern society there are so many different roles to be played and so many different ways are possible. Durkheim believed that human beings are not naturally consensual. He believed that if it is left to our own devices, we are anti-social. He pointed out that during time of rapid social change people become unsure of what is expected of them, and they find it difficult to fashion their actions in terms of conventional norms. Old norms do not seem relevant to current conditions and emerging norms are too ambiguous and poorly formulated to provide effective and meaningful guidelines for behaviours. Under these circumstances, Durkheim believed, an upsurge in deviant behaviour could be expected. The individual has unlimited desires and it can be regulated by a moral force. The moral power is superior to the individual and he must accept the social and moral expectation to maintain social solidarity. But any abrupt transition such as economic disorder, industrial crisis or sudden prosperity can cause a deregulation of a normative structure. As a result the mechanism of solidarity breaks down and normlessness ensures. Durkheim called this situation as **anomie.**

For Merton, social structure consists of culturally approved goals and institutionalized means to achieve the goals. Merton defined anomie as the disjunction between cultural goal and institutionalized means. The process where by exaltation of the end generates a literal demoralization and de-institutionalization (Francis Abraham, 1981: 181). Merton identified the following five responses to the end-means dilemma and the violation of which culturally adopted means leads to anomie (Zonden 1990: 210-211).

1. **Conformity**: It exists when people accept both the cultural goals and the culturally approved means to achieve the goal. Such behaviour is the bed rock of stable society.
2. **Innovation**: The individual accepts the cultural goals but rejects the approved means.
3. **Ritualism**: It involves the abandoning or scaling down of the lofty cultural goals but accept the cultural means.
4. **Retreatism**: Rejection of both cultural goals and cultural means and without substituting new norms for them.
5. **Rebellion**: Rejection of both cultural goals and cultural means and substitute new norms for them.

According to Merton anomie refers to a property of a social system, not to the state of mind of this or that individual within the system.

The concept of **alienation** was first used by Karl Marx. For Marx, the history of mankind is not only a history of class struggle but also the increasing alienation of man. In the capitalist society, the estranged or alienated labour involves four aspects: the worker's alienation from the object he produces, from the process of production, from himself and from community of his fellow men. Marx felt that when the labours are devalued and sink to the level of commodity, he/she will *get* *al.*ienated. Marx has identified two "hostile power" which render labour and its product alien. One is the capitalist who commands production and the other is the economic system which governs the behaviour of capital and the process of production (Marx, 1964: 124).

Treating alienation from the personal standpoint of the actor Melvin Seeman found five basic ways in which the concept of alienation has been used:

1. Powerlessness,
2. Meaninglessness,
3. Normlessness,
4. Loneliness and
5. Self-estrangement (Francis Abraham, 1982: 199).

Scnacht argued that the individual may *get al.*ienated due to loneliness, exclusion from social and cultural participation, lack of identification with other's views, interests and tastes, dissatisfaction in social relations, lack of job satisfaction, feeling of powerlessness, dissociation from popular culture, dissociation from societal values, rejection of societal behavioural norms and incomprehensibility of events (Abraham, 1982: 199).

Application of theory of anomie and alienation to the present study

The contemporary society is a highly complex society. Unlike traditional society the individuals are expected to perform different roles to meet the challenges of life. As a result of urbanization, industrialization, modernization and globalization, the present society is witnessing frequent changes. The rapid changes taking place in the society increase the inequality with unequal distribution of wealth and means to meet the ends. It has the characteristics of materialism, consumerism, exploitation and dehumanization. Modernity eroded the faith in ethics. It has given farewell to God and its related religious faith and moral values and norms. The society became fit for the person who knows the tactics of extracting the benefit without evaluating its morality.

The people, especially the migrants, illiterates, marginalized groups including women and poor, unemployed, and the rich who always have the intention of enjoying all worldly affairs find very difficult to satisfy their needs by using conventional norms. For them, the old norms are unsuitable to earn for their livelihood and/or to satisfy their needs. The emerging new norms are too confusing and it has not helped them for their empowerment and modifies their behaviour. As a result of normlessness the individual gives more importance to fulfill his desires rather than societal expectations.

HIV/AIDS emerged and spread nook and corner of the world as a result of the risk behaviour of individual. These individuals have not given importance to culturally accepted norms in the society. Poverty and other economical crises forced some women to fulfil their goal of survival by violating culturally approved means of earning and taken prostitution as a means for survival. Their sexual involvement with different customers increases the chances of getting HIV infection.

For sex, marriage is the only means which is approved by the society. Sex outside the marriage is considered as deviant behaviour. But the migrants and the others who have sexual impulsion find prostitution as an easily available source to satisfy their sexual urge. It increases the chances of getting and spreading HIV infection. The prevailing normlessness in the society created number of deviants including drug addicts and criminals. They find lot of confusion to match their life with the new norms emerging as a result of modernization.

The survival strategy makes them frustrated and to become addicts either by using heroin or using injecting drugs. They have a false hope that it will help to forget their problems to some extent in subconscious mind. As a result of frustration, the injecting drug users often seek sex with sex workers without realizing their risk and the need for safe sex. Their unsafe sexual behaviour increases the risk of getting HIV infection not only for them but also for the sex workers. If the infected people have other sexual partner/wives or if they get married they will infect the innocent women.

The individual is not the only person responsible for the spread of HIV infections in the world. The society is responsible for individual's risk behaviour. Because the rapidly changing society has increased the gap between rich and poor and it has not distributed the resources equally to all people. The people who have more resources and who have the capacity to control the flow of resources are more powerful and they try to exploit the powerless by devaluing their rights. The present economic system also favours only to the growth and benefit of economically, socially, politically and intellectually wealthy people. The sense of powerlessness, meaninglessness, normlessness, isolation and self-estrangement of the individual causes alienation not only from himself but also from his goal, means and community and the world to a larger extent. The conflict with the present situation forces alienated individual to take another option as means to survival. The poor, poverty stricken and under privileged women who are alienated as a result of their economic suppression and domination of economically powerful people and have chosen prostitution as a alternative means for their survival. Similarly are the exploited, low skilled, unskilled and unemployed people who are involved in migration as a result of the alienation due to their devolution in the local areas. Their separation from the spouses influences them to satisfy their sexual urge through sex workers and get infection.

The infected individuals are isolated from the society. They will not get support and care from their primary relationship and they are excluded from social and cultural participation. They loose their identity with others. The infected individuals also normally develop the feelings of powerlessness and inability to influence others to get support and help. They develop the sense of feeling that their rights are denied and their life is made meaningless by the non infected and so called conservative people in the society. Their disassociation from the normal social network as a result of their infection make them to get al.ienated and forces them even to the extent of committing suicide.

The stigma and discrimination affects different segments of population in different ways. The revelation is based on the nature of infection. The women who got infection through their husbands will easily reveal their status to their family members rather than sex workers and who got infection through their promiscuous relationship and pre marital sex. Though the discrimination have no bond, the house wives may get little support from their parents and sympathy from their relatives, friends and neighbours.

The spread effect is more in India due to the severity of anomie among the infected individual and non-revelation of HIV status in the society.

Jurgen Habermas Neo-Conflict theories or Critical theories

Habermas argued that expecting revolution from the proletariat class in the contemporary society is meaningless. They are now a pampered class of people within the trap of the capitalist class. In such situation, Habermas puts his critical theory of communication and domination. According to Habermas, we must talk to each other in order to find common ground and establish a consensus with the others over meaning. It is because we are capable of being rational and reasonable to co-exist with others in our every day social encounters. So long as the parties to a communicative exchange have an equal opportunity to state their views, so long as they treat each other as equals and honest, the agreement on the issues can be easily obtained. In other words, so long as an encounter is approached rationally with reason, the differences can be overcome (Jones, 2005: 171).

In order to solve the problem of domination, Hebermas suggests the construction of an ideal speech community. His main point is that purposive rationality penetrates every day practices, especially every day communications. His ideal speech community has the features of

(i) all individuals capable of speech can participate in the debate,

(ii) all individuals have equal right to give their reasons for their stated position and

(iii) no individual can be denied the right to participate in the debate (Doshi, 2003: 475-76).

Application of Habermas Neo-conflict theories/ critical theories in the present study

Women are the marginalized segments in the institution of family under the domination of patriarchal culture. The domination of male over the female is also supported by the religion and the commercial economic system of the country. The women are not given much opportunity to express their opinion related to the issues which affect them adversely. As far as sexual relationship is concerned, they are denied the rights of communication with their sexual partners. The lack of communication is the major factor for the spread of infection among the women in India. The communication/information disseminated through various print and visual media has created sufficient knowledge and awareness about AIDS and its implication on the society. No doubt, the women and men have some knowledge about AIDS and its prevention. The communication between spouses or between sexual partners with regard to safe sex is essential to prevent the infection between them. Women should be given equal opportunities to state their views with regard to sex and sexuality. If male partner treat the women as equal and honest they can easily arrive consensus with regard to the use of condom as preventive method for all sexually transmitted infections.

The stigma based hidden status of HIV infection affects not only the infected individual but also their family. The infected individual undergoes traumatic experiences due to non-communication of their feelings and inflectional status either to their marital partners or to their family members. The implication of non-communication with regard to HIV infection at level of individual, family and community may bring adverse impact in the spread of infection to the larger society.

Therefore, communication at all level is the urgent need to prevent and control the rate of HIV infection in all societies.

Significance of Present Study

Women become the epicenter of HIV/AIDS epidemic in India and in almost all parts of the country, the epidemic is feminized without realizing the circumstances leading to infection. The infected women are subjected to discrimination, abuse and violence. The stigma and discrimination may affect their social interaction in the social system. The present study is undertaken to fulfill the research gap by identifying the circumstances leading to HIV/AIDS, socio-economic conditions of women infected with HIV positive, circumstances leading to prostitution, sexual behaviour after infection, changes taken place in the social interaction of the women infected with HIV positive and attitude of infected women towards pregnancy and child birth.

Chapterisation

The present study is comprised of seven chapters arranged in systematic sequence. The First chapter presents an introduction of women infected with HIV positive with a brief account of causes and consequences of HIV on women. The Second chapter presents review of literature related to the study. The Third chapter deals with the methodology adopted to conduct the present study, which includes objectives, operational definition of the concept, sampling procedure and sample size, tools of data collection and method of analysis. A comprehensive view on the global scenario of HIV/AIDS is presented in the Fourth chapter. The Fifth chapter analyses the primary data with a view to derive findings based on the objectives designed for the study. The Sixth chapter contains major findings, suggestions and conclusion of the study. The implication of research in the form of Action Plan towards prevention and control of HIV/AIDS, care and support and relief and rehabilitation of HIV/AIDS affected people with the goal of creating AIDS free society is presented in the Seventh chapter.

2

Review of Literature

It is important to mention various studies and surveys related to HIV/AIDS for making a modest attempt towards greater understanding of the issue focused. The review of literature is focused on the issues related to socio-economic factors and HIV/AIDS, high risk behaviour and HIV/AIDS, stigma and discrimination, violence against women and HIV/AIDS, reproductive health and HIV/AIDS, women's knowledge on HIV/AIDS, impact of HIV/AIDS and intervention taken by both government and non-governmental organizations.

Social and Economic Factors and HIV/AIDS

Prakasa Rao and Nandini Rao (1982: 11-37) described that in India, marriage was treated as an alliance between two families rather than a mere union of two individuals and the traditional normative patterns did not provide any opportunity to the prospective spouses to participate in the decision making process of their own marriage and it is largely arranged by parents on the basis of matching of horoscope.

Ramasamy *et al.* (1988: 179-187) have discussed the relationship between promiscuity and family pathology. They have concluded that promiscuity is deeply ingrained in the personality of the individual and is a product of early life experiences. Thus the family and its impact on the individual are very vital in determining the activities of a person.

Ryder *et al.* (1989: 1637-42) study based in Kinshasa indicates that the deprivations caused by poverty itself lead to faster development of AIDS among women, even increasing the likelihood of that their new born children will be HIV positive.

Luciano Sandala *et al.* (1994: S61-68) studied the relationship between "dry sex" practices and HIV infection in Lusaka, Zambia. A cross sectional study was carried out in a sexually transmitted diseases clinic in Lusaka among 329 women aged 15-50 years. The study identified 58% of seroprevalence among the sample but no practice was statistically significantly associated with HIV.

Alessandro Cozzi Lepri *et al.* (1995: 1151-55) have conducted a study among 854 HIV infected women and men in Italy to evaluate the influence of gender in HIV disease progression. Their findings were:

1. The risk of CD4 lymphocyte count declining below 200 was not significantly different between women and men.
2. Progression to AIDS was slightly slower among women than men. The cumulative mortality from AIDS tended to be lower in women than in men but the difference is not significant.

Gangakhedkar *et al.* (1997: 2000-92) studied the risk of HIV infection among the monogamous married women attending sexually transmitted clinics in Pune, India. The study has compared the incidence of HIV and other STDs among 525 female sex workers with 391 other women (almost all of whom were married and reported only on sexual partner) and identified that 50 per cent of sex workers and 14 per cent of other women were HIV positive. Over all, 43 per cent of the sex workers and 65 per cent of the other women were diagnosed as having one or more genital infections. The study also found that among the sex workers, HIV seropositivity was associated with inconsistent condom use, genital ulcers and genital warts. Among the other women, only having a partner who had been diagnosed with an STD predicted HIV infection. The investigators of the study reported that the married women have a belief that they are at low risk because they have only one partner. The authors concluded that an increasing proportion of women and infants in India will become infected with HIV if we have not heightened efforts to disseminate information about HIV and other STDs.

Schoultz, Ksristan Kay (1998: 1327) have undertaken an exploratory study to understand the ways in which fundamental social structures and cultural factors contribute to different levels of Sexually Transmitted Infection vulnerability in Hausa society in Niamey, Niger. The study results suggest that those Hausa men and women who express the strongest social ties to the systems and beliefs of the modern world are best equipped to protect themselves and are therefore least socially vulnerable to sexually transmitted infections, while those who maintain more traditional beliefs and practices have fewer effective resources upon which to rely for protection from infection and are therefore more socially vulnerable. Within this evolving social stratification, there are important differences between men and women which ultimately place women at an overall disadvantage relative to men in terms of social vulnerability to sexually transmitted infections. The data collected for the study suggest that until efforts are made to address the effects of the social structural and cultural factors which contribute to gender differentials in sexually transmitted infection risk, and individual-action (or "lifestyle") approach to sexually transmitted infection risk reduction is unlikely to be successful.

Rwabukwali, Charles Barwogeza, (1998: 3976) have studied the "Gender, poverty and AIDS in Kabarole, in Western Uganda" to understand and unravel the complex interaction between cultural norms and women's social and economic dependency, and how these limit Batoro women's ability to reduce their risk of HIV infection through safer sexual practices. Specially, the study aims to identify the socio-cultural and sexual behavioral pasterns that influence the vulnerability of Batoro women to increased risk of HIV infection. The study found that most of the women in the sample were complying with government advice to reduce the number of sexual partners, and to be faithful to one's spouse in order to avoid AIDS. However, a range of cultural, economic, and social factors, including gender inequality and male sexual behaviour combine to maintain women's vulnerability to HIV infection. Most women believe that their best chance of avoiding AIDS is to become economically independent of men. Therefore, the author suggested taking socio-cultural and economic factors into account when introducing AIDS control programs, and the need for co-ordination at all levels with regard to service delivery for AIDS control.

Hirve and Sathe (1999: 17) have identified that increased mobility owing to increased urbanization and industrialization is the major cause for higher vulnerability of HIV infection in the regions of Maharasthra and the increased mobility of men and their unsafe sex with sex workers increases women's vulnerability to HIV and other sexually transmitted diseases.

Martin S.L *et al.* (1999: 417-426) studied the domestic abuse in five districts of Uttar Pradesh and found that 18-45 per cent of husbands were physically abused their wives due to poverty and lack of education. Economical backwardness is taken as a tool for men to discriminate the women. The condition become worst if they are infected with HIV/AIDS.

Karen Hardee *et al.* (1999: 52-59) have studied reproductive health policies and programmes in eight countries – three in Asia (Bangladesh, India and Nepal), three in the Middle East and Africa (Jordan, Ghana and Senegal) and two in Latin America and the Caribbean (Jamaica and Peru). It is found from this study that India is targeting on specific method called female sterilization as a family planning programme since 1967. As of 1992-1993, 41 per cent of married women aged 13-49 used a method, with female sterilization accounting for 75 per cent of all modern methods of birth control. It is evident from this study that the Indian women were very conscious to avoid birth rather than infection and once they undergone sterilization they were not bothered about using condom to safeguard themselves from sexually transmitted diseases. Such behaviour among women is also one of the causes for increasing HIV infection among women in India.

Karuppaih (2000) has studied the Socio-cultural and economic correlates of HIV/AIDS in Madras City. His analysis indicated that the economically poor and illiterate and primary school educated people were more vulnerable to HIV/AIDS infection due to high risk behaviour and lack of or poor knowledge on HIV/AIDS and prevention and control measures.

Digumarti Baskara Rao (2000: 101-105) has studied the women's susceptibility to HIV epidemic. His study revealed that the most of the women who are infected by HIV are wives and other partners and these women are becoming infected through sexual transmission at a significantly younger age than men and most of the girls and young women are in their teens and early twenties. The direct function of power relations between men and women and, in particular, or men's sexual identity, illiteracy and lack of access to information are the major factors for the infection of women identified from the study.

Elizabeth Reid (2000: 120) studied the factors affecting the lives of young women which make them vulnerable to HIV infection. According to the study, the prevalence patterns of HIV infection are known to be a factor of poverty, social and geographic mobility, commerce, tourism, social disruption and civil unrest.

Myo Thani (2000: 148) argued that the poor women are severely affected by the AIDS epidemic in Southeast Asia. He says that the AIDS epidemic is becoming a women's disease for two reasons. One is, as the epidemic spreads to more areas and progresses from being a disease of a few subgroups to that of the larger population, more and more women become infected. The second is, the epidemic affects women, especially poor women due to biological, sociological and economic reasons. According to him, epidemiologically, the virus is more easily transmitted from men to women than the other way round and women frequently lack control over their own sexual lives or those of their husbands outside the marriage, even though extra marital relations, as well as intravenous drug abuse or bisexual behaviour, are possible routes for the entry of the HIV into the marital union.

The author also reported that the women's ability to insist on protected sex is affected by socio-cultural barriers to women as decision makers, limited literacy, mobility and access to information and cultural and moral attitudes towards sexuality. According to him women may not be able to discuss sexual matters in public, or even with their husbands and social and sexual passivity make insistence on the use of condoms as protection against HIV infection difficult.

Syamala Nataraj (2002: 36-40) has studied the women in prostitution in Chennai, Tamil Nadu. According to her study a prostitute does not earn only for herself; she sells sex for her children, for her family. A study conducted by her shows that over 60 per cent of the women in prostitution are dalits and 50 per cent maintain independent households. The author has concluded that continuing gender discrimination and the failure of the State to provide opportunities for women to ensure education and economic independence is the single largest factor that fuels the entry of women into prostitution.

Naomi Rutenberg (2002: 3) explored that HIV prevalence is high in communities where early age of child bearing is common. Adolescent boys and girls may place themselves at risk of HIV to realize their child bearing preference.

Kelly and Gray (2003: 446-451) studied the "age differences in sexual partners and risk of HIV-1 infection in rural Uganda" and identified the positive relationship between age of the partners and HIV infections. The study found that the risk of HIV infection doubles for adolescent women with male partners ten or more years older.

Ann E. Biddlecom, (2004: 66-67) explained that certain social, cultural and economic factors are attributed with women which make more vulnerable to HIV/AIDS. Their study shows that sexual activity tends to start earlier for women, particularly because women marry at younger ages (and therefore have more regular sexual intercourse) than men and many young women are married to much older men (often a decade or more older), who are likely to have had sex with several different partners in the past. Some of them will therefore have and STI, including HIV, and may transmit it to their young wives. Their study also reveals that women experiences sexual abuse and rape more than men and poverty push women, especially young women to risk their lives by accepting money or goods in exchange for unsafe sex.

They also stressed the importance of recognizing social constraints in combating the spread of HIV/AIDS. According to them HIV/AIDS is not a disease that individuals can prevent alone and married women have to bear much of the HIV/AIDS burden in many parts of the world, so the ABC approach (Abstain, Be faithful, use of Condom) is generally ineffective for them. Therefore, abstinence does not make sense within marriage, while monogamy and condom use require both partner's cooperation.

The Hindu (2004: November 30) has published the article of David C. Mulford, U.S Ambassador to India. The article argued that HIV/AIDS is the most serious public health a challenge facing India today and India is at critical juncture in the epidemic. The article also revealed that in India 36 per cent of the people estimated to be infected with HIV are women, and it has the potential to have much higher number in future. The same issue also shares that in sub-Saharan Africa, the proportion is 57 per cent. Young girls are particularly vulnerable and in some African communities, as many as 20 per cent of girls aged 15-19 years are infected, compared to just 5 per cent of boys the same age. World wide, almost 50 per cent of HIV positive people are women.

The report further revealed that HIV is spreading rapidly among females for many reasons. The lower status of women and girls and practices such as male infidelity, prostitution, child sexual abuse, and ex trafficking are factors. In addition, male-to-female HIV transmission during sex is twice as likely to occur as female-to-male transmission. The report also indicated that the rate of female injecting drug use, another common way HIV/AIDS is transmitted, is increasing.

The Hindu (2004: December 1) in its editorial on "Women at Risk" argued that women are being infected at an alarming rate primarily because of ignorance, socio-cultural biases, poverty and sexual abuse and violence. The report says that the vulnerability of women to HIV/AIDS is a huge challenge to the societies which have severely discriminatory attitudes towards women. It quoted the *AIDS Epidemic Update 2004* released by the Joint United Nations Programme on HIV/AIDS

(UNAIDS) and the World Health Organistions and reveled that the rise in infection is at its peak in East Asia, Eastern Europe and Central Asia and half of the infected adult population of 37.2 million people (aged 15-49) are women, marking a steady rise from 47 per cent in 1998.

The editorial further revealed that in India, 25 per cent of all newly infected are women and the increasing trend is mainly because of some states inadequate prevention efforts which allowed men to engage in high-risk behaviour to transmit the virus to women with whom they have a regular relationship. These women are often unable to negotiate safe sex, within marriage or outside, for variety of reasons including the transmission from drug injectors. According to the editorial, Chennai has on of the highest HIV prevalence rates among pregnant women in the country, and 64 per cent of drug injectors in the city were also found to be positive in 2003.

The editorial also revealed that the World AIDS Day on 2004 has been dedicated to the concerns of women. The idea is to highlight the links between gender inequality and the epidemic.

The Hindu (2004: December 5) has given an insight with regard to HIV/AIDS epidemic in India. It has revealed that the epidemic in India is no longer confined to high-risk groups or urban populations but is gradually spreading into rural areas and the general population and the younger women are most vulnerable to infection. According to the report, the number of women infected is steadily rising in India and one in every four AIDS reported is a women and 37 per cent of the cases is found among the sexually active age group of 15-29 years. Rural women are particularly vulnerable to being infected as they have less access to health care and information on HIV/AIDS. The report further says that it is the marriage, not promiscuity or other high risk behaviour makes the vast majority of the Indian women vulnerable to HIV.

National Institute of Social Defence (2004: 8) claims that married women in India are more susceptible to HIV/AIDS as they have no control over the sexual behaviour of their husbands. It further reported that increasing levels of HIV infection is found among Indian women, who, are largely in monogamous relationship. It says that these women have virtually no control over their husbands' sexual behaviour and the disease is spreading to rural areas through migrant labourers and truckers. As a large number of women become infected, the number of children infected through vertical transmission is also likely to increase, says the same report.

Kalpana Sharma (2005: 3) studied the contraceptive option available for women to avoid pregnancy and abortions in Uttar Pradesh. The study says that in theory, women are supposed to be given a choice in contraception methods, but in reality, the only choice before them is sterilization through tubectomies. According to the study the total number of sterilizations performed in U.P, 97 per cent are done on women and these sterilized women were never thinks about the need of safe sex.

Thinamalar (2005: January 1) has published that one-fourth of the new infection in India is occurred among women and 90 per cent of these women had sex only with their husbands. Therefore, majority of the married women in India have got infection through their husbands.

High Risk Behaviour and HIV/AIDS

Jeff Goodwin (1978: 17) studied cause for high risk social movements in the Huk Rebellion in Philippines during 1946-54. The study has documented "sex opportunism", which is often described as "sex problem", as a cause for high risk behaviour for the men involved in Huk Rebellion. He described that the men were unhappy without women and the substantial number of married men within the Huk movement were engaged in extra marital sexual relations with women in the Huk camps in the Sierra Madre. It shows the ground reality of men's sex and sexuality in the context of HIV/AIDS.

Potterat (1985: 329) examined the concept of susceptibility and exposure for explaining women's reasons for entering the sex industry. The susceptibility model contends that psychological characteristics (e.g. alienation, feeling of worthlessness) in conjunction with traumatic events (e.g. incest), predispose some women to the lure of prostitution. The exposure model predicts that interpersonal contact with and inducement from significant others involved in the sex industry (eg. friends, family members), lead to personal involvement.

John *et al.* (1987) has described that HIV infection has become rampant among high-risk groups in the coastal states of Maharashtra and Tamil Nadu and among injecting drug users in northeastern India including Manipur and Nagaland. Their report also showed that the spread of infection to the general population is mainly due to the unsafe behaviour of high risk groups.

Hospedales (1988: 32) study explain that heterosexual contacts could become the main source of infection and that it could therefore spread to the general population of Europe and United States. This study also revealed that many homosexuals are often also bisexual and the wives of these men are not aware of these customs and of their risk of infection.

Bongaarts (1988: 4-6) identified that the probability of infection depends on the frequency of sexual contact, prevalence of infection in the contact group, and the rate of partner change. The infectiousness of partner is a function of gender (male-to-female transmission is more efficient), stage of disease (individuals with AIDS or symptomatic HIV disease are most infectious), and the use of condoms.

Schneider (1989: 74) study showed that in the United States and Western Europe intravenous drug users (IVDU) represent a considerable fraction of all AIDS cases. In Italy 62 per cent of all HIV positive cases are found among IVDUs. In the Federal Republic of Germany the relative proportion of female AIDS cases is increasing mainly due to intravenous drug use. Of the AIDS cases among women, 57 per cent had a history of intravenous drug use. In the United States, 8 per cent of diagnosed AIDS cases are among women. Half of these are caused by drug use and 21 per cent of them were sexual partners of drug users.

Bhave *et al.* (1992) report revealed that the seroprevalence is raising among high risk groups, particularly among sex workers. Her survey showed the increasing trend of seropositivity among sex workers by one per cent of infection among sex workers in 1987, 18 per cent in 1990 and 34 per cent in 1992. The survey result revealed the potential risk of spreading HIV infection among general population by increasing the infection rate among women attending antenatal clinics.

Elford *et al.* (1993) has said that the predominant mode of infection in India is heterosexual intercourse. Their article also revealed that India has to face severe impact due to HIV/AIDS as a result of its population growth.

Thomas Cox and Bal. K. Suvedi (1994: 7) have studied the sexual networking in five urban areas in the Nepal Terai. Epidemiological evidence suggests that the principal route of AIDS transmission is heterosexual with commercial sex fueling the current spread of HIV in Nepal. According to their study, high prevalence of sexually transmitted diseases (STDs) and low rates of condom use facilitates HIV transmission in Nepal. In addition, lack of public awareness, related to the country's low rate of literacy, a shortage of appropriate AIDS education message, and strong cultural prohibitions against the public discussion of sex further contribute to the problem. This study also identified that the transport workers are the major clients of sex workers and because of their mobility they became the core group of potential transmitters of HIV.

Jeanette J. Rodrigues *et al.* (1995: 723-25) have studied the risk factors for HIV infection in people attending clinics for sexually transmitted diseases in India among 2800 patients in Pune, India. The study has concluded that in India the prevalence of HIV infection is alarmingly high among female sex workers and men attending clinics for sexually transmitted diseases. It also found high prevalence of HIV infection in monogamous, married women who denied any history of sex working. The study also revealed that high risk sexual behaviour, including lack of condom use and high number of sexual partners are the main cause for the infection of STDs. The dramatic increase in prevalence of HIV-1 in these high risk groups suggests there is an urgent need for comprehensive and national efforts in India to control sexually transmitted diseases and to provide intensive education on HIV and AIDS targeted at changing high risk behaviour.

Hardman (1997: 20) argued that economic vulnerability force women into streets and he also stated that because of women's restricted access to financial and material resources, some women may resort to prostitution as a resistance or response to poverty. In other wards, according to the author, prostitution may be viewed as an active coping strategy in the face of privation.

APAC (1998: 25) has studied the community prevalence of sexually transmitted disease in Tamil Nadu among 2000 people (both male and female) in three districts of Tamil Nadu. The study has concluded that (i) the prevalence of any STD condition in Tamil Nadu was 15.8% and this fell in the high endemic rate for the community and the classical STD remains 9.7% in the study community. (ii) The age group maximum at risk for any STD was 30-39 years. (iii) Prevalence of HIV among women was higher than men. (iv) While all STD were widely prevalent in both rural and urban population, HIV appear to be more prevalent in the rural areas than in urban. (v) Genital discharge and sexual complaints were very common and were reported in upto 38% of the population.

Pottert (1998: 333-40) examined the sequences and timing of prostitution entry and drug use among the women involved in prostitution. The study showed that among the regular drug users, 66 per cent use drug prior to entering prostitution, for 18 per cent drug use and prostitution occurred concurrently and 17 per cent take drug following their entry into prostitution.

APAC (1998) report on third wave surveillance survey among 558 respondents of various risk groups in Tamil Nadu revealed the marital status of the people who had multiple sex partners. The report shows that the majority of the sex workers are married and the level of illiteracy was high among sex workers. Majority of the commercial sex workers are engaged in full-time sex trade. Women engaged in occupation like vegetable/ fruits vendors, house-maid, construction workers, workers in film industry, person in other petty trades also practises commercial sex and they constituted 53% of the commercial sex workers respondents. Majority of the unmarried female factory workers (44.8%), male factory workers (48%), truckers

(42.8%) and helpers 42.8%) are found to be unmarried in this survey. These high risk groups are the potential sources for spreading the dreaded virus HIV into the general population.

APAC report on Sixth Wave with regard to HIV Risk Behaviour Surveillance Survey among 6195 high risk population in Tamil Nadu and 4980 in Pondicherry has captured certain salient findings in which the truckers and helpers perceive that sex with casual partners is not risky and there is an emotional relationship with casual partners and sex becomes more enjoyable without condoms. They also perceive that AIDS is curable as lot of advertisements in the recent days are promoting on remedies. Besides, as far as commercial sex workers are concern that they have perceived that having sex without condom with regular partners is not risky. The intravenous drug users perceived that their involvement in drug decrease their sexual potency and therefore they involved in paid sex. The men seeking sex with men perceived that sex with men is not risky and it is safe and no need of using condom

Krishnamurthy *et al.* (1998: 39-48) study on HIV/AIDS and Safe Sex Practices among Female Sex workers in India is an exploratory study and it explored the profile of female sex workers and their sex practices. As per the study result the female sex workers had a mean age of 31.23 years and more than 60 per cent of them were married. The number of respondents married and living with their husband was almost equal to those respondents were unmarried. Illiteracy is the common features and they had no sources of income other than commercial sex. The study also revealed that the commercial sex workers are part of the floating population in many towns, especially where commercial sex activity is seasonal. Many commercial sex workers go to tourist centers, places of pilgrimage and large towns. The commercial sex workers interviewed for this study engage in different patterns of soliciting as all of them move around in different places. The brothel based commercial sex workers reportedly used public places for direct soliciting. However, 52 per cent of the commercial sex workers reported that soliciting is done at bus stands, 36.3 per cent from the streets and 33.4 per cent from other public places like railway stations, parks beaches, temples and cinema theatres. Indirect soliciting was through pimps, 16.3 per cent through brothel keepers, three per cent through auto drivers, clients, friends and relatives and through phone calls 18.4 per cent. It was found that most of the commercial sex workers did not feel it necessary to use condoms with regular partners and they used to have a sexual intercourse with clients though they have symptoms of infections.

Lakshmi Bai *et al.* (1998: 59-64) study on "High Risk Behaviour" stated that many men knowingly or out of sheer ignorance pursues such risks unmindful of the consequences. Hetero-sexuality is one such risky activity where man indulges for temporary pleasure. This illicit or extra marital indulgence is an open invitation to a dreaded scourge, may be STD or AIDS or it may be both, which would ruin him physically and mentally. These groups are not only exposed to this risk but are also spreading these diseases to their wives and children and other sexual partners. This group consists of truck drivers and their associates who stay away from the warmth of their family for week operating goods transport services from one end of the country to another.

Benedict B.B. Naanen (1999) has studied the women involved in prostitution in "Itinerant Gold Mines" of Cross River Basin of Nigeria. He concluded that colonialism, under-development, class kinship and sexual exploitations, and a tradition of sexual freedom contributed in varying degrees to increase cross river prostitution in Nigeria. He identified very poor knowledge on safe sexual practices among the women involved in sex work in Nigeria. According to Naanen, the unsafe sexual practices among the women in prostitution and their sexual partners increase the chance for spreading the sexually transmitted diseases like STD/HIV/AIDS through the river basin of Nigeria.

Vijaya Srinivasan (1999: 5) summerised the risk factors predisposing individuals to STD infections including HIV infections. The major factors are female gender, age at first intercourse, number of sex partners, sex with low paid sec workers, high level of partner mixing through a core group of infected transmitters and heavy petting and foreplay. Besides, low socio-economic status, drug abuse and presence of other intercurrent STD conditions, poor treatment seeking behaviour of the STD patients also increases HIV positive status and reinfection among STD core groups. According to the author, the asymptomatic groups are an independent cohort which poses special threat to the community in spread of STD infections.

Jagatheeswary, *et al.* (2000) have studied the relationship between HIV and STD. They have conducted the study among patients attending the STD clinic at the Governmental Central Hospital in Chennai between January 1993 and September 1997. The study revealed that the incidence of HIV among STD patients has been increasing since 1992 (from 8% to 14.2%). This study also revealed that the incidence is higher in male than in female.

Sivaramamurthy *et al.* (2000) have studied the sexuality, sexual behaviour and awareness about HIV/AIDS among rural men near Salem, Tamil Nadu. This study found that most of the men are enjoyed paid sex and among them many have the perception of having sex with virgin girl will cure AIDS. It also revealed that the men have first sexual experience with women other than their wife and pre marital and extra marital affairs are prevalent among the rural men in Salem. It is also identified from the study that as the educational level increases, the age at which the first sexual encounter also increases and even though 99% of men are aware of AIDS, only 18.2% know all methods of transmission and 37.9% do not know anything about modes of transmission.

Panda *et al.* (2000) studied the transmission of HIV from injecting drug users to their wives in Manipur in India in 1996. HIV status was determined by ELISA test and found that positive association between injecting drug users and HIV positive status of their wives. The study identified 45% of the injecting drug users wives were HIV positive and only 15% of the couples reported regular usage of condoms during intercourse. The researcher suggested improved control of STDs, condom promotion, and improved blood screening in Manipur to control the spread of HIV among the wives of injecting drug users.

Praveen Sethi (2000) has studied the relationship between tourism and prostitution. According to Praveen Sethi sex tourism is a major component of International travel to South-east Asia and has been given both overt and covert encouragement by government as a source of foreign exchange. His study explored that many tourist from western countries are visiting to South-east Asian countries just to enjoy sex and the control of sexuality is vested with the men of foreign travellers. The women in sex work have no power and the controlling mechanisms on sexuality are dominated by masculinity. It lead to unsafe sexually practices which is the main route cause for the transmission and the spread of HIV/AIDS. The sex tourism is the main cause for the spread of HIV in South-east Asian countries, especially in Thailand.

Joyce V. Lyons (2000: 79) studied the behaviour patterns of Thai long-haul truck drivers and identified that they use to take amphetamines (in pill form) and alcohol and engage in sex with sex workers to release the amphetamine effect. These long-hauls truck drivers have belief that sleeping with prostitutes in brothels is perfectly natural and their habits of drinking alcohol make the prostitutes find very difficult to convince the truckers to use condoms. The study has concluded that long-haul truck drivers behaviour exposed them to a significant risk of contracting the HIV and they are the core group to transmit the virus to their wives and to the general population.

Richa Singh (2001: 1944) has identified that marginalized groups, living in economically unstable/disadvantageous social settings have been particularly vulnerable to HIV/AIDS infection. He has studied one such vulnerable group workers in Wazirpur Industrial area, New Delhi. He identified that the most of the workers are migrants, particularly from Bihar, Uttar Pradesh, Madya Pradesh, Orissa, Nepal and West Bengal and they are working as a casual labourers in temporary jobs. Among them majority of them were from rural areas and they stay far away from their families, living with friends and relatives or kins from their village. They often speak about their loneliness and anxieties of being away from their families. The author has argued that social identities are important determines of sexual behaviour and the notion of masculinity, i.e., "being man" forces the workers to involve in instable sexuality–sex with multiple sexual partners which heightens not only their vulnerability to HIV/AIDS infection and also their womenfolk.

Dinesh Varma (2004) has reported the Behaviour Surveillance Survey (BSS) conducted by AIDS Prevention and Control Project (APAC) run by Voluntary Health Service in Chennai, Tamil Nadu. The survey covered a sample of 1,600 men students and 6,000 women students in schools and colleges of Madurai, Coimbatore, Salem, Vellore and Nagercoil. According to the survey, though the urban youth seemed to have a clear idea of the risk of paid sex, they have low risk perception of having sex with casual partners. The survey also found that the school drops and youth in urban slums are engaged in "high-risk" behaviour by spending money on commercial sex workers.

Rochelle Dalla (2004: 190) has identified the positive relationship between childhood sexual abuse and prostitution in her study entitled "I fell off (the mothering) track: Barriers to effective mothering among prostituted women". The study revealed that childhood sexual abuse results in separating emotions from sexual activity on the victims begins to view herself as debased, the process referred to as "mortification of self". It facilitates her identification with prostitution.

Krishnamuthy (2005: 5) has conducted a study with AIDS Prevention and Control (APAC) to assess the prevalence of sexually transmitted infections in Tamil Nadu and identified the prevalence rate of 10.6 per cent in the State. The study shows that the prevalence of sexually transmitted infection among men was 9.2 per cent and women was 11.5 per cent. Asymptomatic infections were high among both sexes. The infection rate among two high risk groups – prostitution and truckers and helpers showed that the STI prevalence in the first group was 56 per cent and it was 15 per cent in the latter group. The study showed the need to track emerging misconceptions and counter them through multiple channels of communication.

Ramya Kannan (2005: 8) has reported the outcome of the research conducted by Chennai Corporation AIDS Prevention and Control Society between April 2002 and March 2005. It has surveyed 3,699 street children in Chennai, of whom 409 had to be treated for STD. It also identified two children (one boy and one girl) as HIV positive. According to the study, living on and off the streets is the biggest risk factor for children to acquire sexually transmitted infection. It also revealed that children sleeping on the streets at night are sexually abused periodically by strangers which led to the infection of STD.

Stigma and Discrimination

Jacob *et al.* (1987: 412-413) have indicated that the social stigma not only affectthe life of the patient profoundly but also cause serious problems for those with whom the patient has personal, intimate, familial and occupational ties.

Richard W Goodgame (1990: 383-389) has explained some important cultural factors which made hindrance in revealing HIV status to the infected persons in Uganda. This is due to the feeling that providing this information is cruel in the cultural context. Africans are averse to talk about death or dying. Another cause for concern about informing patients of their diagnosis is the fear of an adverse reaction such as suicide or a decision to spread the infection purposefully. Therefore, according to him considering cultural factor is important in dealing with the social dimension of any disease.

Young *et al.* (1991: 777-986) have studied the effect of family structure on the sexual behaviour of adolescents and they found significant relationship between parents / single parent family and the adolescent sexual behaviour such as age at first sex experience, frequency of intercourse and the level of sexual activity. It is commonly noticed that the influence on the child by both the parents is greater and stronger when compared with that of a single parent.

McEwan (1992: 577-584) and Jemmolt *et al.* (1993: 41-53) have investigated sexual behaviour under the influence of alcohol and the relationship between drinking habits and unsafe sex. They have shown in their study that alcohol and drug users during sexual activity are predictors of the HIV risk related behaviour. Their study revealed that there is a significant relationship between alcohol and unprotected coitus and failure to use condoms. Therefore, in the socio-cultural context, it is observed that the various habits formed during different stages of one's life influence the total attitude of a person including his /her inclination to sex.

Francois-Xavier Bagnoud Center for Health and Human Rights (1995: 10-36) has given many conditions under human rights perspectives which can influence a person's well-being. Such conditions include access to medical services and access to healthy physical, biological and social environment. According to this center, discrimination and lack of respect for human rights and dignity are the root cause of the HIV/AIDS pandemic. Therefore, the center has suggested perceiving the health action programmes under human right perspectives in the context of HIV/AIDS. It also stated that HIV prevention and care for HIV infected people and people with AIDS are closely related activities. So, caring for HIV infected people includes counseling and support to help to prevent further transmission of HIV.

Machika TANNO, *et al.* (1997: 223) have conducted a case study to identify the agony of a family of AIDS patients. From the experiences of the study, the agony of the family was summarized as below:

1. Fear of Infection.
2. Fear of being known to others.
3. Damage to family bondage.
4. Fear of being neglected by nurses.

Reid and Jeanette Brown (1998: 971) studied the emotional impact of two young women whose mothers are HIV- infected. The researcher say that because of the stigma and prejudices attached to HIV/AIDS, it appeared that young people who lived in families affected by HIV/AIDS were susceptible to psychological distress and may have been in need of special services. The study came out with the finding that young peo0ple affected by HIV/AIDS were significantly emotionally impacted. Some of the more imposing manifestations of the emotional impact were anger, depression, withdrawal, anxiousness, fear, shame, helplessness, and hopelessness. The emotional impact was also manifested in behaviour problems such as violent behaviour, combativeness and non-compliance with authority figures and truancy from school. The narrative analyses of the study revealed five distinct themes or patterns that reflected these young women's life experiences. The themes that emerged were: emotional distress, wall of silence, mother/daughter relationship issues, physical problems and school problems. The major recommendations from this study were for mental health services such as family counseling, support groups for HIV-infected parents, and peer support groups for the young people affected by HIV/AIDS to be provided through a community mental health clinic.

Francis Lobo (1999: 3) argued that the stigma of HIV/AIDS is intensified because of the behavioural actions (example, sexual and drug activities linked to morality and sin) and the illness progression (example, debilitating, disfiguring and fatal manifestations) associated with the disease. According to him these conditions lead people who are diagnosed with HIV/AIDS or who are significant others of people with the illness to experience severe social distancing. In the case of multiple stigma, social distance is added with each successive stigma which led to feelings of emotional and social isolation.

Jocop K. John (2000) from Christian Medical College, Vellore, Tamil Nadu has studied the problems faced by the infected people in the society. The study identified many personal and social implications due to HIV/AIDS. The issues such as death, sex, drug abuse etc. have been associated with significant psychological and social distress. It is found from the study that most individual with HIV/AIDS consider suicide is a best means to escape from the societal discrimination and stigma.

Meena Gopal (2000: 7-8) has studied gender and disease in India. Her study concluded that because of gender implication women who are diseased has to undergo greater suffering both in the house and in the community. In the case of communicable diseases, the women were more stigmatized and they were isolated often from all activities within the household such as cooking, child-care etc.

Tokunbo Simbowale Osinubi (2003: 32) studied the people attitudes towards the prevalence of HIV/AIDS and their perception towards AIDS victims in Ibadan, Southwestern Nigeria. The study was carried out among 2,500 household and revealed that most of the respondents do not believe in the existence of the HIV virus or AIDS. Most of them do not have adequate knowledge on how the virus is contracted, spread and how to avoid it. Most of them believe that the AIDS or HIV virus can be contracted through social contact like eating, conversing and associating with an AIDS patient. This belief has an adverse impact on the sexual relations in families with AIDS victims.

Ann E. Biddlecom *et al.* (2004: 66-67) expresses that women who test for HIV infection may face serious consequences from husbands and partners – stigma, rejection, domestic violence and economic reperc-ussions, including those related to inheritance and divorce. They also reported that fear of these consequences my keep women from seeking testing and thus help the virus to spread and many women are still on the short end of the ARV receiving line.

The Hindu (2004: December 5) published the study on discrimination against women with HIV/AIDS which is sponsored by UNIFEM and jointly conducted by CFAR and a Positive Women's Network, Chennai in 2002 in three districts of south India – Kerala, Karnataka and Tamil Nadu. The study revealed that the stigma and discrimination appeared on top of the list of problems with women facing harassment and violence within and without family. The study also revealed that the women are negatively impacted by humiliation at both individual level – within the marital and natal homes – and lack of programmatic responses from the States have driven women to destitution. According to the study, torture by in-laws, rejection by parents and denial of property rights to positive women worsened the situation.

Besides, outside the family, the reluctance of the community to let positive women rent property or use community property while performing last rites were listed out as most commonly faced problems by the women infected with HIV positive in this study.

Meena Menon (2005: 13) argued that the poor services provided by the hospitals influenced higher suicidal rate among the HIV positive patients in Mumbai hospitals. She says that there are two reasons for these suicides. One is people feel that they will not be cured and there is a feeling of neglect by the hospital staff. Another one is that there is a psychological breakdown to induce the people with HIV positive to get suicide.

George Paul (2005) described that the HIV/AIDS patients are discriminated by the doctors due to the most outrageous attitude of refusing treatment on the perception that they are going to die anyway. He also described that the discriminatory practices in the health care sector leads to hiding of HIV status by the patients while taking treatment in the hospitals.

Violence Against Women and HIV/AIDS

Friedlan *et al.* (1991: 144) studied the survival status of AIDS patients in United States and found poor survival of women than men due to poor use of antiretroviral treatment.

Fleming *et al.* (1993: 61) reported that the half of the HIV cases in the developing world are women and most of them are belong to ethnic and racial minorities. Social, economic and cultural discrimination against the minority groups facilitated the infection of HIV/AIDS.

Deepa Punia *et al.* (1996: 17) described the sexual victimization of women, young girls and female children. In their article they argued that the female children are abused and discriminated at every step and as a result they their physical, social and psychological developments were adversely affected in several ways. According to them, in every day many women were subjected to rape, kidnap, abduction, eve-teasing, molestation etc. and many women face such sexual atrocities from their men either within the family or close to their family.

Risa Deneberg (1997: 2-4) found strong association between sexual abuse including abuse in childhood and risk of HIV infection for women. According to the author, childhood sexual abuse was significantly associated with: use of intravenous drug use, exchange of sex for drugs, money or shelter, higher number of sexual partners and have a sexual relationship with a person at high risk for HIV. The report further revealed that the HIV positive women have to face increased risk of domestic violence as a result of her HIV status.

Martin (1999: 1967) studied the relationship between the domestic violence and reproductive behavioural health variables in five districts of Uttar Pradesh. The data on spousal abuse were collected in 1995-96 from 6,695 married men aged 15-65 years. Significant bivariate associations were found between abuse and reproductive health and behaviour variables. It is found that the variables of men who had pre and extra marital sex, STD symptoms, not practicing condom and experienced an unplanned pregnancy have strongest association with nonconsensual sex followed by physical abuse and then by forced sex.

Martin (1999: 44) studied the cause for physical and sexual abuse of women in the marital life in five districts of Uttar Pradesh and data on spousal abuse were collected in 1995-96 a part of a survey on male reproductive health that included 6,695 married men aged 15-65 years. The study has identified significant association between wife abuse and reproductive health behaviour of husband. The study also found significant association between poverty, low education and abuse of women by their husbands.

News Today (2002: February 10) reported that violence against women is increasing in India in the form of rape including custodial rape and trafficking of women. The report also says that custodial offence is increasing in India and sex workers are the main victims.

Nahid Tobia, *et al.* (2004: 19) studied female genital mutilation/cutting (FGM/C) and described that it is a traditional social practice that involve cutting or removing parts of the external genitalia of girls or young women. They reveal that the purposes of the practices of FGM are cultural: a rite of passage to womanhood and of curbing female sexuality and it is practiced predominantly and in various forms in at least 25 African countries and some Asian communities. According to them FGM is associated with both long term and short term health complications. The short term effects can includes great pain, excessive bleeding, infection and shock, most due to unsanitary conditions, failed procedures by inexperienced circumcisers and inadequate medical services afterward. Long term complication includes urinary tract infections and painful sexual intercourse and its related problems including STD and HIV/AIDS.

Anandhi Subramanian (2004: 4) argued that one in three women throughout the world will suffer violence in her lifetime. She will be beaten, raped, assaulted, trafficked, harassed or forced to submit to harmful practices such a female genital mutilation and in majority of the cases, the abuser will be a member of the woman's own family or someone known to her. According to her violence against women is pandemic that knows no boundaries of culture, geography, age or wealth and the abuse of women stems from a multiplicity of cultural circumstances influenced by power relations which is inherent in social structure and is reinforced by politics.

Ranjita Biwas (2005: 4) found that trafficking of women and girls is a major problem in eastern India. Her articles reveal that feminization of poverty has blurred the line between what is right and what is wrong even for the women involved and in majority of the cases the girls are trafficked by known persons, relatives, lovers, and even family members. Her report found that 75 per cent of the trafficked women have direct link with the traffickers and it explored that the main method of coercion which includes kidnapping, promises of jobs in cities and false marriage. Natural disasters will also increases trafficking of women and girls due to poverty and death of parents and these women have no voice to insist safe sex.

Reproductive Health and HIV/AIDS

Frances A. Althaus (1997: 130-39) has discussed the female circumcision, which is practiced in 28 countries in North Africa in the context of human rights and reproductive health.

According to his study, female circumcision is practiced in male dominated society with a view to control female sexuality and fertility.

Laurie Schwab Zabin and Karungari Kiragu (1998: 210-32) have reviewed the literature on health consequences of adolescent sexual behaviour and child bearing in sub-Saharan Africa, and the social and cultural context in which they occur. Their article has explained the most reproductive health problems experienced by adolescents. They argued that because of age related customs (for example, female circumcision and early marriage) or age-related vulnerability (for example, to economic pressure and to male domination), the health problems are often exacerbated among adolescents. The article also reveals that the biological and social factors often create excess risk for adolescence. Declining ages at menarche are likely to contribute to increase reproductive health risk for young women, whether in the context of traditional early marriage and childbearing or in the context of growing rates of out-of-wedlock sexual activity, sexually transmitted diseases and abortion.

Young Mi Kim (1998: 4-11) have studied the women's ability to take decision with regard to the adoption of contraception in 25 service deliver sites in Kenya. The study has adopted structured observation techniques followed by counseling sessions. The result of the study revealed that many of the women in marital life have very poor knowledge on their reproductive health and they have little choice to choose contraceptive methods to avoid birth. The study also revealed that these women have better knowledge on oral contraception rather than condom which is suggested both for family planning and prevention of sexually transmitted diseases.

John C. Caldwell *et al.* (1998: 149) studied the adolescent sexuality and reproduction in the changing world. The study results revealed that the adolescent women's sexual behaviour has changed from the traditional sexual behaviour as a result of massive economic, institutional and social changes in the context of global economy and society. The Western concept of companionate heterosexual relations before and during marriage is getting more popular as a result of globalization which brought easy movements of films, magazine, novels and girls are more affected by these influences than the boys, and wives more than husbands.

Karen Hardee *et al.* (1999: S2-3) evaluated the reproductive health policies and programmes in eight countries such as Bangladesh, India, Nepal, Jordan, Ghana, Senegal, Jamaica and Peru. The evolution report revealed that while all countries have adopted the ICPD definition of reproductive health and all have initiated policy reforms to reflect a new focus, less has been accomplished in implementing integrated reproductive health programmes. Several challenges are faced by all countries including improving knowledge and support among stakeholders, planning for integration and decentralized services, developing human resources, improving quality of care and maintaining a long-term perspective regarding the implementation of the Cairo agenda.

Susheela Singh *et al.* (2000: 21-28) have studied the gender differences in the timing of first intercourse in 14 countries throughout the world. According to the authors, early initiation of intercourse and the context within which sexual activity begins are key indicators of adolescents' potential risk for unplanned pregnancy, abortion and sexually transmitted diseases. The study has collected data from nationally representative surveys of reproductive behaviour of 15-19 year old boys and girls. The result of the study showed that in most countries, roughly one-third or more of teenage women have had sexual intercourse, in four countries (Ghana, Mail, Jamaica and Great Britain) about three in five are sexually experienced. Between about one-half and three-quarters of adolescent males in seven countries have ever had intercourse, but the proportion is one-third or less in Ghana, Zuimbabwe, the Philippines and Thailand. In most countries, sexual intercourse during the teenage years occurs predominantly outside marriage among men but largely within marriage among women.

Evasius K. Bauni *et al.* (2000: 69-80) studied the adoption of family planning and sexual behaviour of women at the age group of 18-39 years through focus group discussion in Nakuru district,

Kenya. The researcher argued that the twin risks of unwanted pregnancy and HIV/AIDS infection remain central concerns of reproductive health programmes. The findings of the study reflected that:

(i) The presence of STDs is increasing in the study area and the study groups have estimated that the prevalence of STDs within the range of three to seven persons infected out of every ten residents.

(ii) Many infected men seek treatment without their partners' knowledge.

(iii) It is estimated that every ten homes, seven will have a girl or woman who has experienced an unwanted pregnancy.

(iv) Although knowledge of condoms is widespread in the study area, their acceptability and use is not so widespread.

(v) Most married couples are not using condom due to opposition by spouse.

(vi) The women in the study area believed that condoms are known and used by men in their extra marital affairs and if they insist it in the marital life, the person would be considered promiscuous.

(vii) Condom use and disposal is embarrassing for many married women.

(viii) Many women have no idea to protect them from the risk of HIV/AIDS and they have justified their passive response with their husbands.

Nancy L. Sloan *et al.* (2000: 55-58) studied the STD and the ability of women to understand the symptoms of STD in developing countries. The result of the study showed that they women are less able to recognize the symptoms of STD and its risk factors.

Kim Best (2001: 8-10) has analysed the reproductive behaviour of women in some African countries including Zimbabwe and Yaounde. The analysis showed that about third of the HIV infected mothers passes the virus to their newborns without taking treatment. Because, most HIV infected women do not know their HIV status before they conceive and some prepare pregnancy even if they know their HIV status due to their desire to have children which is rooted in social system with regard to motherhood. The analysis also revealed the antiretroviral drug is beyond the reach of many women during pregnancy to prevent mother to child transmission and they also depend breast feed for their babies which provide another root of transmission for children.

Kim Best (2001: 12) studied the fertility status of HIV infected women in sub-Saharan Africa and identified lower fertility rate among the HIV infected women than the uninfected women. The study revealed that many women, due to their HIV status, may abstain from sexual relations, use contraception or have abortions to avoid giving birth to children.

The Hindu (2002: November 17) reported the Behavioural Surveillance Survey (BSS) carried out by the Central Government of India in 2000-01. The report revealed that overall awareness about HIV/AIDS among young people in the reproductive age group (15-49 years) was 76.1 per cent, higher among men than among women and also better known in cities than villages. The same report further revealed that only around one-third of rural women in Bihar, Gujarat, Uttar Pradesh, Madhya Pradesh and West Bengal ere aware of the disease.

ICPD–The International Conference of Population and Development (2004: 11) defined reproductive health as a state of complete physical, mental and social well being and not merely the absence of disease or infirmity, in all maters relating to the reproductive system and to its functions and processes. According to ICPD, reproductive health therefore implies that people are able to have a satisfying and safe sex life and that they have the capability to reproduce and the freedom to decide if, when and how often to do so. "Implicit in this last condition are the right of men and women to be informed and to have access to safe, effective, affordable and acceptable methods of family planning of their choice, as well as other method of their choice for regulation of fertility which are not against the law, and the right of access to appropriate health-care services that will enable women to go safely through pregnancy and child birth and provide couples with the best chance of having a healthy infant.

ICPD also defined reproductive health care in the line of above definition. It defined reproductive health care as the constellation of methods, techniques and services that contribute to reproductive health and well-being by preventing and solving reproductive health problems. It also includes sexual health, the purpose of which is the enhancement of live and personal relations, and not merely counseling and care related to reproduction and sexually transmitted diseases.

Any Coen and Geeta Rao Gupta (2004: 15) described that gender equality cannot be achieved without honoring reproductive rights. According to them, gender inequality compromises women's sexual and reproductive autonomy. They also felt that women must depend on men for food or shelter because they have no property or inheritance rights under law and the resulting power imbalance makes it impossible to demand safe sex or make other reproductive choice for women.

Feffrey O'Malley (2004: 60-62) has stressed the importance of integration of Sexual and Reproductive Health and Rights (SRHR) services and HIV/AIDS issues and its related programmes. The author projected that the overwhelming majority of HIV infections are sexually transmitted or associated with pregnancy and breastfeeding, so both HIV prevention and SRHR efforts must focus on sexuality and reproduction. He also expressed that both sexual and reproductive ill health and HIV are rooted in the same social pathologies, including unequal gender relations, sexual violence, and discrimination against sexual minorities, conflict and poverty.

Amanda Kolburn Kawal and Lynn Blinn Pike (2004: 377) examined the role of older siblings in protecting adolescents from engaging in unsafe sexual practices. The study has included 297 participants with the age of 17 years from Midwestern high school. The result of the study showed that siblings discussion about safe sex in conjunction with parental discussion predicted better attitude towards safe sexual practices for adolescents which include safe sex, self-efficacy for refusing sex, self-efficacy for communication about condom use and self-efficacy for buying and using condom.

Women's Knowledge on HIV/AIDS

Singh and Malavia (1990: 103) has conducted a survey among female sex workers in Delhi in 1998 and identified very low per centage (5%) of awareness on AIDS and usage of condom (20%). The same study also identified increased awareness on AIDS (70%) and usage of condom (70%) after intervention programmes.

Chuttani (1991: 20-22) conducted a survey among 669 men and 829 women in the villages in and around Delhi and Haryana. The study identified very less awareness (12%) on HIV/AIDS among the women than men (50%).

National Family Health Survey (1993: 2-3) explains the Knowledge of AIDS among the women of Tripura State, India. The report shows that the knowledge of the existence of Acquired Immuno Deficiency Syndrome (AIDS) is limited in Tripura. Only 13% of the ever married women age 13-49 have heard about AIDS, the per centage of misconceptions about different ways of getting AIDS ranges from 35% who think that it can be contracted from shaking hands with some one with AIDS, 82% have thought that AIDS can be contracted thought mosquito , flea, or bud bug bites. 41% of women have thought it is curable and 3% have believed that and AIDS vaccine exists. Only 30% correctly thought that AIDS can be avoided by using condoms during intercourse and 35% have thought that it can be prevented by practicing safe sex. Others modes of avoidance of AIDS such as checking blood prior to transfusion, sterilizing needles and syringes for injections and avoiding pregnancy when infected with AIDS are mentioned by only 13% of fewer women who have heard about AIDS.

McGrath (1993: 55) study on AIDS and the urban family showed that many women were not aware of their sexual partner's HIV infection. This lack of knowledge may be attributed partly to reluctance in AIDS patients to acknowledge their illness themselves or disclose it to their wives.

Gladys Baingana *et al.* (1995: S32) have assessed the knowledge of a partner's AIDS diagnosis, perceived risk of HIV infection, need for HIV testing and future support plans among women partners of male Ugandan AIDS patients. They have conducted a cross-sectional descriptive survey at New Mulago Hospital, Kamala, Uganda among wives of 177 male AIDS patients in 1992. The study revealed that many women are not aware of the risk of getting infection from their male partners. Their survey also identified that an overwhelming majority of subjects (88%) were not aware of their husbands or main sexual partner's infection status. The study also identified the significant relationship between women's financial independence and their knowledge about their sexual partner's HIV infection status. The findings suggested that the women's economic liberation of women should be considered as an important factor for HIV prevention.

Geeta Bhave *et al.* (1995: S21-25) have studied the level of knowledge on HIV and use of condoms among the sex workers in Bombay with a view to develop and test HIV intervention programmes targeting sex workers and madams in the brothels of Bombay. In a controlled intervention trial, with the measurements before and after the intervention, 334 sex workers and 20 madams were recruited from an intervention site, and 207 and 17, respectively from a similar control site, in red light areas of Bombay. The study found that the base line level of knowledge about HIV and experience with condoms was extremely low among both sex workers and madams. But after intervention, the use of condom level has increased and they were willing to refuse clients who would not use them. But in the same time they were concerned about losing business if condom use was insisted upon. This study also confirmed high rate of HIV prevalence among female sex workers in Bombay. They stressed the strengthening the intervention programmes with regard to condom use to prevent and control the transmission of HIV and sexually transmitted diseases.

Banatuvala (1995: 104) studied the causes for increasing the risk of HIV infection among heterosexual men and women. According to the study, lack of awareness with regard to infection status of the infected people increases the risk of spreading infection to the general population.

Rajkumar (1996: 13) carried out a survey to assess the awareness about HIV/AIDS among women in different population sub groups and identified low level of knowledge in Tamil Nadu and Maharastra were the infection is high.

Thomas William (1996: 33) studied the HIV/AIDS awareness among 80 college students of North Arcot Ambedkar District of Tamil Nadu. The study has revealed that the male students have good knowledge on the general aspects of AIDS (prevention and control) and the female have insufficient knowledge both on the basic preventive aspects of the disease.

Hirve and Sathe (1997: 17) have surveyed 4976 women of currently married and in the age group of upto 47 years in the rural areas of three rural coastal districts of Western Maharashtra, an area with a high potential for spread of HIV/AIDS. According to their study only 35% of women were aware about AIDS, and among them knowledge about sexual route of transmission was the most common (75%) followed by the use of contaminated needles and blood transfusion (40%). Mother to child transmits was mentioned only by about 15%. This study showed that age had an inverted 'U' shaped statistically significant relationship with AIDS awareness, with awareness of AIDS being lower in the younger and the higher in the higher age group. A statistically significant increasing trend in awareness about AIDS was seen with increasing literacy levels. According to the study, television played a major role in conveying information about AIDS to the public in general and women in particular.

Suresh K Anjum (1998: 21) has cited the survey conducted by the U.S. based East-West Center with regard to knowledge of HIV/AIDS among Indian women. According to the article, 30,000 married women were interviewed by the organisations and the report of the survey showed that most rural women were not even aware of the disease. The report revealed that only 19.1 per cent between 25-29 years of age had heard about AIDS and only 20.4 per cent between 30-34 years and 14 per cent between 45-49 years knew about the hazards of AID. Among the communities, 40.2 per cent are Christians, 16.5 per cent are Hindus and 10 per cent are Muslims.

Arrow for Change (2000: 3) has conducted a research on among young Filipinas in Australia in order to examine the interplay between young women's knowledge and attitudes about sex and sexuality, the influence of culture and the social context in which sex occurs. The study found low level of knowledge on sexually transmitted diseases among majority of the young women and the women have adjust between two sets of cultural values – their native culture and the culture of the country where they live. The research has suggested the need of health education specifically migrant women who face this conflict.

The Hindu (2004: November 30) has reported the women's awareness on HIV/AIDS in India. According to the report, in India, awareness of HIV/AIDS among women is distressingly low – only 20 per cent of women in some areas have correct knowledge about the disease.

Sharma. K. (2005: 3) has argued that in majority cases, the woman would not have known about the possibility of contracting the diseases through sexual relations with her husband and even if she knew, and was aware of the precautions that ought to be taken, she would not have been in a position to insist due to her subordinate position as a woman and as a wife.

Impact of HIV/AIDS

Berkley *et al.* (1990: 1237) has conducted a survey in Uganda during 1997-98 to identify the impact of HIV on women. The survey concluded that the women are increasing infected by HIV mostly through their AIDS affected sexual partners and they are struggling to cope not only with their spouse's illness but also with her own potential risk of HIV infection and with her family future well-being.

Wendy Ledger (1997: 3-24) has described AIDS as a national calamity of Kenya. He described that the virus is affecting the society in a variety of interrelated ways and it has generated worst impact on the national economy and development by taking the lives of economically productive youth, increasing the expenditure on identifying vaccine for AIDS and giving treatment for the infected, and implementing intervention programmes for prevention, control and care.

Pushpa Khurana (1998: 80) explored the social and economic impact of HIV/AIDS on women. She argued that the women should bear the double burden in the family by taking the care of the entire household and the sick who are affected by HIV and other illness. In addition the infected women give birth to 30-40 per cent infected babies and the babies and they will be orphaned due to the narrowing life expectancy of their parents as a result of AIDS.

Basia Zaba and Simon Gregson (1998: S41-50) have measured the impact of HIV on fertility in Africa. The study has identified the lower fertility among HIV infected women in all age groups. Lower fertility amongst HIV positive women cause a population attributable decline in total fertility of the order of 0.4 per cent for each per centage point of HIV prevalence in the general female population. The study argued that in populations that do not use contraceptives, HIV positive women have lower fertility principally as a result of fetal losses consequent to infection with HIV and co-infection with other sexually transmitted diseases and behaviour factors with regard to avoiding pregnancy to prevent infants from HIV infection enhance this differential.

Syed V. Naveed (1998: 133) has studied the interpersonal relationships among the relatives/friends of HIV/AIDS patients in a metropolitan city - Hyderabad in India. He also examined the process of change in relations with reference to personal factors. The study revealed that the large number of respondents have very poor interest to have an international relationships with the HIV/AIDS patients. Besides, the nature of change of interpersonal relations is positively related to the level of misconception about transmission of disease. When a person's level of misconception is high he/she is likely to have a negative change in his/her relations with the patients.

UNDP (1999: 4) has described AIDS as development issue. According to the report, HIV/AIDS presents major challenges to human survival, human rights and human development, with implications far beyond the health sector and the social and economic consequences of the epidemic are one of the most serious threats to sustainable human development.

Inn Mackinnon and Adam Piore (2001: 5-8) argued that the HIV infected women are more stigmatized and discriminated in India than the men. According to the author, most of the infected women are innocent victims and they have to face more violence both in husbands' family and her own natal family.

UNAIDS (2002: 1-19) report says that the HIV/AIDS epidemic is the fourth biggest global killer and it is now the leading cause of death in sub-Saharan Africa. The report also revealed that in many countries, AIDS is erasing decades of progress made in extending life expectancies. The impact on life expectancy signifies a major blow to a society's development. The UNAIDS has projected that in the 45 most affected countries, between 2000 and 2020, 68 million people will die earlier than they would have in the absence of AIDS.

UNAIDS report further explained that the impact of HIV/AIDS is severe on households by leaving the children as orphaned due to the death of their infected parents, and lose of income and increased expenses for medical treatment and giving care to the infected persons push the affected household deeper into poverty. Besides, the government has to deal the problem of additional/huge expenses on the health sectors. In addition to this, AIDS weaken economic activity by squeezing productivity, adding costs, diverting productive resources and depleting skills. The epidemic's potential impact on the rule of law has challenged the social cohesion in many countries in which the stability and progress of country depend.

The Hindu (2004: July 12) has reported the U.N. Secretary-General Kofi Annan in the International AIDS Conference. The report revealed that the world leaders have not done enough to combat the history's biggest epidemic and the Asian countries, including India and China stand to lose more than 18 million workers to AIDS over the next decade including huge losses of households and business and stifling economic growth.

The Hindu (2004: July 11) has published the ILO's ominous estimates in the impact of HIV/AIDS on the globe. According the report of ILO (International Labour Organisation) 35.7 million people between the ages of 15 and 49 years could be affected with HIV, 26 million of who are workers. While tens of millions of workers have already died, millions more are dropping out of the labour force. The ILO estimates that in 2005, two million workers globally will be unable to work-up from 500,000 in 1995. By 2015, the number will double to four millions.

The same report also revealed the study carried out by four organisations of people infected with HIV/AIDS in India (the Delhi, Manipur and Maharashtra Network of Positive People, and the Positive Women's Network of South India). The study found that about one-third of respondents were unemployed because of ill-health and a third still worked but had disclosed their HIV status (38 per cent) fearing job loss and only about a third has revealed their status.

National Institute of Social Defence (2004: 1) stated that the rate of increase of HIV/AIDS is on the rise and, as per an estimate, there could be 100 million people testing HIV positive by the year 2010 and lack of proper and adequate medical facilities in the developing world makes the survival of infected people very lean. The news letter of National Institute of Social Defence also revealed that the largest spread of HIV/AIDS is found among the mot sexually active population in the age group of 15-49 year and out of 14,000 new HIV infections occurring daily, a whopping 12,000 persons are from this age group alone. Unprotected sex and injecting drug use are the two chief modes of transmission of this disease in the Asia Pacific regain. The news letter suggested considering the issue of adolescent sexual and reproductive health as central theme of HIV/AIDS prevention and controlling intervention programmes.

Intervention

World Health Organisation (1988) reports on the social aspects of AIDS stress that persons suspected or known to be HIV positive should remain integrated within the society and help to assume responsibility for preventing HIV transmission to others.

Foley M *et al.* (1994: 1483-1487) have emphasized on the importance of family support to HIV/AIDS patients in their paper on family support for heterosexual partners suffered from HIV infection. They found that awareness and family support were associated with gender of the family members, HIV sero-positivity and sex education. Further, they suggested that family support is very essential to arrest the spread of sexually transmitted diseases as well to discourage the people without HIV/AIDS.

Asian Red Cross and Red Crescent Regional AIDS Task Force (1997: 18) has organized Regional workshop on Home and Community Care for people infected with HIV/AIDS (PLWHA) in Thailand. The workshop has stressed the importance of providing family and community care to PLWHA to prevent and control the spread of HIV. According to the report of the workshop, the discrimination and stigma associated with AIDS can be overcome if the public are motivated to accept the PLWHA by providing care and support.

Riedel, Marion C (1998: 4813) have explored the relationships between family role tasks and the mental health and custody plans of AIDS-affected youth. They interviewed women with AIDS and their adolescent children in New York city. In this study most of the women were contracted HIV through sexual contact with an IV drug-using partners. The study found that the women were experiencing g relatively high rates of AIDS-related physical distress and less than a third of the mothers had formal custody plans for their adolescent children, but almost all had made some informal arrangements. Prospective guardians were mostly maternal kin-mothers and sisters. The infected women's mental health distress was associated with higher role task performance toward siblings, in the household and overall, though only the first relationship was significant. These relationships were moderated by the youths' gender, mothers' level of illness, residential stability, the age of the adolescent, and number of siblings.

Tamil Nadu State AIDS Control Society (1998: 41) expressed that HIV infected persons can live upto ten years or more without developing AIDS, if provided they are cared for and given support, not just medical but emotional too.

Michal C Latham and Elizabeth A Preble (2000: 525) have described that HIV and AIDS have seriously affected women of reproductive age in sub-Saharan Africa and it increases mother to child transmission mainly through breast milk. Therefore, the researchers have suggested formula milk instead of breast milk for the infants. According to the authors, the infected mothers living in poor households in developing countries prepared the breast milk to feed the infant due to the expensive cost of formula methods. They have stressed the importance of exploring the possibility of alternative feeding methods to safeguard the infant from infections.

Lawyers Collective (2000: 3) has expressed that the best way of preventing the spread of HIV/AIDS infection is to promote and protect the right of affected populations, so that they are empowered to protect themselves. Promoting the protecting of the HIV infected with help them to choose safer behaviours and to access services like information, counseling and healthcares, without the fear of discrimination or penal sanctions. It is more important in the control of the epidemic. According to them, exclusionary approaches to single out the vulnerable population may motivate them to move underground and they may not observe changes in their behaviour for preserving the social health of the society. It makes the control of epidemic impossible and it increases the vulnerability and it affects all intervention programmes.

Indian Express (2001: May 29) has reported that there is no time scale to say when a person could become sick and it depends on the body's immune power-how long it can fight against opportunistic diseases. According to the report, an HIV positive person can live for a long period, as long a the person takes responsibilities for self, that is, leading a quality life, avoiding stress and strain, taking proper medicines, avoiding smoking and consumption of alcohol, ensuring adequate sleep and exercise with proper emotional supportive counseling.

Thinathanthi (2003: January 1) has reported the marriage between HIV infected man and women in Ernakulam in Kerala, India. This news indicates that the infected persons should be denied to get marriage, but they should be advocated to choose partners among HIV infected persons.

The Hindu (2003: December 1) reported the decision taken by the government with regard to free antiretroviral drugs to the HIV/AIDS patients at free of cost through government hospitals and antenatal clinics. According to the report, Tamil Nadu, Andhra Pradesh, Karnataka, Maharashtra, Manipur and Nagaland have given priority for free antiretroviral drugs scheme. The report also further revealed that the supply would be initially to be three categories of patients: children of parents infected with HIV, women having the infection and men who suffer from full-blown AIDS.

The Hindu (2004: November 30) reported that NGOs are playing a vital role in providing care and support of people infected with HIV/AIDS and creating attitudinal changes with regard to positive people in the public. It has cited the work rendered by the CHESS (Community Health Education Society), a Chennai based NGO in providing care to the pregnant woman who was negated by the hospital for delivery and isolated by the neighbours. The CHESS has admitted her in their hospital and helped to deliver a baby and the baby was given sufficient care by the staff which made the neighbours to change their mind and accommodate the positive women to live along with them.

The Hindu (2004: December 1) published that the HIV positive patients are not receiving adequate medical care and support after they are discharged from hospitals and they are abandoned by relatives. In order to provide them good care, the State Government of Tamil Nadu is launching the project in which the village Health Nurses will visit patients' homes to render personal care with the objective of follow-up care.

The Hindu (2004: December 6) reported the six significant concerns identified by the positive women to safeguard their right and lives and it includes health care and treatment, property succession and inheritance within natal and marital homes, access to reproductive rights and health, livelihood opportunities, decision-making powers and access to state-sponsored benefits.

The New Indian Express (2004: 7. December 1) has reported the movement of People Infected with HIV in India (INP+) in Chennai for promoting care and support of the affected community. The net work has stressed to facilitate and improve the access to treatment and information for people infected with HIV. It also advocated the promotion and protection of human right of people infected with HIV with active involvement of affected people at all levels of decision making. The positive net work also demanded social acceptance and life free from stigma and discrimination.

Thinamalar (2005: June 14) reported the 'team sex' which influence the girls who are studying in various colleges of Salem in Tamil Nadu. The report revealed that the girls who are in need of money for their lavish life are influenced by the prostitution net work and they take these girls for paid sex in team like a tourist.

Robert Szabo and Roger V Short (2000: 1592) studied the relationship between male circumcision and risk reduction of HIV/AIDS. According to the study, no new infection occurred among any of the 50 circumcised men over a period of 30 months, whereas 40 of 137 uncircumcised men became infected during the same period. The study revealed that the inner surface of the foreskin, which is rich in HIV receptors, and the frenulum, a common site for trauma and other sexually transmitted infections, must be regarded as the most probable sites for viral entry in primary HIV infection in men. He argue in the light of his evidence of the study, advocating male circumcision may be treated as new preventive strategies to prevent and control the spread of infection both for male and female.

Grosskurth *et al.* (2000: 1981) critically evaluated the findings of two studies carried out in Mwanza and Rakai with regard to the control of sexually transmitted diseases as a means for decreasing the incidence of HIV-1 infection. These studies reported a statistically significant 38% reduction in HIV-1 infection among the patients who have treated for syphilis. The authors assert that the results from these studies are complementary to each other, and provide important insights into current thinking on the management of STD in the context of AIDS prevention.

WISE Words (2000: 1) argue that women are not only biologically more susceptible to contracting HIV, but they also face social barriers that prevent their access and use of available prevention methods and the recognition of gender-related constraints for HIV prevention has led for female controlled and initiated methods of protection including female condom. The article revealed that the female condom is generally accepted and used by the women in Brazil, Thailand, South Africa and Zimbabwe. But the cost of female condom prohibits many women, especially poor women, around the world from using them.

Peter Piot (2000: 1), the Executive Director of the Joint Nations Programme on HIV/AIDS in UNAIDS stressed the addressing of gender inequality in HIV/AIDS prevention programmes. According to him women's economic dependence on men makes women less able to protect themselves while social norms limit their access to information about sexual matters. He also expressed that the greater social acceptance of high-risk male sexual behaviour can expose both men and their partners to infection.

William R. Finger (2001: 14) stressed the importance of encouraging the young women to use condom and to develop skills to refuse unwanted sex. He stated that the young women are often inexperienced with condoms and also feel invulnerable to risk and these factors challenges the intervention programmes which are targeted on adolescent girls. The article also revealed that in addition to condom use, the women and girls should be given knowledge on the early detection of sexually transmitted infections and its cure and prevention. The author has suggested the integration of family planning programmes with HIV/AIDS intervention programmes to make the people to receive condom without the fear of stigma.

The Hindu (2004: April 22) expressed the article of The United Nations' General Assemble global response for combating HIV and AIDS. The news revealed that about $9 billion is required annually to combat HIV and AIDS and half of which would be needed in sub-Saharan Africa. According to the article, about $4.8 billion would be required for prevention, including interventions focusing on youth, workplace programmes, mother-to-child transmission and condom distribution and another $4.4 billion would be needed for treating opportunistic infection to which HIV patients become susceptible. The article further revealed that since 15,000 new infections occur each day, the annual resources needed for an expanded global response would increase from $3.2 billion in 2002, $4.7 billion in 2003, $6.8 billion in 2004 to $9.2 billion in 2005.

According to the article, the level of spending by 2005 would provide prevention services for over 22 million, and voluntary counseling and testing for nine million. An additional 35 million women would receive testing at prenatal clinics and 9, 00,000 would receive antiretroviral drugs to prevent mother-to-child transmissions. Special prevention programmes would reach almost sex million sex workers, 28 million men who have sex with men and three million injecting drug users. These costs would include funds for over six billion condoms.

The Hindu (2004: December 2) reported that the main challenge for India is to break down the barriers of denial and the denial of epidemic has led to inaction. It has an view that the AIDS pandemic is one where the media has an important role, and may even save more lives, than doctors.

Ramyakannan (2004: 5) report in Hindu says that the members of the positive community throughout the state have brought several complaints of harassment and discrimination by medical and para-medical personnel in both the government and private health sectors. Her report also reveals that stigma over HIV/AIDS still exists in the medical community and doctors are often hesitant to treat patients, who reveal their HIV status.

The Hindu (2004: July 12) published the talk of the Union Minister for Health and Family Welfare, Anbumani Ramadoss at the second Asia-Pacific Ministerial meeting on HIV/AIDS in Bangkok. According to the report, India has taken political commitment to control the spread of HIV/AIDS. The report also revealed that India had identified cases of 5.1 million HIV infections, accounting to less than one per cent of the population and anti-retroviral therapy (ART) had been introduced in India in April 2004 at free of cost, through the public sectors.

The Hindu (2004: December 1) says that economic dependence has rendered millions of women vulnerable because they are unable to set the terms of their relationship with men. Violence and coercion within marriage, and lack of access to property, basic education and employment opportunities are important factors that subjugate women. Therefore, it has suggested reviewing the laws to empower women and liberal approach in funding employment ventures on the line of health education on HIV/AIDS. The report also stressed that the 'APC' approach to prevention–Abstinence, Being faithful and reducing the number of sexual partners, and Condom use–will have only a limited impact if the underlying socio-economic and cultural cause are not addressed.

National Institute of Social Defence (2004: 8) published press clippings with regard to the survey conducted by ORG-MARG (Operation Research Group-Marketing and Research Group) to assess the condom usage among the couples in urban India (*India Today*, 2004: Oct. 4). The survey identified the drastic decline of condom use in Urban India due to the barrage of publicity surrounding condoms and HIV/AIDS prevention. According to the survey, many people have a feeling that condom is only for high-risk groups and not for non-risk groups.

The Hindu (2005: February 8) quoted the Union Health and Family Welfare Minister, Anbumani Ramadoss statement and reported that India has began human clinical trial of an investigational vaccine designed to prevent Human Immuno-deficiency Virus infection and Acquired Immunodeficiency Syndrome at the Pune-based National AIDS Research Institute and if the trial is successful, a vaccine against the disease would be available within eight years.

The Hindu (2005: February 10) reported that the senior Vatican official has supported the use of condoms to fight Africa's AIDS pandemic, contradicting the Catholic Church's official position. According to the statement given by the Cardinal Georges Cottier, though contraception is officially forbidden by the Catholic Church, the use of condom in some situations can be considered morally legitimate. He also warned that sex with condoms is not safe.

Prasad (2005: 13) revealed that there has been a positive correlation between circumcision and reduced risk of HIV infection. He has quoted the trial carried out among 3000 heterosexual male volunteers in South Africa and revealed that the incidence of HIV infection in circumcised volunteers was three times lower compared with uncircumcised men. He suggested that inclusion of male circumcision in intervention strategy may help to prevent infection through sexual contact.

Research Gap and Present Study

Review indicates the issues involved in HIV/AIDS infection and its transmission to vulnerable groups in terms of socio-economic factors, high risk behaviour and HIV/AIDS, stigma and discrimination, violence against women, reproductive health, women's knowledge on HIV/AIDS, impact of HIV and intervention. However, these revelations and expositions are inadequate to understand comprehensively the various problems of HIV infected women. Accordingly a comprehensive attempt focusing on the various circumstances leading to HIV positive for women, influence of socio-economic factor leading to the infection of women, discrimination due to HIV infection, sexual behaviour of women after infection, impact of HIV/AIDS on social relationship of women and their attitude towards pregnancy and child birth after infection with sociological overtone was felt and found as research gap with special reference to women in larger cities.

Accordingly, to fulfil this research gap the present study is formulated to conduct the same in Chennai City, the Capital of Tamil Nadu with a strong methodological support and also specific research questions of:

1. What is the socio-economic background of women infected with HIV positive?
2. Why the infection rate is high in monogamy relationship?

3. **Whether HIV infection increases the rate of widowhood?**
4. **Is there any change in the sexual behaviour of sex workers and housewives after infection?**
5. **Why the sex workers remain in sex work even after knowing their infection?**
6. **What is the impact of HIV on social relationship of women after infection?**
7. **Are the infected women revealing their HIV status to others?**
8. **Is there any gender discrimination in treatment?**
9. **Is there any economic change in the life of women after infection?**
10. **How women perceive pregnancy and child birth after infection?**

3

Research Methodology

Over View of HIV/AIDS as Social Problem

HIV/AIDS is not an individual problem. But it is the problem of entire society. It affects the public at large. If it is an individual problem, we can find solution very easily within the framework of individual's life style. Since it affects larger society, HIV/AIDS should be treated as social problem. Therefore, controlling the situation is always beyond the ability of one or few persons. This responsibility should be placed upon society at large. Collective efforts are needed to restore social ethics which describes human conduct as right and wrong in group relations.

Social disorganisation is the major factor for the infection and spread of HIV virus into the general population. Social disorganisation is a condition of society, community or group in which there is a break down of social control, or of social order, or of formal and informal norms that define permissible behaviours. It is characterized by impersonal secondary relations, anonymity, loneliness, high mobility and extreme specialization, contradictions in social systems, malfunctioning of economic systems, defective functioning political systems, lack of co-operation, breakdown of social values, lack of unity, indiscipline, unpredictability, lack of consensus and integration of institutions and inadequate social control.

Social problem will emerge when there is a change in the equilibrium forces of the social structure. The traditional norms and values and practices become ineffective due to the intervention of new life style as a result of modernization, westernization and globalization. The disruption in the traditional values brought changes in the social and economic life of the people. Many become impoverished as a result of technological transformation and modernization. The technological transformation in the field of economy and modernization in all sphere of the structure led to migration and unemployment of unskilled, semi skilled labourers. Prostitution and paid sex, drug abuse are the direct impact of migration and unemployment which is identified as major risk factor for infection and the spread HIV/AIDS.

The phenomenon of cultural lag is another important factor which prevents the practice of intervention programmes implemented by the government and non-governmental organisations to control and prevent further spread of infection. With the influence of various mass media, the people are exposed to sex and safe sex knowledge. But the conservative attitude of the people creates fear among them to use condom as a means of safe sex whenever they have heterosexual experiences. The conservative thought and its related fear act as barriers to practice the intervention programmes in their life style.

The prevailing value conflict between male and female with regard to breaking the silence surrounding the sex and suggesting and adopting condom during sexual encounter is another important cause to increase the women' vulnerability towards HIV/AIDS. A value is a generalized principle of behaviours to which the members of a group feel a strong, emotional, positive commitment. The values provide a standard for judging specific acts and goals. Each member of the group is expected to remain committed to the values accepted by the group. The value of Indian culture expects women to be submissive and men to be aggressive in sex and sexuality. Such expectation made Indian women to be ignorant about sex and safe sex and its related implication on their life.

Personal deviation and peer group pressure is another important variable for the behaviours of injecting drug use, prostitution, promiscuous relationships, pre and extra marital behaviours. Deviation is non-conformity to social norms.

Personal deviancy develops because of either an individual's inability to follow generally accepted norms or an individual's failure to accept generally accepted norms. A deviant behaviour of the individual is either directly or indirectly related to deficiency in socialization. The deviants, though they have learnt norms and values of the society, they are unable to put them into practice. The deviants as a result of their peer group pressure used to engage in high risk activities which bring all infections including HIV. These deviants also act as carrier as well as transmitter of virus to their innocent sexual partners.

Risky behaviours in the context of AIDS refer to behaviours that increase the chances of getting infected by HIV or transmitting the virus. Such behaviours include having sexual intercourse without condom (male or females), practicing anal sex, sex with several partners, having sex with sex workers, injecting drug use and using unclean equipment, and if HIV positive going through pregnancy, child birth and breast feed with voluntary counseling and testing and other interventions. Vulnerability to HIV infection arises from circumstances that are beyond the direct control of the people involved. Such circumstances include poverty, low social status, gender discrimination, social discrimination, marginalization and criminalization. These circumstances also reduce or deny a person's access to HIV information, services, means of prevention and support. Gender inequality increases the vulnerability of both men and women to HIV infection.

Women and children, injecting drug users, poor people, refugees, migrants, prisoners, homosexual men, injecting drug users, sex workers are considered as vulnerable population. These vulnerable populations may face increased stigma and discrimination as a result of their HIV status.

The AIDS epidemic claimed 2.9 million lives in 2003, and an estimated 4.8 million people acquired HIV virus in 2003. As on December 2003, 37.8 million (range 34.6-42.3 million) of people are globally living with HIV positive. Among the global total one-third of the people living with HIV are young people between

15-24 years. The UNAIDS Global report on HIV/AIDS 2004 reveals that half of all people infected with HIV/AIDS are women. As on December 2003, of the total 37.8 million of people living with HIV positive, 17 million are female. The new infection included 800,000 children. Among them more than 90% have infected through parent to child transmission (PTCT). About 90% of the infection through PTCT occurred in Sub-Saharan Africa, but the number of such infection is increasing in other regions, particularly South-East Asia.

No country is free from HIV infection. South Africa remains the world's worst affected region of the world. It has 10% of world's population, but is the home for 70% global infection. Women in Africa are being infected at an earlier age than men. Asia has 60% of the world's population. Now it becomes the home for fastest growing AIDS epidemic in the world. In Asia, an estimated 7.4 million people (range 5.0-10.5%) are living with HIV. Around half a million (range 330 000-740 000) are believed to have died of AIDS in 2003, and about 1.1 million (range 610 000-2.2 million) become newly infected. In Asia HIV/AIDS is concentrated more in India, China, Philippines, Thailand, Myanmar, Indonesia, and Nepal.

India has the largest number of people living with HIV next to South Africa. It is estimated that 5.1 million people living with HIV in 2003. Most infections acquired sexually, but injecting drug use dominates in the north-east of the country. In this area, infection level of 60-75% has been found among injecting drug users using non-sterile injecting equipment. In India's southern states of Andhra Pradesh, Karnataka, Maharashtra and Tamil Nadu, HIV is transmitted through heterosexual sex, and is largely linked to sex work. In many states infection level among pregnant women in sentinel antenatal clinics have found to be more than 1 per cent. This suggests that sex workers' clients may have passed HIV to their wives. In many parts of India, HIV transmission through sex between men is also a major concern. The homosexual men may also have sex with women - wives or other female sexual partners.

The Government of India has taken tremendous efforts through NACO and State AIDS Control Societies to disseminate the knowledge related to HIV/AIDS to the public in general and high risk groups in particular. But the level of knowledge is still inadequate and incomplete. The people of India have not taken the issue as serious social problem. The information with regard to HIV/AIDS, safe sex, preventive mechanism, its impact has not reached many parts of rural India where the epidemic has taken its entry through rural to urban and urban to rural migration. As a result of cultural constrains, women, girls and adolescents have limited access to gain knowledge about sex, safe sex, reproductive health, condom use, antiretroviral therapy, voluntary testing, treatment etc. The poor knowledge and increasing risk behaviours among youth and risk groups further fuel the epidemic in India.

Statement of the Problem

In India, the HIV infection has engulfed all parts of the country irrespective of its socio-economic developments. HIV/AIDS is no longer a problem restricted to specific groups with high risk behaviours in India. The epidemic has reached to the level of infecting non-risk groups including women and children. In India women are increasingly at greater risk of getting infection due to cultural constraints in the male dominated patriarchal society.

The ratio of infection between male and female is 3 :1. The majority of the infection occurs in young women with the age group of 15-24 years. Heterosexuality is identified as major risk factor for women's infection in India. Many women have infected with the risk behaviours of others especially from their husband in the marital life. Discrimination, poverty, gender based violence and conservative culture and traditional norms, attitude towards parenthood are the important factors which fuel the epidemic among the women and now it is feminized in India. The Indian women either know nothing or too little about HIV and various mechanisms to protect themselves from infection. Even if they know some thing about HIV and safe sexual practices, it is often rendered useless by the discrimination and violence they face in the society.

The 'ABC' approach – Abstain, Be faithful and use Condom has not produced significant impact in the control and prevention of HIV among women and adolescent girls. This is mainly because the success of the approach entirely depends on the behaviours of the men in Indian social context. The persisting gender inequality has taken the dreaded disease called AIDS into a socio-economic crisis.

In India, women living with and affected by HIV/AIDS have to face lot of consequences including taking care of ill and AIDS related stigma and discrimination throughout their life. In many cases they are blamed by their husband and in-laws for being the "vectors" or "carriers" of HIV. Though they are shouldering the responsibility of taking care of other infected persons in the family, for example husband and children, they find no one to take care of them when they fell ill and the society has no care and support mechanisms for the victims of HIV/AIDS.

The socio-cultural values and religious norms in India prevent women to use female control protection method. They have no right to get free from these harmful traditional practices, violence and to exercise control over their own bodies. In the Indian context, women's sex and sexuality is controlled by men due to the rights given to them in the patriarchal family system.

The violence against women is major human right and public health problem in India. It increases female vulnerability to HIV. Rape, sexual abuse, trafficking, sex trade and exploitation of women are frequently reported by various media (print and visual). The sexual abuses increase women's vulnerability towards HIV.

The Indian women suffer with restricted economic option. Illiteracy, ignorance, lack of skill and limited or lack of opportunities to acquire skill pushes them into the trap of poverty, violence and homelessness. The Indian social structure never encouraged women to possess and inherit property. Her economic insecurity increases her personal insecurity in the form of domestic violence, unsafe sex and other HIV related risk factors. The feminization of poverty as a result of rapid economic changes and introduction of mechanization forced marginalized women to engage in unsafe sex for money and other survival needs which increases their vulnerability to the infection sexually transmitted infections including HIV/AIDS.

Tamil Nadu has highest number of infection in India. The infection rate is steadily increasing among the STD patients and pregnant women. Young girls are under the threat of infection due to the prevailing myth that the sex with virgin can cure the infection. As a result of increasing migration from rural to urban the increasing number of innocent housewives are getting infection from their husbands with risky behaviour. The people in general and risk group in particular are hesitant to undergo HIV test. They have a fear that if they take up HIV tests they will be labeled as promiscuous. The stigma and discrimination associated with HIV/AIDS also enable women to become the victim of HIV/AIDS.

There is no legal mechanism in India, to know the HIV status of the individual before marriage. Since most of the marriages are arranged based on the horoscope in the Indian families, the marrying partners have no chance to know their own HIV status which increases the risk of both men and women in the marital life.

In this context the present study makes an attempt to expose the plight of women living with HIV positive in Chennai city, Tamil Nadu.

Objectives

The objectives of the present study are as follows :

1. To study the social and economic background of women living with HIV positive.
2. To analyse the marital status of women and vulnerability to HIV infection..
3. To examine the circumstances leading to HIV infection and related behaviour on women.
4. To investigate the sexual behaviour of women after infection.
5. To analyse the impact of HIV status on social relationships of women.

6. To expose women's attitude towards pregnancy and child birth after infection.
7. To suggest suitable measures and prepare a plan of action leading to prevention and control of HIV in society in general and women in particular.

Significance of the Study

Many studies have revealed the causes and social and economic implication of HIV/AIDS in general. Many studies have not examined the problems of women living with HIV positive in the patriarchal society like India where women have limited access to gain reproductive knowledge, less control over their body and more subjected to sexual abuse and violence. It is a social responsibility to protect women from the dreaded disease of HIV/AIDS and its related stigma and discrimination. It is more essential to identify the plight of women living with HIV positive in the Indian society which give more importance to moral values and family ethics so that positive measures can be initiated to ensure HIV free society.

Operational Definition of the Terms used in the Topic

Women living with HIV positive

The term refers to the female who are living with HIV status.

Chennai

Chennai is the City which is in the capital of Tamil Nadu State.

Tamil Nadu

Tamil Nadu is one of the southern States in peninsular India.

Research Design

The nature of the present study is diagnostic. The study is diagnostic because it exposes the important problems experienced by the women living with HIV in various social and economic spheres. There is no need for specific hypothesis for this study, since the objectives are conceptually clear.

Selection of the Study Area

Table 3.1. Aids Cases in Tamil Nadu
(Districtwise - cumulative)
(Reported up to September 2001by Tamil Nadu State AIDS Control Society, 2001)

Sl. No.	*Name of the District*	*Male*	*Female*	*Total*
1.	Chennai	2876	867	3743
2.	Thiruvellore	436	132	568
3.	Kancheepuram	335	95	430
4.	Vellore	513	176	689
5.	Thiruvannanmalai	387	120	507
6.	Villupuram	603	205	808
7.	Cuddalore	480	129	609
8.	Dharmapuri	354	112	466
9.	Salem	774	241	1015
10.	Namakkal	703	200	903
11.	Erode	619	183	802
12.	Coimbatore	271	61	332
13.	The Nilgiris	24	1	31
14.	Perambalur	212	78	290
15.	Trichy	596	203	799
16.	Ariyalur	23	15	38
17.	Karur	238	54	290
18.	Pudukkottai	92	29	121
19.	Thanjavur	152	54	206
20.	Tiruvarur	39	9	45
21.	Nagapattinam	54	14	68
22.	Dindigul	312	95	407
23.	Madurai	521	168	689
24.	Theni	170	37	207
25.	Sivagangai	69	24	93
26.	Virudhunagar	64	11	75
27.	Ramanathapuram	38	12	50
28	Tirunelveli	165	33	198
29.	Thoothukudi	128	27	155
30.	Kanyakumari	23	5	28
	Address not known	272	40	312
	Other States	60	17	77
	Total	11601	3453	15054

Chennai city in Tamil Nadu is purposively selected on the basis of reported AIDS statistics available in the Tamil Nadu State AIDS Control Society. The prevalence of HIV in Chennai is also confirmed by survey of literature, pilot studies and interaction with Government and Non-Governmental Organisations. Besides, homosexual activities are increasing in Chennai and the report of the Indian Community Welfare Organisation revealed that there are 7,000 homosexuals identified among the estimated 65,000 people in Chennai City. Since homosexual men are often functionally heterosexual, the risk of STD and HIV spreading to males as well as females is very high (*Indian Express*, 1999. Oct. 14). Chennai Corporation of AIDS Prevention and Control Society (CAPACS) is established in 1998 with the objectives of strengthening the activities related to awareness, accessibility and action. The Organisation was established as per the direction of National AIDS Control Organisation (NACO) exclusively for Chennai in view of the high density of floating population which the city attracts regularly.

Besides, being the capital city, Chennai is a well known place for multi sectoral activities with increasing urbanization, modernization, industrialization and commercialization. Floating and migratory population from various parts of the state, country and world are the common feature of Chennai. The city oriented life encouraged multisexual activities, both pre-marital and extra marital sex. Many attractive tourism spots including Mahabalipuram and Kanchipuram are located close to Chennai. The well organized road transport, air ways and sea port influences tourists from all over the world. As a result of population growth and movements, the sex industries have well organized underground net work to encourage prostitution which are responsible for the spread of sexually transmitted diseases including HIV/AIDS.

So, Chennai is purposely selected for the study. As for the respondents are concerned, purposive sampling is adopted to select 200 women living with HIV positive by applying snowball technique with the support of Non Governmental and Governmental agencies.

Pilot Study

The pilot study has been conducted by the researcher in the districts of Chennai, Dindigul and Madurai in order to obtain general view with regard to women living with HIV. In addition to interaction and focused discussion with HIV infected women, the researcher also referred the relevant articles and annual reports related to the prevalence of high risk groups and sexual behaviours of those groups in their respective working areas.

Universe

According to AIDS cases surveillance report by Tamil Nadu State AIDS Control Society, as on October 2001, the total number of samples screened for HIV in Tamil Nadu was 8,15,922 and among them number of persons found seropositive were 20,051 with 2.45 seropositivity rate per thousand. The estimation of State wise HIV prevalence report of the NACO from 1998-2003 reveals the HIV prevalence rate in Tamil Nadu during 2001 is high based on the prevalence rate of various risk groups including patients attending STD clinics (12.60%), Women attending antenatal clinics (1.13%), Intravenous drug users (24.56%) and men seeking men (MSM) with 2.40%.

High secrecy is maintained by the Government of Tamil Nadu in keeping the records of reported cases as well as revealing their address to the public. The current prevalence rate of HIV is an estimated figure based on the sentinel surveillance data on the selected sites according to UNAIDS/WHO criteria, it is highly difficult to obtain exact number of people living with HIV/AIDS in general and women in particular for all districts of Tamil Nadu. Therefore due to this limitation, universe is not taken into consideration for this study.

Sample Design

The available data based on Tamil Nadu AIDS control Society on the reported cases of AIDS in various districts in Tamil Nadu suggested that the HIV prevalence rate is high in Chennai. Therefore, purposive sampling technique is adopted to contact the respondents by resorting to snowballing procedure. Accordingly 200 HIV infected persons representing cross sections living in Chennai city were interviewed for the purpose of empirical investigations. The respondents were identified with the support of Governmental and Non-Governmental Organisations (NGOs) in Chennai city.

Sources of Data

The present study has used both primary and secondary sources of data. The primary data were collected directly from the respondents (women living with HIV positive) by the researcher.

The main instrument for the collection of primary data was the interview schedule which was structured in order to collect relevant data. Though the interview schedule was constructed in English, the interview was conducted in Tamil, which is the regional language of Tamil Nadu. The interview schedule administered with the women living with HIV positive consisted the questions intended to elicit information regarding personal data, family particulars, socio-economic status, marital details, circumstances leading to HIV positive, circumstances leading to commercial sex work, sexual behaviour after HIV infection, details about HIV testing and pre and post test counseling, social relationship of the respondents in the family, in neighbourhood, in work place, and among relatives and friendship, the discrimination experienced in treatment and in work place and their perception of pregnancy after infection.

The secondary data were collected from sources like journals, magazine, newspapers, books, articles, pamphlets, reports, web sites etc.

Tools for Data Collection

Personal interview was carried out with the structured interview schedule in order to collect required information from the respondents in consonance with the objectives formulated for the study. Observation techniques (both participatory and non-participatory), and focused group discussion with the women living with HIV positive also used to supplement and strengthen the primary data.

Discussion was also held with the Government Organisation especially with the officials of Tamil Nadu State AIDS Control

Society in Chennai, Non-governmental Organisations working in AIDS Prevention and Control Activities and Funding Agencies like AIDS Prevention and Control Project (APAC).

Pre-test

The constructed interview schedule was put to field test with few women living with HIV positive in order to test its suitability and relevance. Later, the schedule was edited and standardized based on the results of the pre-test.

Data Editing, Coding and Analysis

After collecting data from the respondents, the interview schedule was scrutinized and edited for checking the errors and omissions. After editing, the collected data were coded to enter into the master table for classification of data for tabulation. Conventional statistical tools such as average and per centages were employed for data processing and analysis.

Scope and Limitations

As the present study is based on the sample of women living with HIV positive, it is bound to be limited in its scope and applicability. As far as scope is concerned, it is mainly focused on the discrimination faced by the women in various socio-economic spheres in terms of comparison with their male infected partners. The study also focused on the perception of infected women towards their pregnancy and transmission of HIV to the infants. The research also further focused on the possible ways and means to prevent and control the spread of HIV infection in the form of suggestion of an action plan.

Reluctance, hesitation, fear, anger and sickness to cope with the interview on the part of the women living with the HIV positive are the major limitations of the study while collecting sensitive and crucial information. However, the researcher has taken a number of visits to meet the respondents in order to persuade and motivate to collect reliable data.

Reference Period

The reference period of the present study was 2001 to 2005.

4

HIV/AIDS: A Global Scenario

Tracing the History of HIV/AIDS

The Human Immuno Deficiency Virus (HIV) started threatening the entire world since early 1980s. It is a retrovirus that infects the immune system, mainly CD4 cells and macrophages, which is the key components of immune system. It destroys or impairs the functions of immune system, leading to "immune deficiency" called AIDS – "Acquired Immune Deficiency Syndrome". The word acquired was chosen because the illness was neither genetically determined nor, the result of other conditions. In other words, it was acquired during the normal life and the term AIDS is used when the disease has progressed and the person develops one or more serious infections or conditions (Thomas, 1997: 2). The majority of people infected with HIV, if not treated, develop signs of AIDS within eight to 30 years. Symptoms of AIDS generally appear when the numbers of CD4 white blood cells decreases to 200 per cubic millilitre (ml^3) of blood (UNAIDS, Q&A, 2004: 3).

A century ago, that is in 1884 itself, the German bacteriologist Robert Koch in his key paper on tuberculosis he spelled out the three criteria for proving a microbe guilty of causing a disease. First, the germ must be found growing abundantly in every patient and every diseased tissue; second, the germ must be isolated and grown in the laboratory; and third, the purified germ must cause the disease again in another host. Together, these came to be known as Koch's Postulates (Ellison and Duesberg, 1994: 21). The scientists agreed that the evidence on the link between HIV and AIDS passes this test. There is a clear correlation of clinical findings of AIDS and the identification of HIV in the blood (UNAIDS Q&A, 2004: 3). Search for tracing the virus followed the Robert Koch's postulates.

Biologists estimated that the first HIV cases occurred in Africa in the 1930s and then for many unknown reasons, it burst out of its African origins and transmitted throughout the world without leaving any place with AIDS free status (Zhu *et al.*, 1998: 94-99).

Chronologically speaking, the origin of HIV may be traced from 1950s where the similar appearance of AIDS is noticed in some African region after World War II (Thomas, 1997: 26). AIDS like symptom in patient was identified as early as 1959 (Sabatier, 1988).

In 1959 a British sailor with Kaposi's Sarcoma and pneumocystis died in Manchester. In 1969, a 15-year old black US boy died with Kaposi's Sarcoma and opportunistic infections in St. Louis (Thomas, 1997: 26). In the late 1970, the first clue of a strange new disease began to turn up in certain European hospitals. A 47-year old Danish doctor, Dr. Grethe Rask, had practised medicine in a remote hospital in Zaire, died in Denmark in 1977. A biopsy showed that the cause of death was the rare Pneumocystis Carinii Pneumonia (PCP) (Singhal: 2003: 48). In 1978, a 27-year old Rwandan mother developed the immunodeficiency symptoms and died. In the same year a 34-year old Zairean women died due to opportunistic infection in Kinshasa. In 1979 a 44-year old homosexual man died with Kaposi's Sarcoma in New York city (Thomas, 1997: 26). Kaposi's Saracoma is a kind of cancer found very common among AIDS patients in the West.

A dozen AIDS cases were retrospectively identified in the United States and Haiti between 1972 and 1976 (Korber *et al.*, 2000: 1789-96). An Air Canada flight steward called Gaetan Dugas who was identified as homosexual frequently visited Paris and played a vital role in transmitting the virus in the United States (Shilts and Randy, 1987).

In 1980 the first unusual immune system failure was documented by Dr. Michael S. Gottlieb, a young immunologist at University of California, Los Angeles in the United States. His first patient sought medical care because of weight loss, candidiasis (Singhal, 2003: 49), yeast infection, and Pneumocystis carinii pneumonia which is the disease rarely struck anyone but cancer patients (Ellison and Duesberg, 1994: 103). The report on the new symptom of disease made the local physicians in Los Angeles to refer several similar cases to Gottileb and it was found that all were active homosexuals (Ellison and Duesberg, 1994: 103).

The opportunistic infections of these patients led Gottlieb to suspect problems with their immune systems, and he found that the men had a deficiency of T lymphocytes (Arvind Singhal, 2003: 49). In 1981 the Centre for Disease Control's (CDC) weekly medical surveillance report called Morbidity and Mortality Weekly Report cited a cluster of cases of Karposi's Saràcoma, a rare type of skin cancer usually found among elderly men of Mediterranean ancestry. All of the individuals in the cluster were young gay men. Similar cases were also reported gay men from New York, San Francisco and Los Angeles (Maclure, 1998: 467-73).

The epidemiologist of the CDC started to search the causes and means of transmission of this strange new disease of immune suppression. They assumed that a virus was being transmitted through sexual contact among gay men and it caused immune deficiency in the human body which allowed to acquire various opportunistic infection. In the beginning, the disease did not have an official name and it was called by "Gay Related Immune Deficiency Syndrom" (Singhal, 2003: 50). By July of 1982 the CDC decided to call it the Acquired Immune Deficiency Syndrome (AIDS) (Ellison and Duesberg, 1994: 105).

By 1983, scientists in France discovered virus which caused AIDS and showed that it was undeniably a new virus. At first, different names were given to the AIDS virus by the French and the American workers and ultimately, the International Committee on the Nomenclature of Viruses intervened and the name 'human immunodeficiency virus or HIV' was accepted

(Pavri, 1992: 4-5). HIV-1 was identified by Dr. Robert Gallo at the National Cancer Institute in Bethesda, Maryland and HIV-2 by Dr. Luc Montagnier of Pasteur Institute in Paris in 1983 (Singhal, 2003: 46).

These two human HIV viruses are distinguishable by their genome makeup but are believed that it had a common ancestor in Africa. Scientist believed that HIV-2 was transmitted to humans from a simian source, probably the sooty mongabeys that are hunted for food in Senegal, Guinea, the Ivory Coast, and Gambia. HIV-1, which is more lethal, is closely related to Simian Immunodeficiency Virus and it was transmitted from the Central African Chimpanzee called 'Pan troglodytes. HIV-1 mutates very rapidly, and Simian Immunodeficiency virus crossed over to humans as Human Immunodeficiency Virus (Arvind Singhal, 2003: 46). While HIV-1 is found worldwide, HIV-2 is mostly found in West Africa and now the cases have been reported from East Africa, Europe, Asia and Latin America (*The Week*, 2001: 6).

In the course of the year, three modes of transmission– contaminated blood and blood products transfusion including contaminated needles, sexual intercourse, and mother to child transmission were described (UNAIDS, Q & A, 2004: 1).

The Current Feature of HIV/AIDS

HIV is currently spreading at the rate of one new infection in every fifteen seconds, according to Dr. Michael Merson, head of the Global Programmes on AIDS at the World Health Organisation. The virus is also spreading geographically beyond the urban areas and reaching deeper into the countryside. No country is exempted from infection and it has covered all directions of the world -East and West, North and South. Every day, throughout the world, an estimated 16,000 people become infected with the HIV (UNAIDS REPORT, 1999)

Young male and female are increasingly affected by HIV and every day, 7000 people between the ages of 10-24 worldwide acquire the virus. This means 2.6 million new infections a year (Avert Organisation, 2005). Approximately one-quarter of those living with HIV/AIDS are men under age 25. More than 70% of HIV infections worldwide are estimated to result from sex between men and women. Ten per cent can be traced to sexual transmission between men, and 5 per cent of infections are due to needle-sharing by people who inject drugs and four out of five injecting drug users are men (Parliamentary Forum on HIV/AIDS, 2004)

Another disturbing trend is the growing proportion of women infected with HIV, over 15,000 women become infected every week and in many countries women surpassing the rate of men's HIV infection, according to Merson. HIV is also spreading into the general population in many parts of the world, and is no longer linked to groups with high risk behaviours.

Global Patterns of HIV Infection

Three categories of global pattern and the countries are given below: (Pavri, 1992: 16).

Table 4.1. Global Pattern of HIV Infection

Pattern I	Extensive spread of HIV began in the late 1970s/ early 1980s. Homosexual male and intravenous drug users have been predominantly affected populations, but heterosexual transmission is increasing. Western Europe, North America, some areas in South Africa, Australia, New Zealand.
Pattern II	Extensive spread of HIV began in the mid-to-late 1970s/early 1980s. Heterosexual transmission has continues to predominate. Africa, Caribbean, some areas in South America.
Pattern III	Introduction and/or extensive spread of HIV did not occur until mid-to-late 1890s. Extensive spread of HIV is now being documented in several countries in South East Asia, but the prevalence of HIV, in most countries classified within this pattern, remains relatively low. Countries in Asia are included in Pattern III, where HIV was introduced late. Asia, the Pacific region (minus Australia and New Zealand), the Middle East, Eastern Europe and some rural areas of South America.

Trends of Global HIV Infection

The following estimated figures reflect the increasing trends of HIV infection in the world (Table 4.2):

Table 4.2. Global Summary of AIDS Epidemic (1996-2004)

	1996	*1999*	*2000*	*2001*	*2002*	*2003*	*2004*
No. of infection (in million)	29.4	33.6	34	35	37	38	39.4

Source: UNAIDS Global summary of the *AIDS Epidemic Update*, December 2004.

It was estimated that around 29.4 million HIV infection in 1996 and the current estimates of 2004 shows that around 39.4 million people were living with HIV through out the world. It is almost an increase of 10 million within eight years that is from 1996-2004 (UNAIDS, 2004: 6). It shows that the number of people living with HIV continue to rise, despite the fact that all countries have effective prevention strategies.

Mode of Transmission of HIV/AIDs

Table 4.3. Hiv/AIDs – Region wise mode of Transmission

Regions	*Epidemic Started*	*Mode of Transmission*
Sub-Saharan Africa	Late 70s and early 80s	Heterosexual
South and South East Asia	Late 80s	Heterosexual
Latin America	Late 70s and early 80s	Male to male, Intravenous drug use, and Heterosexual
America, W. Europe, Australia/New Zealand	Late 70s and early 80s	Male to male, Intravenous drug use, and Heterosexual
Caribbean	Late 70s and early 80s	Heterosexual
Central/Eastern Europe, Central Asia	Early 90s	Intravenous drug use, Male to male
East Asia, Pacific	Late 80s	Male to male, Intravenous drug use, and Heterosexual
South Africa, Middle East	Late 80s	Intravenous drug use, heterosexual

Source: Digumarti Bhaskara Rao, (2000: 211)

Worldwide, between 75 and 85 of every 100 HIV infection in adults have been transmitted through unprotected sexual intercourse including oral, vaginal or anal sex. Heterosexual (male-female) intercourse accounts for more than 70 per cent of global adult HIV infections and homosexuals (male-male) intercourse accounts for 5-10 per cent. HIV is more likely to be transmitted through intercourse when either one or both partners have a classic Sexually Transmitted Disease (STD). Around 25-35 per cent of all infants born to HIV infected women themselves become infected with the virus before or during birth, or through breast-feeding. This mother-to-child (vertical) transmission accounts for more than 90 per cent of global infections in infants and children (Digumarti Bhaskara Rao, 2000: 209).

The sharing of HIV infected injection equipment by drug users resulting in blood borne HIV transmission, which accounts for 5-10 per cent of all adult infections. This proportion is growing in many areas of the world. Transfusion of HIV infected blood or blood products accounts for 3-5 per cent of all adult HIV infections. In many parts of the world HIV transmission through the transfusion of infected blood has been reduced by the use of voluntary blood donors, the routine screening of donated blood for HIV, and more rational use of blood aimed at reducing the number of transmission (Digumarti Bhaskara Rao, 2000: 209).

A Global Overview of the AIDS Epidemic

Table 4.4. Regional HIV and Aids Statistics and Features, end 2002 and 2004

Regions	*Adult and children living with HIV (in million)*	*Adult and children newly infected with HIV (in million)*	*Adult prevalence %*	*No. of women (15-49) living with HIV (in million)*	*Percent of adult (15-49)women living with HIV*	*Adult and children death due to AIDS (in million)*
Sub-Saharan Africa						
2004	25.4	3.1	7.4	13.3	57	2.3
2002	24.4	2.9	7.5	12.8	57	2.1
North Africa and Middle East						
2004	540 000	92 000	0.3	250 000	48	28 000
2002	430 000	73 000	0.2	200 000	48	20 000

South and South East Asia						
2004	7.1	890 000	0.6	2.1	30	490 000
2002	6.4	820 000	0.6	1.8	23	430 000
East Asia						
2004	1.1	290 000	0.1	250 000	22	51 000
2002	760 000	120 000	0.1	160 000	21	37 000
Oceania						
2004	35 000	5000	0.2	7100	21	700
2002	28 000	3200	0.2	5000	18	500
Latin America						
2004	1.7	240 000	0.6	610 000	36	95 000
2002	1.5	190 000	0.6	520 000	35	74 000
Caribbean						
2004	440 000	53 000	2.3	210 000	49	36000
2002	420 000	52 000	2.3	19 000	49	33000
Eastern Europe and Central Asia						
2004	1.4	210000	0.8	490 000	34	60 000
2002	1.0	190000	0.6	330 000	33	40 000
Western and Central Europe						
2004	610 000	21 000	0.3	160 000	25	6500
2002	600 000	18 000	0.3	150 000	25	6000
North America						
2004	1.0	44000	0.6	260 000	25	16 000
2002	970000	44000	0.6	240 000	25	16 000
Total						
2004	39.4	4.9	1.1	17.6	47	3.1
2002	36.6	4.5	1.1	16.4	48	2.7

Source : UNAIDS *AIDS Epidemic Update*, December (2004 :7-9).

The number of people living with HIV has been rising in every region and no country in the world remains unaffected. The epidemic is not homogeneous within and between the countries. The epidemic has steepest increase in Sub-Saharan Africa, Caribbean, East Asia and in Eastern Europe and Central Asia. In other regions of the world the epidemic is gradually increasing not only among risk groups but also among general population.

UNAIDS and WHO have divided the globe into 10 epidemic zone in order to obtain easy estimation of HIV/AIDS in different regions of the globe. These zones are Sub-Saharan Africa, East Asia, South and South East Asia, Oceania, Eastern Europe and Central Asia, Western and Central Europe, North Africa and Middle East, North America, Caribbean and Latin America.

It is evident from Table 4.4 that the Sub-Saharan Africa has the largest number of people living with HIV positive followed by South and South East Asia. Latin America, Eastern Europe and Central Asia, East Asia and North America. Western and Central Europe, North Africa and Middle East, Caribbean and Oceania regions have low level of infection rate in 2004. But the comparison of rate of infection in 2004 with the 2002 and 2001 shows that these regions will also soon comes under the heavy epidemic regions.

Women and Aids

The women are increasingly infected in many regions. AIDS is affecting women more severely where heterosexual is the dominant mode of transmission. Globally, half of all people living with HIV positive are female. UNICEF survey says that above 50% of young women in high prevalence countries did not know the basic facts about AIDS (UNAIDS AIDS Epidemic Update, December 2004: 8). Women's HIV infection has its roots not only from women's ignorance about HIV/AIDS and sex and sexuality but also from their disempowerment. Most women around the world become HIV infected through their partners' high risk behaviours where women have either little or no control.

In 1996 it was estimated that 42 per cent of the 21.8 million adult living with HIV/AIDS are women, and the proportion has increased to 47 per cent in 2004 (UNAIDS AIDS epidemic update, 2004: 5).

Socio-economic inequality, gender discrimination, poverty, illiteracy and lack of skills, multiple partner relationships, transactional sex, intergenerational sex, violence against women, cultural backwardness are some of the major causes for increasing infection among women in all parts of the world.

The prevalence of HIV infection among women is concentrated more in Sub-Saharan Africa, Caribbean, Latin America, Eastern Europe and Central Asia and Asia.

The Trends of Adult Women (15-49 Years) Living with HIV in High Concentrated Regions

Table 4.5. Percentage of Infection among Adult Women from 1985-2004 in High Prevalence Regions

Regions	*1985*	*1990*	*1995*	*2000*	*2004*
Sub-Saharan Africa	49	54	56	57	57
Caribbean	45	50	47	48	49
Latin America	18	22	30	34	36
Eastern Europe and Central Asia	0	23	28	32	34
Asia	0	19	22	27	30

Source: *UNAIDS AIDS Epidemic Update, 2004: 7.*

Table 4.5 reflected that the HIV prevalence among women is rapidly increasing year by year in the above mentioned regions. Hetero sexual contact is the major mode of transmission in Sub-Saharan Africa and Caribbean. Three quarters of all women with HIV worldwide live in Sub-Saharan Africa. Adult women in Sub-Saharan Africa are upto 1.3 times more likely to be infected with HIV than their male counterparts and the infection is greatest among young women aged 15-24 years. In South Africa, Zambia and Zimbabwe the young women (aged 15-24) are three to six times more likely to be infected than young men. Women constitute nearly half of the 420 000 adults living with HIV in the Caribbean, where young women 15-24 years of age are almost twice as likely to be infected than are young men (*UNAIDS AIDS Epidemic Update*, 2004: 8).

Women represent 36% of the 1.7 million adult living with HIV in Latin America. In this region the epidemic is centered largely among men who have sex with men and injecting drug users. The risk groups normally have sex with sex workers and they also mostly have wives or other sexual partners. In Eastern Europe, the AIDS epidemics are spreading within and between particular population groups such as sex workers or injecting drug users and then into the general population. In these regions women and girls are increasingly affected. In East Asia women comprise 22% of all adults living with HIV and 28% of young people (aged 15-24 years) living with HIV. In South and South-East Asia, 30% of adults and 40% of young people living with HIV are women and girls. Women accounted for more than one quarter of new HIV infections in India and HIV transmission between spouses has become a more prominent cause of new infections in countries such as India, Cambodia, Myanmar and Thailand (*UNAIDS AIDS Epidemic Update*, 2004: 8).

In the industrialized countries of Western Europe and North America, one quarter of people living with HIV are women and the infection is increasingly lodged among women of marginalized sections of populations, including minorities, immigrants and refugees. African American and Hispanic women represent less than one quarter of all women in the United States of America, but accounted for 80% of AIDS cases reported among women at the turn of this century (*UNAIDS AIDS Epidemic Update*, 2004: 9.).

Sub-Saharan Africa

Sub-Saharan Africa is located in the south of the Sahara desert, in Africa. It is the worst-affected region in the world by the AIDS epidemic. The region has just over 10% of the world's population, but is home to over 60% of all people living with HIV. In 1996 14 million people were estimated as HIV positive. However, in 2002, 24.4 million adult and children and in 2004, 25.4 million were estimated as HIV positive. It has almost 11 million of increased infection from 1996. The per centage of adult infection rate in 2002 is 7.5 where as it was found to be stable (7.4%) in 2004. Less than one million (783,700) AIDS deaths were estimated during 1996. But the death rate of adult and children due to AIDS has increased to 2.3 million in 2004 from 2.1 million in 2002. An estimated 3.1 million adults and children became infected with HIV during the year 2004. This brought the total number of people living with HIV/AIDS in the region to 25.4 million by the end of the year 2004.

Many African countries are experiencing generalized epidemics. This means that HIV is spreading throughout the general population, rather than being confined to populations at higher risk, such as sex workers and their clients, men who have sex with men, and injecting drug users.

All the countries in Sub-Saharan Africa have prevalence rate about 17% with Botswana and Swaziland having about 35%. In West Africa HIV prevalence is much lower and no country in this region have prevalence rate above 10%. Adult prevalence rate in central and East Africa is estimated as 4-14 per cent (*Report on the Global Epidemic*, 2004: 7-8).

Women at greater risk in Sub-Saharan Africa

Sub-Saharan Africa ranks first in Women's HIV infection. In the beginning of the era of AIDS epidemic, which was in 1985 the per centage of adult women's (15-49 years) was estimated as below 50%. But it has increased to 57% in 2004 (*UNAIDS AIDS Epidemic Update*, December 2004: 11). Among them 76% of young people are aged between 15-24 years. African women are being infected at an earlier age than men, and the gap in HIV prevalence between them continue to grow. At the beginning of the epidemic in sub-Saharan Africa, women living with HIV were vastly outnumbered by men. But today there are, on average, 13 infected women for every 10 infected men when compared to 12 infected women for every 10 infected men in 2002.

The difference between infection levels is more pronounced in urban areas, with 14 women for very 10 men, than in rural areas, where 12 women are infected for every 10 men. Adult women in Sub-Saharan Africa are 1.3 times more likely to be infected than their male counterparts (*UNAIDS Report on the Global Epidemic*, 2004: 11-12).

The difference in infection levels between women and men is even more pronounced among young people aged 15-24. Today, there are 13 infected women for every 10 infected men in Sub-Saharan Africa. It has its ranges from 20 women for every 10 men in South Africa, to 45 women for very 10 men in Kenya and Mali (*UNAIDS Report on the Global Epidemic*, 2004: 7-8). In Sub-Saharan Africa, heterosexual transmission is by far the predominant mode of HIV transmission. Unsafe injections in health-care settings are believed to be responsible for around 2.5% of all infections.

HIV has spread rapidly among people with high-risk behaviours and widely among those assumed to be at lower risk. Prevalence among urban sex workers ranges from 20 per cent to 50 per cent in various countries of Sub-Saharan Africa. Infection rates among women attending antenatal clinics have grown rapidly to high levels in some areas, have stabilized at lower levels in others and appear to be declining in some areas like Kampala and Uganda. An estimated two-thirds of all new cases of mother-to-child transmission worldwide occur in sub-Saharan Africa (Ramamurthy, 2000: 111).

Median HIV prevalence in Pregnant women attending antenatal clinics in Sub-Saharan Africa from 1998-2003

The prevalence of HIV among antenatal women in different countries of Sub-Saharan Africa shows that the rata of infection is rapidly increasing among the women in African countries (Table 4.6).

In Southern Africa, the epidemic is rapidly increasing among the antenatal women whereas in Eastern Africa the epidemic remain constant and it shows certain declining trends in Uganda. The low prevalence is found in Western Africa, especially in the regions of Ghana, Nigeria and Senegal. But the region of Cameroon and Cote d'ivoire has higher prevalence of infection in Western Africa. In these regions, the median HIV prevalence levels have reached to 10% among pregnant women.

Table 4.6. Percentage of HIV Prevalence Among Pregnant Women from 1997-2003

Regions	*1997-98*	*1999-2000*	*2001*	*2002*	*2003*
SOUTHERN AFRICA					
Botswana	37	38	40	40	39
Mozambique	No data	10	15	15	—
South Africa	20	23	25	27	30
EASTERN AFRICA					
Ethiopia	13	10	10	10	9
Kenya	13	14	10	9	9
Uganda	10	5	6	5	—
WESTERN AFRICA					
Ghana	3	3	6	5	—
Cote d'ivoire	10	9	10	10	—
Nigeria	—	5	6	4	5
Senegal	0	0	4	0	—

Source: *UNAIDS AIDS epidemic update*, 2004: 20.

Causes for Women's HIV infection in Sub-Saharan Region

Poverty, lower status of women, female circumcision, involvement in sexual activities at early ages, pre marital sex to overcome financial strain are the major factors for women to get infected by the dreaded virus HIV. The culture of silence surrounding sexuality, exploitative transactional and intergenerational sex and violence against women within the relationship are the other important causes for African's women's vulnerability towards HIV/AIDS.

Impact of HIV/AIDS on Africa

HIV/AIDS has a widespread impact on many sections of society.

- In many countries of Sub-Saharan Africa, AIDS has reduced the life expectancy of the people. Millions of adults are dying at young or in early middle age. Average life expectancy in Sub-Saharan Africa is now 47 years, when it could have been 62 without AIDS.

- The toll of HIV/AIDS on households can be very severe. Many families are losing their income earners. Many of those dying have surviving partners who are themselves infected and in need of care. They leave behind children grieving and struggling to survive without a parent's care. HIV/AIDS strips the family assets further impoverishing the poor.
- In all affected countries, the HIV/AIDS epidemic is bringing additional pressure to bear on the health sector.
- A decline in school enrolment is one of the most visible effects of the HIV/AIDS epidemic on education in Africa.
- HIV/AIDS dramatically affects labour, setting back economic activity and social progress. The vast majority of people living with HIV/AIDS in Africa are between the ages of 15 and 49 - in the prime of their working lives.

Caribbean

The Caribbean is the second most affected region in the world with regard to women's infection with the adult prevalence rate of 2.3 per cent. It was estimated that 270,000 people were living with HIV AIDS in 1996 (Digmarti Bhaskara Rao, 2000: 217), but the infection has almost doubled in 2004. Among adult in the age group of 15-44, AIDS has become the leading cause of death (*UNAIDS Global Epidemic Update*, 2004: 35). Among young people 15-24 years of age, an estimated 3.1% of women and 1.7 of men were living with HIV in 2004. In five countries such as **Bahamas, Belize, Guyana, Haiti and Trinidad** and **Tobago** the national prevalence exceeds 2%. The adult prevalence is almost stabilized in Caribbean.

In this region, 12 countries face a generalized epidemic, with 1% prevalence among pregnant women. Heterosexual transmission is the main mode of transmission and it is only in Puerto Rico that injecting drug use drives the epidemic. **Haiti** is the most affected country, with 30,000 AIDS related deaths a year and 120,000 orphans due to AIDS. Its adult prevalence rate remains stable at 5% to 6% (WHO, 2003: 7).

HIV infection among Women in Caribbean

The highest infections among women in the Americas are in Caribbean countries. Women constitute nearly half of the adult living with the HIV positive. Young women are 2.5 times more likely to be infected than young men in the Caribbean island. The women in several countries like Barbados, Bermuda, Dominican Republic, Jamaica and Trinidad and Tabago and territories which depend on tourism are severely affected by HIV infection (*UNAIDS Global Epidemic Update*, 2004: 11).

In 2002-2004 around 49% of all people living with HIV positive in Caribbean are women. In 1985 the rate of infection among women was identified as 45%. But now it has increased to 49%. The ratio of infection between men and women is 2: 1. Women younger than 24 years in the Dominican Republic were almost twice as likely to be HIV infected than their male counterparts. In Jamaica teenage girls are 2.5 times more likely to be infected than boys in the same age group of 10-19 years.

Haiti continues to have the largest number of people living with HIV in Caribbean. It has 280 000 (range 120,000-600,000) people living with HIV in 2003. The median HIV prevalence among women (25-49 years) attending antenatal clinics has fallen from 4.5% in 1996 to 2.8% in 2003-2004. HIV prevalence among pregnant women aged 15-24 years appears to have declined from 3.6% to 2.8% in 2003-2004. The over all infection among pregnant women varies between 1.8% and 7.0% in different parts of Haiti.

Jamaica has an estimated 22000 (range 11 000-41 000) people living with HIV in 2003. HIV prevalence among pregnant women attending antenatal clinics is found to be at 1.4% in 2002. But it has increased to 2.7% in St. James and 1.9% in Kingston and St. Andrews. High HIV prevalence is also observed among patients at sexually transmitted clinics in 2002. Almost 8% of men and 5% of women in sexually transmitted clinics are infected by HIV.

In **Bahamas** where an estimated 5000 people were living with HIV in 2003 and the HIV prevalence among pregnant women fall from 4.8% in 1993 and 3.6% in 1996 to 3.0% in 2002 due to stronger preventions techniques.

In **Barbados** region, declining trend in HIV infection is observed. HIV infection among pregnant women dropped from 0.7% in 1999 to 0.3% in 2003. Mother-to-child transmission also reduced due to the expansion of voluntary counseling and testing services and the provision of anti retroviral treatment. In Bermuda, the number of AIDS cases decreased by almost half (19 to11) between 2000 and 2002.

HIV prevalence in **Guyana** was the second highest in this region (2.5%) in 2003. The epidemic is serious in Dominican Republic with HIV prevalence among pregnant women higher than 2%. Most of the infections are due to unprotected sex. HIV prevalence is very low in Cuba .But now it has observed rising trends in HIV infection as a result of sex between men.

Factors influencing Women's HIV Infection in Caribbean

The causes for their infection are due to the fact that some girls have sexual relationship with older men who are more likely to be HIV infected. The same trend has also been documented in several countries of Caribbean regions. This trend is due to large proportion of men who have sex with men, also have sex with women. This is partly responsible for the increasing feminization of the epidemic.

Latin America

All the main modes of transmission exist in most countries of Latin America along with significant levels of risky behaviours–such as early sexual entrance, unprotected sex with multiple partners and the use of unclean drug-injecting equipment. HIV prevalence rate is increasing in many Latin American Countries.

Around 1.7 million people are living with HIV in Latin America in 2004 compared with 1.5 million in 2002 and 1.3 million in 1996. In 2004 it is estimated that 95 000 people have died due to AIDS. The mortality rate is higher when compared to the mortality rate of 2003 (84 000) and 2002 (74000) and 1996 (70,000). Among young people 15-24 years of age, 0.5% of women and 0.8% of men were living with HIV in 2003. The adult's prevalence rate is 0.6% in 2004.

Several Central American countries, such as **Belize, Honduras, Guyana and Suriname** have an estimated HIV prevalence of 1% or more among pregnant women. The infection among Latin American women was estimated around 15-20% in 1985 and it was increased to 35% in 2002 and 36% in 2004. The ratio of men with HIV infections to women with HIV infections has narrowed considerably to about 3 to1. This is partly because a large proportion of men who have sex with men, also have sex with women.

National HIV prevalence is now estimated to be 1% in Belize, Guyana, Honduras and Suriname. In most countries HIV infection is not generalized but is highly concentrated in populations at particular risk. Despite a national prevalence below 1%, Brazil has 40% of people living with HIV in Latin America. In some Brazilian cities, more than 60% of drug users are HIV positive.

In most **South American countries**, almost all infections are caused by contaminated drug-injecting equipment or sex between men. **In Puerto Rico,** more than half of all infections in 2002 were associated with injecting drug use, and about one-quarter were heterosexually transmitted (UNAIDS report on the global epidemic, 2004).

In **Central America**, injecting drug use plays less role, and the virus is spread predominantly through sex. HIV prevalence among female sex workers ranges from less than 1% in **Nicaragua,** 2% in **Panama,** 4% in **El Salvador** and 5% in **Guatemala,** to over 20% in **Hondura** (UNAIDS report on the global epidemic, 2004).

Unsafe sex among men who have sex with men is common across the whole region. The 13% of HIV prevalence in **Honduran** and the 8 to 18% of infection in Central America was among men who have sex with men. In Honduras 7% of male prisoners were infected with HIV infection. Unsafe sex is the major cause for the infection in the **Andean countries** of South America. In these places, prevalence rates have ranged from 14% in Lima, Peru to 20% in Bogotá in **Colombia** and 28% **Guayaquil** in **Ecuador.** In these regions, the large per centages of men who have sex with men also have unsafe sex with women which ultimately increase women's vulnerability to HIV/AIDS.

The spread of HIV through the sharing of drug injecting equipment is of growing concern in several countries, notably **Argentina, Brazil, Chile, Paraguay, Uruguay** and the northern part of **Mexico.** Injecting drug use accounts for an estimated 40% of reported new infections in **Argentina** and 28% in **Uruguay**. In both of these countries a growing number of women with HIV are injecting drug users or the sexual partners of men who are injecting drug users.

The increasing infection in Latin America is mainly due to low rates of condom use, and high numbers of sexual partners and low perceptions of risk.

Provision of anti-retroviral

Countries in Latin America for example Brazil, Argentina, Chile, Mexico and Uruguay, Colombia, Costa Rica and Paraguay are making efforts to provide antiretroviral drugs to patients with HIV/AIDS related illnesses. The Brazilian government has estimated that antiretroviral treatment has contributed to a 50% fall in mortality rates, a 60-80% decrease in morbidity rates and a 70% reduction in hospitalizations among HIV-positive people. Argentina reported decreasing numbers of deaths between 1999 and 2004 with stabilization over the last two years (Rob Noble, 2004: wp1).

East Europe and Central Asia

The infection is drastically increasing in East European and Central Asian countries. The infection was estimated as just 50,000 in 1996. But it has increased to 1.4 million in 2004. Around 210 000 people were newly infected with HIV during 2003 and 60 000 people have died due to AIDS till 2004 as against 1000 people in 1996. Like other countries, in these regions also the infection is found in higher per centage among the young people with the age of 15-24 years. Among them, the estimated rate of infection for women is 0.8% (0.4-1.6%) and for men it is found to be around 1.7% (0.8-3.7%). In both the regions, the women's HIV infection was estimated as 20% in 2001. But it has increased to 21% in 2002 and 34% in 2004 (UNAIDS Global Epidemic Update, December 2004: 52-60).

Eastern Europe

In the Eastern Europe, Ukraine is the worst affected region and Russian Federation is the home to the largest epidemic in the entire region. In 2001, the Russian Federation has 55% of infection in the Eastern European countries. But it has increased to 70% in 2004 mainly due to the activities of commercial sex and injecting drug use. In other regions of Eastern Europe, the epidemic is in its early stage (*UNAIDS AIDS Epidemic Update*, 2004: 52).

Across the continent, HIV infections through heterosexual contact are increasing steadily and women account for a rising proportion of HIV diagnoses. Most of the infections are among adult below the age of 30 years. In Ukraine 25%, in Belaras 60% are aged between 15-24 years. Most of the drug users are under the age of 19 years of age (30% in St. Petersburg, 20% in Ukraine, and 12% in Moscow). The use of unclean equipment, sharing of drug injecting equipment is the common norm among the drug users (Avert Organisation.2004: 1).

Social and economic transition forced large number of youth towards injecting drug use and commercial sex activities. Around 81% of women entered into prostitution at their younger age of 15-39 years. Therefore, the rate of infection is higher (64%) among the women at the age group of 20-24 years. Around 30% infection in Ukraine among women is heterosexual in 2003. It is three times higher than the documents of 1997 (11%). In Eastern Europe, 40% of infected women were at their reproductive age and 60% are under the age of 25 years. Nearly 1% of pregnant women were tested HIV positives in these regions. The increasing trend of infection among women shows the increasing trend of mother-to-child transmission. In 2001 around 27% of child infection is through mother-to-child transmission. But it has decreased to 12% in 2003 as a result of effective intervention programme (*UNAIDS AIDS Epidemic Update*, 2004: 52-60).

Central Asia

Kazakhstan, Kyrgyzstan, Tajikistan, Turkmenistan and Uzbekistan are the five countries associated with Central Asian Republics (Jawahar, 2004: 1). The number of reported cases of infection is still low in Central Asia. But the infection is dramatically increasing. Officially reported cases in the five countries of Central Asia jumped from about 500 in 200 to over 12000 in 2004. Unreported cases are higher in these regions. The Centre for Disease Control and Prevention in Central Asia has estimated that around 90000 people are living with HIV in these regions. One third of all identified cases were detected only in 2003. The rapid increase is between 2000 and 2003 is three fold in Kazakhstan, nine fold in the Kyrgyz Republic, 17 fold in Tajikistan and 16 fold in Uzbekistan. The male-female ration was greater than 4: 1 in all countries. The rate of infection is higher among the prisoners (8%). The infection among pregnant women in the entire region is found to be below 1% and among drug users is around 2% (The World Bank Group, 2005: 1).

In Central Asia, the epidemic is driven by injecting drug use and unsafe sex and it is concentrated among young people. Therefore, drug users and prostitutes forming the largest risk groups. According to World Health Organisation, 70% of all new infection in Uzbekistan are among injection drug users. The impact of stigma with regard to HIV/AIDS is higher in Central Asian Countries. The prevailing stigma reduces the harm reduction programme for drug users, prostitutes and other higher risk groups. The stigma also prevents high risk people from taking HIV test (Naz Nazar, 2004: 1).

Central Asian countries are located on both the sides of major drug trafficking routes into the Russian Federation and Europe. Young people particularly economically marginalized are more vulnerable. In Kazakhstan, for example, three quarters of people diagnosed with HIV were unemployed. In Kazakhstan and Kyrgyzstan 70% of all HIV positive persons are under 30 years of age. Condom use is generally low among the young people in Eastern Europe and Central Asia and it increases the rate of infection among the general population in general and women in particular (Avert Organisation, 2004: 1).

Asia

The Asian continent comprises of South and South East Asia and East Asia. In East Asia 22% of the adults living with HIV/AIDS are women. Among them 28% are young people aged between 15-24 years. In South and South East Asia more than a quarter of adults and 40% of young people living with HIV/AIDS are women. Until now the mode of infection in Asia is mainly through injecting drug use and sex work. Factors affecting the spread of HIV/AIDS among women and girls in the regions are poverty, early marriage, trafficking and sex work, migration, lack of education, gender discrimination and violence. HIV transmission between spouses has become a more prominent cause of new infection in countries such as Cambodia, Myanmar, Thailand anu India. Injecting drug use is the major mode of transmission in countries such as Indonesia, Nepal and Bangladesh.

Table 4.7. HIV and AIDS Statistics and Features end of 2002 and 2004

Year	*Adult & Children living with HIV (in million)*	*No. of Women living with HIV (in million)*	*Adult & Children newly infected with HIV (in million)*	*Adult prevalence (%)*	*Adult & Child death due to AIDS (in million)*
2004	8.2 (5.4-11.8)	2.3 (1.5-3.3)	1.2 (720 000-2.4 million)	0.4 (0.3-0.6)	540 000 (350 000-810 000)
2002	7.2 (4.6-10.5)	1.9 (1.2-2.8)	1.1 (540-2.5 million)	0.4 (0.2-0.5)	470 000 (300 00-690 000)

Source: UNAIDS Global Epidemic Update, December 2004: 36-49.

National HIV infection level in Asia is low compared with some other continent like Africa. The latest estimate shows that 8.2 million people are living with in 2004. Among them 2.3 million are adult women. The new infection during 2004 is 1.2 million. AIDS claimed 540 000 lives in 2004. Among young people 15-24 years of age, 0.3% of women and 0.4% of men were living with HIV by the end of 2004.

Classification of Asian regions

Asian countries can be divided into several categories according to the epidemic they are experiencing (UNAIDS AIDS

Epidemic Update, (2004: 36). They are classified as:

Table 4.8. Classification of Regions Based on Prevalence of HIV

Early Hit countries	Cambodia, Myanmar and Thailand
Low prevalence countries	Bangladesh, East Timor, Laos, Pakistan and the Philippines
High prevalence countries	Indonesia, Nepal, Vietnam, China and India

Early Hit Countries

Early hit countries are located close to "Golden Triangle" which is known for drug trafficking. Sex industry flourished in these regions due to widespread poverty. Ignorance, gender inequality, lower status, poor knowledge on AIDS, and poor education causes for the spread of epidemic in early hit countries.

Cambodia

The UNAIDS statistics of global over view of AIDS epidemic states that the Cambodia's national HIV prevalence is around 3% — the highest rate of infection in Asia (UNAIDS, 2002). According to UNAIDS statistics of 2003, there were 170 000 people between the age group of 15-49 are living with HIV. Among them women and children accounted for 51,000 and 7300. The adult prevalence rate is 2.6% and the AIDS death in 2003 is 15,000. The women attending anti natal clinics accounted for 2.2% (http: /hivinsite.ucsf.edu/global).

HIV was first detected in 1991 during serological screening of donated blood in 1991 and the first cases of AIDS were diagnosed in late 1993 (Arvind Singhal *et al.*, 2003: 111). Active commercial sex and "bridging" networks played a major role in the rapid spread of HIV, with a large portion of HIV incidence comprising transmission from sex workers to their male clients (Ramamurthy 2003: 13). HIV Sentinel Surveillance (HSS) data of Cambodia reveals that the sexual contact, both homo (14%) and hetero sexual is the major cause for the spread of epidemic followed by injection drug use. HIV prevalence rate is suspected to be high on the Thai border. The results provided the first evidence of a highly disseminated HIV epidemic, with prevalence of HIV upto 38% among female sex workers, 8% among police and the military and about 2.5% among women attending antenatal clinics (WHO, 2003: 26).

A survey of female sex workers by the Government of Cambodia in 1995 revealed that 38% were HIV positive. Therefore, Cambodia has borrowed the idea of 100 Percent Condom Programme and implemented in all regions of Cambodia. As a result condom use by brothel-based commercial sex workers has increased from 53% in 1998 to 78% in 1999 the increased condom use reduced the infection among brothel-based sex workers from 43% in 1998 to 29% in 2002. There have also been sustained declines in prevalence among their customers, who include urban policemen, military conscripts and motorcycle taxi riders (Singhal *et al.*, 2003: 112).

Table 4.9. Percentage of HIV Infection among Different Risk Groups from 1999-2002

Risk groups	*1999*	*2000*	*2001*	*2002*
Direct Sex Workers	13	9	8	6
Indirect Sex Workers	5	5.5	4	3
Police men	2.5	2	1.5	1
Pregnant women	1	2	1.5	1

Sources: UNAIDS AIDS epidemic update, 2004

The above table shows that the rate of HIV prevalence is decreasing among female sex workers, both direct and indirect due to the impact of various intervention programmes with regard to safe sex by using condom.

Myanmar

Geographical mapping of officially reported AIDS cases show that the eastern states/divisions have been the hardest hit by the epidemic. The central and delta regions have moderate rates of infection, with the lowest found on the western borders. The UNAIDS global report of 2003 reveals that an estimated 320,000 adult with the age of 15-49 are living with HIV positive in 2003 with the adult prevalence rate of 1.2%. Among them the women with the age of 15-49 living with HIV positive in 2003 is found to be 97,000. The children infected with HIV are estimated as 7600 in 2003. AIDS mortality is accounted for 20,000 in 2003 (UNAIDS, 2004).

HIV/AIDS situation in Myanmar is 'explosive' and it becomes a major contributor to the erosion of the well being of the general population. The infection has moved towards general population from most vulnerable sub -populations, such as injecting drug users and sex workers. HIV in Myanmar is mostly spread by injecting drug use and risky sex, both heterosexual and between men. The prevalence among injecting drug users is found in large area- from Yangon to the Shan State (Taunggyi, Lashio and Muse), bordering India, and Myitkyina in Kachin State.

The first HIV positive case in Myanmar was found in 1988 and the first AIDS case in 1991. UNAIDS (2002) data shows that the infection rate among commercial sex workers is (CSW) 33.5%, blood donors accounted for 1.1%, new military recruits have 2.2% and pregnant women's infection is around 2.2%. The official reported HIV cases show 30% are due to injecting drug use and 68% are due to unprotected heterosexual transmission (Myanmar Business Coalition of AIDS, 2002: 1). In some places, 78% of drug injectors tested positive in 2003. Each year the infection rate among injecting drug users are found to be around 45% to 80%. HIV infection among the patients attending sexually transmitted clinics have increased from 6% to 9% in 2003 (UNDIAD, December, 2004: 43).

The epidemic has been able to spread quickly throughout Myanmar due to several reasons. These include low awareness of HIV/AIDS amongst the general population' improper STD care, irregular HIV testing, low use of condoms, and large commercial sex business hidden from public life which makes it harder to control HIV/AIDS among commercial sex workers.

Thailand

Thailand has around 570,000 people living with HIV/AIDS including 200 000 women and 12,000 children. The estimated adult prevalence rate in 2003 is 1.5% (0.8-2.8%). The number of people died due to AIDS in 2003 is accounted for 58,000 (UNAIDS, Dec 2004: 44). Hetero sex, much of it between commercial sex workers and their customers (Celentano *et al.*, 2000: 535-40) and sharing needles among the injecting drug users are the main mode of HIV transmission in Thailand.

The first case of AIDS was reported in Thailand in 1984, (Phanuphak *et al.*, 1985: 195-199, Limsuwan *et al.* 1986: 164-169). In 1988-89 in the first major wave of the epidemic exploded among injecting drug-users, and found 40% in 1989. The second wave of infection spread among sex workers. In 1989, it was found that 44% of sex workers in Chiang Mai, in the north, were infected with HIV. The third waves of the epidemic identified among male clients of sex workers, their wives and partners, and their children (Weniger, 1991: S71: S85).

An estimated 200,000 of Thailand's 63 million people are commercial sex workers. During 1989 to 1995, 600,000 Thai men became HIV positive and the figure gone upto 984,000 in 2002 (Singal *et al.*, 2003: 103). At present it is estimated that one fifth of all new HIV infection is occurring among injecting drug users and in Northern Thailand 30% of drug injectors are infected with HIV and in other parts it was around 51%. The HIV prevalence is found to be 17% among men who have sex with men. Most of the men who are visiting brothel based sex workers, homosexuals and injecting drug users have wife and girl friends. Therefore, increasing number of women is infected by their husbands and the infection levels among pregnant women remain high in many parts of the country including the South, where they exceeded 2% in 2002 (UNAIDS, Dec. 2004: 44).

A massive intervention programme with strong political commitment (through mass media and other Government and non-governmental agencies) to control HIV has reduced men's visits to commercial sex workers by half, raised condom usage, and decreased STDs (Sexually Transmitted Diseases) and achieved substantial reductions in new HIV infections (World Bank, 2000: 1) from 140,000 in 1991 to 29000 in 2001 (Ramamorthy, 2000: 115) to 21,000 in 2003 (UNAIDS, July 2002: 31-32).

The main routes of HIV transmission occurred through commercial sex has been changed due to Thailand's massive 100% condom programme with the aim of 100% condom use for all commercial and casual sex. As a result by 1992, condom use in brothels had claimed to 90% and the rate of sexually transmitted diseases among males dropped to 90% and the infection rate among conscripts in the Royal Thai Army has decreased from 4% in 1993 to 1.3% in 1999 (Ainsworth et, 2000: 6).

But steady transmission of HIV from the infected male clients of female sex workers, and from infected male injecting drug users to their regular sex partners (wives and girlfriends) is observed in Thailand (World Health Organisation, 2001: 21-23). Now half of the newly identified infections are occurring among the wives and sexual partners of men who got infected several years ago (UNAIDS 2002: 10).

Though the rate of HIV infection among commercial sex workers was reduced from 50% in 1991 to 20% in 2001 still there is evidence that HIV prevalence is on the rise among sex workers in some parts of the country, particularly in Bangkok (World Bank, 2000: 2). The unsafe sexual behaviour is increasing among young people in Thailand and the rates of infection among teenagers have increased to 17% from 11% (WHO, 2001: 21-23). Still one-in 100 Thais are infected with HIV, and AIDS has become the leading cause of death (Ramamorthy, 2000: 115). Poverty, injecting drug use and a flourishing sex industry provided fertile conditions for rapid spread of the virus in Thailand.

Low Prevalence Countries

The rate of HIV/AIDS is found to be less in some of the Asian countries which are given in Table 4.10:

Table 4.10. Low Prevalence Countries

	Bangladesh 2002	*East Timor 2003*	*Mongolia 2003*	*PDR Lao 2003*	*Pakistan 2003*	*Philippines 2003*	*Sri Lanka 2003*
Female Sex workers	0-07%	3%	0	0-1.1%	0	<1%	0-02%
Men who have sex with men	0-0.2%	0.9%	—	—	—	0	—
High risk men	0	0	0	0	—	0	0
STI clinic clients	0	—	0	—	—	—	0-1%
Drug injectors	0.4%	—	—	—	0	0	—

Source: UNAIDS Epidemic. Update: December, 2004: 45

High risk men include truck drivers, launch workers, boyfriends of sex workers, taxi drivers and soldiers, military recruits, transport workers and male military.

Hetero sex and injecting drug use are the main mode of HIV transmission in low prevalence countries. Female sex workers are infected more in these regions when compared to other risk groups. HIV/AIDS is not yet documented properly in Maldives and Buttons. The threat of continued growth in HIV prevalence in these regions depends on the proportion of people engaging in unprotected sex with infected partners, its spread to pregnant women and their babies, and the proportion exposed to unsafe blood-related procedures. Sri Lanka, Maldives, Philippines, Malaysia, Bangladesh and Japan are encouraging tourism to increase its national income. In these regions sex work is flourishing and the culture of injecting drug use is increasing as a result of tourism. It also increases rural to urban migration (Ramamurthy, 2003: 236).

Sex work is the predominant cause for the spread of HIV in Bangladesh and Philippines. Malaysia's HIV infection is largely derived from injection drug users. In Malaysia 55% of people detected with HIV between 1998 and 2001 were drug injectors. Migration is identified as the major cause for the spread of HIV infection in East Timor and Pakistan. In Japan, HIV prevalence is steadily raised among male blood donors and men who have sex with men. These men might also be transmitting the virus to female sex workers (*UNAIDS, AIDS epidemic Update*, December, 2004: 45-46).

The low prevalence countries the adult prevalence rate varies from 0.1% to 0.4%. The number of HIV infection also varies from 500 to 38,900. The highest number of women living with HIV/AIDS is found in Pakistan (38,900) and Malaysia (8500). The lesser number of infected women is identified in Sri Lanka (600) and PDR Lao (<500) (UNAIDS report 2003).

Poverty, gender inequalities and low level of education and literacy contribute to HIV vulnerability to women. In low prevalence countries women in general have lower socio-economic status, less mobility and less decision making power. Women in these regions have low awareness on HIV/AIDS, its implications and safe sex practices. Besides, safe sex matters are not discussed at interpersonal level. It increases their HIV vulnerability. Illiteracy makes an obstacle for HIV/AIDS prevention in general and much harder to reach women than men with information about how they can protect themselves from HIV infection. The economic and social dependency on men and social restriction on their mobility often make it difficult for women to obtain access to health and social services and access to basic reproductive health care. Their restricted decision making power in the family again make an obstacle to negotiate with their partners for safer sexual practices. These marginalized people enter into prostitution for their livelihood and they are more vulnerable to HIV infection and condom use among them is relatively low. Their low awareness of the implications of unsafe sex increases their vulnerability to HIV (Ramamurthy, 2003: 123-240).

High Prevalence Countries

High prevalence countries in Asia are identified as China, Nepal, Indonesia and India.

China

China is experiencing one of the most rapidly expanding HIV epidemics in the world. It has 30% of annual rate of increase since 1999. Based on this calculation it is estimated that the number of people living in China will exceed 10 million by 2010, if there is no sufficient control on epidemic. The most frequent mode of HIV transmission has been injecting drug use in Southern and Western China and unsafe practices paid blood donors in other regions. Hetero sexually transmitted HIV is occurring primarily in the Eastern provinces of China, fueled by an increasing commercial sex trades and by large number of migrants moving to other provinces in search of labour. The per centage of female prostitute not using condom is identified as 66.7% in 1999 and 37.4% in 2001. HIV prevalence among injecting drug users is found to be 35-80% in Xingjian and 20% in Guangdong. The estimated injecting drug users in China range from a low of about less than half million to three million. These infected injecting drug users have transmitted and can be expected to transmit their infection to a large proportion of their sex partners (WHO, 2003: 53) In rural areas, where people earned money by donating blood plasma in early 1990s, infection level of 10 to 20 per cent have been found, rising to 60% in certain communities (Rob Noble, September, 2004).

In China, its 31 provinces, autonomous regions and municipalities are witnessed the rapid spread of HIV transmission. China has a larger population than any other country in the world at 1.3 billion, 720 million of whom are aged between 15 and 49, the period of greatest sexual activity and drug use. China has become more of a market-lead economy in the last decade, and these economic changes have had social repercussions. Sex before marriage is now more socially acceptable, especially to young people, and there has been a rapid rise in commercial sex. As a result of the increase in sexual freedom, STDs have risen at a rate of about 30% each year for the past ten years.

According to UNAIDS statement, the estimated number of HIV/AIDS in China is 2003 is 840 000. Among them the adult with the age 15-49 years accounted for 830 000 and the estimated adult prevalence of HIV/AIDS in 2003 is 0.1%. The women living with HIV/AIDS accounted for 190 000 in 2003. The estimated number of AIDS death in 2003 is found to be 30 000.

Nepal

In Nepal, the topography, environmental degradation, poverty and economic migration are linked together and they combine with other factors to increase vulnerability to HIV. The predominant mode of transmission is sexual contact, most likely heterosexual. Highest rates of HIV have been identified in injecting drug users (IDUs), commercial sex workers, their clients, labour migrants and youth and young people. The rate of infection is high among the adult population between the ages of 15-49. Increasing levels of sexually transmitted diseases and limited information about homosexual and bisexual transmission facilitate the rapid spread of infection in all regions of Nepal.

The first cases of AIDS were reported in Nepal in 1988. But the Government of Nepal has identified only 0.5% of HIV prevalence among general population in June 2002. . The infection among adult with the age group of 15-49 is found to be 16000 in 2003 (UNAIDS 2004) and the number of adult and child mortality due to HIV/AIDS is 3100 in 2003. Among the people living with HIV, the IDUs accounted for maximum per centage (68%) in 2002. The report published by the Nepal Government in 2000 says that the HIV prevalence among the sex worker was 17.3%, among the people affected by sexually transmitted diseases accounted for 0.7-6.6%, followed by the blood donors (0.28-0.48%) and the infection found among the anti natal care women was only 0.2%. (Ramamurthy, 2003: 174).

One in 200 adult in Nepal is living with HIV positive and nine people a day died of AIDS in 2003 (Mennonite Central Committee, 2005). It shows that HIV is increasing in Nepal as a result of unemployment, migrant labor, civil unrest, drug use and prostitution. Intravenous drug users have highest risk of contracting HIV infection in Nepal followed by commercial sex workers, their clients and migrant labourers.

Nepali Capital, Kathmandu, is host to a great influx of of people from various parts of the country for seeking employment in industries, such as carpet, transport, stone quarries and constructions. The use of commercial sex is high among men who come to the city alone. Many women coming to the city fall into prostitution as a way to earn money for basic survival (Mennonite Central Committee, 2005)

The rate of HIV prevalence is high among the general population in Kathmandu Valley due to widespread commercial sex work and larger per centage (40.4%) of youths involvement in taking intravenous drugs. In 2000, it is found that among intravenous drug users in Nepal, 40% are HIV positive. It is also estimated that as many as 70 per cent of commercial sex workers returning from India are HIV positive. Estimates of the number of Nepali men working in India are around 1 million and above. Many of these men are contracting HIV/AIDS in

India and bringing it back to their wives in Nepal. It is estimated that 10% of HIV infection is found among the men returning from Mumbai to Nepal. Many of these infected people do not know that they are infected and many of them may be engaging in unsafe sexual practices. Such kind of unsafe sexual behaviours and intravenous drugs using habits among the youth has taken the country to the "concentrated epidemic" zone where HIV/AIDS prevalence consistently exceeds 5% in one or more subgroups. (Ramamurthy. V, 2003: 175-178)).

Due to their highly marginalized status in society, sex workers have little access to accurate information about reproductive health and sexually transmitted infections. Truckers and migrant workers are their main customers and it is found that 10.2% of truckers are infected with sexually transmitted infections and 1.5% is infected with HIV. Condom usages are very limited among these marginalized segments (Ramamurthy, 2003: 186).

Indonesia

It is estimated that about 110 000 (0.1%) of HIV infection is found in the age group of 15-49 years. HIV/AIDS data collect in Indonesia from all sources indicated that HIV prevalence rates were higher among female sex workers and it ranges from 1% to 5% in several areas of Indonesia. HIV prevalence is also increasing among injecting drug users in Jakarta (over 35% in 2000). During 1990s, most HIV infections in Indonesia could be attributed to infections acquired outside the country and to a pocket of epidemic heterosexual transmission in areas such as Merauke. Since the late 1990s, there has been an explosive HIV epidemic in injecting drug use populations in Indonesia. As of 2003, the most common pattern of HIV transmission in Indonesia has been from HIV infected persons to their spouses or regular sex partners and this will continue tc be the predominant pattern of HIV transmission in Indonesia. Indonesia is now classified as a country with a concentrated HIV epidemic, primarily among injecting drug use population (WHO, 2003: 60).

Indian Scenario on HIV/AIDS

Table 4.11. Important Landmarks of HIV Infection in India

Year	*Events*
April 1986	First cluster (ten prostitutes) of HIV seropositives detected in Madras, Tamil Nadu.
May 1986	First patient of final stage disease detected in Bombay, Maharashtra (recipient of unscreened blood transfusion during cardiac surgery in USA).
Dec. 1986	First seropositive male detected from STD clinic in Tamil Nadu.
July 1987	First seropositive blood donor in Vellore, Tamil Nadu (retrospective detection subsequent t to the recipient's illness).
July 1987	Spouse to spouse transmission is identified (the same donor's wife).
Oct. 1987	Detection of a seropositive infant (born to the abovementioned parents).
June 1988	First AIDS death (sex workers in Kamathipura, Mumbai.
April 1988	First indigenous case of full-blown HIV disease in an Indian.
Jan. 1989	Evidence of HIV antibodies in indigenously produced blood products.
Jan. 1989	Evidence of exposure to HIV among a high proportion of donors used by commercial manufacturers followed by a government ban on production.
July 1989	Government gazette notification for mandatory screening of blood donors for freedom from HIV antibodies.
Jan-Feb. 1990	Recognition of a cluster of seropositives in IV drug users in north-east India.
July 1992	Constitution of the National AIDS Control Organisation (NACO); at state levels also.
Oct. 1992.	Establishment of the National AIDS Research Institute, Pune by Indian Council of Medical Research (ICMR).

Year	*Events*
Dec 2004*	Free Antiretroviral drugs are given to the people living with HIV positive in the high prevalence states
July 2005*	India has begun human clinical trial of an investigational vaccine designed to prevent Human Immunodeficiency Virus (HIV) and Acquired Immuno-deficiency Syndrome (AIDS).

Sources: Khorshed M. Pavri, (1992: 17).
**The Hindu*, December 2004 and July 2005.

Like most countries in Asia, India is included in the Pattern III distribution of HIV disease. Although HIV begins in late 1980s, all the known modes of viral spread have been identified within the short period. There is not “one” single HIV epidemic in India. The spread of HIV in India is diverse and many states of India have low rate of infection. The epidemic is extreme in Southern states. As of December 2004, 92% of all nationally reported AIDS cases have been found in 10 of the 28 states and 7 Union territories. The greatest numbers were in Maharasthra and Gujarat in the West; Tamil Nadu and Andhra Pradesh in the South; Manipur and Nagaland in the North East (NACO, March 2005). In Southern States, the epidemics are mostly due to hetero sexual contract, while infections are mainly found amongst injecting drug users in Manipur and Nagaland (UNAIDS/WHO, 2004) and one-fourth of the HIV positives throughout the world may live in India (Sinha, 1999: 81).

India has a population of one billion, and around half of this population is in sexually active age group of 15-49 years (NACO, 1998: 15). The first AIDS patient in India was diagnosed by Dr. Suniti Soloman, a microbiology professor at the Madras Medical College in Chennai in 1986. The initial cases of HIV was identified among the sex workers in Chennai while the police involved in sending their assigned quota of 100 commercial sex workers per month to the city prison. Dr. Suniti Soloman has collected the blood sample from one month's batch of 100 sex workers. Among them six were identified as HIV positive in the test Enzyme Linked Immunosorbent Assay (ELISA) at the

Christian Medical College in Vellore and the result rechecked with the Western Blot analysis in the United States. All the six are confirmed HIV positive and none of them have non-Indian customers. This shows that HIV was already circulating within India (Arvind Singhal *et al.*, 2003: 115).

From 1986 to mid 1990s the Indian government proclaimed that AIDS was a foreign disease, and that the epidemic could never spread in a family-centered society like India. However, in 1999, 1400 Indian citizens were being infected each day and by 2002 this figure had jumped to 5000 (Arvind Singhal *et al.*, 2003: 115).

Within a short period AIDS has emerged as one of the most public health problem in the country. During the recent years the occurrence and spread of HIV/AIDS in the country has shown the following trends and shift in paradigm (NACO, 1998: 15):

1. HIV is prevalent in almost all parts of the country.
2. HIV/AIDS is spreading from urban to rural areas.
3. HIV/AIDS is also spreading from high risk behaviour groups to general population.
4. One in every four cases reported is a woman.
5. More and more women attending antenatal clinics are sero-converting to HIV positive, leading to the added risk of prenatal transmission.
6. Highest per centage of infection is reported to occur through the sexual contact.
7. About 89 per cent of the reported cases are from sexually active and economically productive age groups of 15-49 years.
8. Migration and mobility has increased the chances of the disease spreading to other areas/persons.
9. The social stigma attached to sexually transmitted infection also hold good for HIV/AIDS with more disastrous consequences.

(A) Causes for the rapid spread of HIV/AIDS in India

(a) India is believed to be moralistic society as a influence of religion. Due to various reasons, the gradual decline in moral value increased pre-marital sex and in turn it has increased the rate of sexually transmitted infection.

(b) For economical reasons, mobility and migration has increased among migrant labour, truckers, helpers, uninformed personnel from rural area to urban area which lead to lack of spousal sex. Most of the migrant workers are highly mobile and often live in unhygienic conditions in urban slums. Long working hours, relative isolation from the family and geographical mobility may foster casual sexual relationships and make them highly vulnerable to STDs and HIV/AIDS (Ekstrand M *et al.*, 2003: 56). Migrant workers tend to have little access to HIV/STD information, voluntary counseling and testing and health services.

(c) Flourishing sex industry and its extension beyond red light areas is another important reason for the spread of HIV infection. In Mumbai alone have 15,000 sex workers (Gomare *et al.*, 2003), and 70% of the sex workers in Mumbai are HIV positive (Shankaran, 2002).

(d) Increasing culture of using drugs among the youth also yet another cause for the spread of infection into the general population. Injecting drug use is a major problem in northeastern states, Mumbai, Kolkata, Delhi and Chennai (Reid G. and Costigan G, 2002: 81).

(f) The most vulnerable groups are known for their illiteracy/poor education and low socio-economic conditions. They have very poor knowledge of safe sex and condom use.

(b) Mode of spread of HIV infection in India

The predominant mode of transmission of HIV in India is hetero sexual contact (85.7%), followed by injecting drug use (2.2%), blood transfusion (2.6%), prenatal transmission (2.7%) and other route which is not able to specify the people living with HIV positive (NACO, July 2004: 14).

Table 4.12. Routes of HIV Transmission, end of December 2004 and 31 March 2005

Transmission Categories	*2004 (in %) **	*2005 (in %) ***
Sexual	85.83	85.76
Blood and blood production	2.07	2.03
Intravenous drug users	2.70	2.55
Prenatal	3.45	3.58
Unidentified	5.95	6.08

Sources: * Monthly update on AIDS, NACO, 31 August 2004
**Monthly updates on AIDS, NACO, 31 March 2005.

(c) Pattern of HIV epidemic in India

India's epidemic seems to be following the Type 4 pattern, like in Thailand. In the **first wave,** HIV infection is seen amongst sex workers or intravenous drug users (IDUs) that are also known as the **core transmitters or core groups.** In the **second wave,** the epidemic spreads from these groups at highest risk to bridge populations (clients of sex workers, patients of sexually transmitted infections, partners of drug users, mobile populations such as truck drivers, single male member migrants etc.). When evidence suggests affliction of spouses and children of the clients of sex workers, the HIV epidemic is understood to have reached its **third wave.** Recently a **fourth wave** comprising of adolescents has been proposed to indicate the severity of the epidemic.

(d) HIV/AIDS prevalence in India

The HIV prevalence in adult population can be broadly classified into three groups of States/Union Territories in the country (Ramamurthy.V, 2003: 51).

Group I (High prevalence/generalized epidemic): States like Maharasthra, Tamil Nadu, Karnataka, Andhra Pradesh, Manipur and Nagaland where the HIV infection has crossed 1 per cent or more in antenatal women.

Group II (Moderate prevalent/concentrated epidemic states): States like Gujrat, Goa and Pondicherry where HIV infection has crossed 5 per cent or more among high risk groups but the infection is below 1 per cent in antenatal women.

Group III (Low prevalent states): Remaining states and Union Territories where the HIV infection in any of the high risk groups is still less than 5 per cent and is less than 1 per cent among antenatal women.

(e) HIV Estimate in India

Richard Feacham, head of the Global Fund to Fight AIDS, Tuberculosis and Malaria made a statement that India is surpassed South Africa in the number of HIV infected people, and HIV/AIDS epidemic was growing very rapidly in India and it was out of control (The Hindu, 2005: 14). Table 4.13 reveals the seriousness of the epidemic in India by showing increasing trend every year.

Table 4.13. HIV Estimates: India from 1990—2005

	No of HIV infection – year wise								
Year	1990	1994	1998	1999	2000	2001	2002	2003	2005*
In millions	0.2	1.75	3.5	3.7	3.86	3.97	4.58	5.106	5.134

Source: NACO, annual report (2004: 15).
*NACO monthly update on HIV/AIDS, March. 2005.

India is categorized as a low prevalence nation. But in a view of large population, a mere 0.1% increase in the prevalence rate would increase the number of living with HIV by over half-million (NACO, July 2004: 14). HIV prevalence across the country is about 0.98% in the age group of 15-49 years, just below the "tipping point' of 1% where the disease will become much more difficult to control. The UNAIDS/WHO estimated that 5,100,000 people are living with HIV in India. Among them 5,000,000 are adult, 1,900,000 are women and 120,000 are children (UNAIDS/WHO, 2004).

In India, every day approximately 1500 people become infected with HIV and of that number, young people below 25 years of age account for over 50% of the infections. About 90 per cent of the infected people themselves are not aware of their HIV status and may therefore be transmitting the virus to their partners. Low awareness is the main causes for the rapid spread of HIV infection in India (Parliamentary Forum on HIV/AIDS, 2004).

According to the latest (May 2005) data released by the Ministry of Health and Family Welfare and the National AIDS Control Organisation (NACO), the number of new infection for the year 2004-05 has increased by only about 28,000 as against 5.2 lakhs in 2003-04. The total infection figure now stands at 5.134 million in comparison to 5.106 million reported in 2003-2004. In absolute numbers, India continues to have the most number of cases after South Africa, which has 5.3 million HIV infected persons. In terms of per centage, India has an HIV prevalence of 0.91 per cent among the adult population as compared to 21.5 per cent in South Africa (Aarti Dhar, 2005: 15).

While 1,114 HIV/AIDS related deaths were reported in 2004-05, 1514 deaths were reported in 2003-04. The decrease in the number of fresh cases can be attributed to major steps taken by the Government in creating awareness and introducing the Anti-Retroviral Therapy (ART) treatment. The trends across the country show that there is no galloping HIV epidemic in India as there is no evidence of an upsurge in HIV prevalence. However, there are regional epidemics in various parts, with high prevalence of HIV among both the Sexually Transmitted Diseases (STD) clinic attendees and antenatal clinic attendees (Aarti Dhar, 2005: 15).

The surveillance data on 2004 reveals that 69.3 per cent of the new cases were from six "high prevalence" States, 28 per cent were from "low prevalence" States and the remaining were from "medium prevalence" States. Of the 1.3 lakhs "known HIV positive cases", 8000 were receiving treatment in government hospitals. "About 44,000 causes are reported from Tamil Nadu alone because of better treatment facilities and greater awareness in the State (The Hindu, 2005: 15).

(f) Recorded AIDS cases in India

The data published by Tamil Nadu AIDS Control Society in June 2003 reveals the following reported AIDS cases by NACO from 32 States of India. The following table reveals that the prevalence of AIDS cases is high in Tamil Nadu, Maharashtra, Andhra Pradesh, Gujarat, Karnataka and Manipur.

Table 4.14. AIDs Cases in India (Reported by NACO) from May 1986-June 2003

Sl. No.	*State*	*1996*	*1997*	*1998*	*1999*	*2000*	*2001*	*2002*	*2003*	*2005*	*HIV % 2003*
1.	Tamil Nadu	199	521	532	2730	3866	7354	21813	24667	48180	0.75
2.	Maharashtra	520	930	824	64	279	6454	9234	9234	12963	1.25
3.	Karnataka	12	55	39	47	541	1261	1654	1707	2343	1.25
4.	Manipur	55	147	0	61	344	1033	1238	1238	2866	1.25
5.	Madya Pradesh	6	68	76	116	279	759	972	996	1314	0.00
6.	Gujarat	104	6	2	1	245	1259	2474	2660	5406	0.40
7.	Delhi	27	90	13	0	64	642	766	807	950	0.13
8.	Uttar Pradesh	48	53	16	41	93	461	845	983	1383	0.00
9.	Chandigarh	0	0	0	124	93	427	684	733	1119	0.50
10.	Kerala	26	3	1	0	56	267	267	267	1769	0.33
11.	Rajastan	0	51	25	27	53	248	666	751	1153	0.13
12.	Pondicherry	24	8	9	0	0	141	157	157	302	0.13
13.	Punjab	0	0	48	52	31	135	231	248	292	0.00
14.	Assam	0	9	3	11	62	125	149	171	225	0.00
15.	Nagaland	0	6	0	19	43	211	319	331	736	1.25
16.	West Bengal	11	7	0	0	0	725	930	930	2397	0.50
17.	Orissa	0	0	0	0	49	82	82	82	128	0.00
18 .	Andhra Pradesh	19	15	7	2	0	1265	3341	3707	11,280	1.25
19.	Haryana	0	0	0	0	47	189	271	271	440	0.25
20.	Himachal Pradesh	0	0	0	15	16	91	109	112	223	0.00
21 .	Bihar	1	1	0	0	36	92	148	152	155	0.00
22.	Goa	0	0	0	7	10	75	155	194	508	0.50
23 .	Mizoram	0	5	0	7	3	20	47	50	106	1.38
24.	A & N Islands	0	0	0	0	9	17	24	27	33	0.00
25.	Meghalaya	0	8	0	0	0	8	8	8	8	0.00
26.	Jammu & Kasmir	0	0	0	0	0	2	2	2	2	0.00
27.	Sikkim	0	1	1	0	0	4	6	8	8	0.13
28.	Daman & Diu	0	0	1	0	0	1	1	1	1	0.50
29.	Dadra & Nagar Haveli	0	0	0	0	0	0	0	0	0	0.13
30.	Arunachal Pradesh	0	0	0	0	0	0	0	0	0	0.38
31.	Lakshadweep	0	0	0	0	0	0	0	0	0	0.00

Sl. No.	*State*	*1996*	*1997*	*1998*	*1999*	*2000*	*2001*	*2002*	*2003*	*2005*	*HIV % 2003*
32.	Tripura	0	0	0	0	0	0	6	6	5	0.00
33.	Uttrakhand									0	0.00
34	Ahemdabad Mun.Corp.	—	—	—	—	—	—	—	—	520	—
35	Chennai M.C.	—	—	—	—	—	—	—	—	—	—
36	Mumbai M.C	—	—	—	—	—	—	—	—	7042	1.25
	Total	*1052*	*1984*	*1597*	*3325*	*6218*	*31336*	*46599*	*50500*	*1,03,857*	

Source: *Monthly updates on AIDS, NACO, 31 August 2004: 1.
**Monthly updates on AIDS, NACO, 31 March 2005: 2

As per standard AIDS case definition, only 1052 cases were reported to NACO from all over the country during 1996. It has increased to 96,978 in December 2004 which include 69,559 male and 27,419 female (NACO, August 2004). But in March 2005, the NACO has recorded the higher number of AIDS cases (1,03,857) with the infection of 74,020 males and 29,837 females. The year wise reported AIDS cases clearly indicate the increasing trends of HIV infection in India.

(g) Age and sex-wise distribution of AIDS cases in India

Table 4.15. Age and Sex-wise Distribution of AIDs Cases in India end of March 2005

Age group	*Male*	*%*	*Female*	*%*	*Total*	*%*
0-14	2,651	3.6	1,836	6.3	4,487	4.3
15-29	20,665	27.9	13,211	44.2	33,866	32.6
30-49	45,024	60.8	13,215	44.3	58,239	56.1
>50	5,690	7.7	1,575	5.2	7,265	7.0
Total	74,020	100	29,837	100	103,857	100

Source: *Monthly updates on AIDS*, NACO, 31 March 2005: 2.

The epidemiological analysis of reported AIDS cases reveals that AIDS is increasingly affecting young people in the sexually active age group of 15-49 years including 68.7% of male and 27% of female. Around 89% of the reported cases are occurring in sexually active age and economically productive age group of 15-44 years (Parliamentary Forum of HIV/AIDS, 2004). Children accounted for 4.3% of total AIDS cases in India.

(h) HIV prevalence among various risk groups

Table 4.16. HIV Prevalence among various Risk Groups - State-wise in 2003

Sl. No.	*State / Union Territories*	*Percentage of HIV prevalence*					
		FSW	*MSM*	*IDU*	*STD*	*ANC-Urban*	*ANC-Rural*
1.	Andhra Pradesh	19.4	13.2	—	19.6	1.25	0.75
2.	Arunachal Pradesh	—	—	—	0.0	0.00	0.00
3.	Assam	—	—	—	1.20	0.00	0.00
4.	Bihar	4.8	1.6	—	0.40	0.00	0.00
5.	Chhattisgarh	—	—	—	2.27	0.25	0.00
6.	Delhi	2.0	—	14.4	7.20	0.13	0.00
7.	Goa	30.1	—	—	14.30	0.50	0.19
8.	Gujarat	—	—	—	4.50	0.40	0.00
9.	Haryana	—	—	—	1.20	025	0.33
10.	Himachal Pradesh	0.4/8	—	—	0.80	0.00	0.50
11.	Jammu & Kashmir	—	—	—	1.86	0.00	0.00
12.	Jharkhand	—	—	—	0.13	0.00	0.00
13.	Karnataka	14.4	10.8	2.8	10.40	1.25	1.00
14.	Kerala	2.29	—	—	4.00	0.33	0.00
15.	Madhya Pradesh	—	—	—	1.20	0.00	0.00
16.	Maharashtra	—	—	—	10.00	1.25	0.00
17.	Mumbai	54.9	18.8	24.8	18.40	1.25	N.A
18.	Manipur	12.4	29.2	24.4	13	1.25	0.40
19.	Meghalya	—	—	—	0.40	0.00	0.00
20.	Mizoram	—	—	6.4	3.80	1.38	0.00
21.	Nagaland	4.4	—	12.9	0.90	1.25	1.20
22.	Orissa	—	—	—	2.40	0.00	0.00
23.	Punjab	—	—	—	1.60	0.00	0.13
24.	Rajasthan	—	—	—	3.70	0.13	0.12
25.	Sikkim	—	—	—	0.00	0.13	0.00
26.	Tamil Nadu	8.8	4.4	—	9.20	0.75	0.50

Sl.	*State/Union Territories*	*Percentage of HIV prevalence*					
		FSW	*MSM*	*IDU*	*STD*	*ANC-Urban*	*ANC-Rural*
27.	Tripura	—	5.26	—	0.00	0.00	0.00
28.	Uttar Pradesh	—	—	—	0.55	0.00	0.00
29.	Uttrakhand	—	—	—	0.00	0.00	0.00
30.	West Bengal	6.45	—	2.70	1.45	0.50	0.50
31.	A & N Islands	—	—	—	1.60	0.50	0.25
32.	Chandigarh	1.20	—	—	1.66	0.50	0.00
33.	D & N Haveli	—	—	—	—	—	0.00
34.	Daman & Diu	—	—	—	—	—	0.00
35.	Lakshadweep	—	—	—	0.00	0.00	0.00
36.	Pondicherry	—	—	—	2.60	0.13	0.14

Source: NACO – Facts and Figures, 2004.

Table 4.16 reveals that the Female sex workers (FSW) and Injecting Drug Users (IDU) are the major transmitter of HIV virus to the general population. The table also reveals that STD patients are getting infected by HIV in many States. Ante-natal women, both in urban and rural areas are also under the threat of HIV infection almost in all states.

(i) STATE WISE DISTRIBUTION OF AIDS CASES

Table 4.17. Distribution of Reported AIDs Cases by State at the End of December 2003

States	*Percentage*
Tamil Nadu	44.7
Maharashtra less Mumbai	16.7
Andhra Pradesh	7.9
Gujarat	6.5
Mumbai	4.7
Karnataka	3.2
Manipur	3.2
Madhya Pradesh	1.9

States	*Percentage*
West Bengal	1.7
Delhi	1.5
Nagaland	0.6
Others	8.4

Source: NACO, Annual Report, 2004: 24.

In India Tamil Nadu has higher per centage (44.7%) of reported AIDS cases followed by Maharashtra (16.7%). The numbers of AIDS cases are increasing in Andhra Pradesh, Gujarat, Mumbai, Karnataka, and North Eastern States.

(j) Women living with HIV/AIDS in India

The estimates by UNAIDS/WHO shows that the number of women infection is steadily rising. One in every four AIDS cases reported are woman (Sinha, 1999: 89) and 90% of women with HIV having only one sexual partner in their lives (Parliamentary Forum of HIV/AIDS, 2004). Every year HIV infection among married women is increasing as a result of marital partner's unsafe sexual contact with sex workers and use of injecting drug use. Cultural degradation is witnessed as influence of western culture. Many married women are exposed to extra marital relationship and are subjected to HIV infection. Many of these women have no knowledge about HIV and its implication and the necessity of safe sex (Break-through organisation, 2005: wp13).

For millions of Indian women, sexual intercourse is not a question of choice but rather one of survival and duty. Fertility and her relationship to her husband are often the source of an Indian woman's social identity. HIV/AIDS epidemic in India as inextricably tied to the social and cultural values and economic relationships between men and women and within communities. While social inequalities facilitate its spread in the country, the virus, in turn, reflects and reinforces these inequalities. Women are the least powerful because Indian society praises patriarchy and male sexuality and mourns the births of daughters. In addition, there is an absence of choice at the individual and systemic levels, whether it is the choice to use a condom or even to have sex.

For women, low economic and social status, abuse and violence, as well as limited legal and social protection increase their vulnerability to HIV/AIDS. Knowledge of HIV/AIDS continues to be surprisingly low. The National Family Health Survey, 1998-99 shows that only four out of 10 women of reproductive age have heard of AIDS. Awareness is much lower among rural and less educated women. Only 18 per cent of illiterate women have heard of AIDS, compared with 92 per cent of women who had at least completed high school (Population Reference Bureau, 2005: wp1)

The virus has expanded the boundaries of high-risk groups to adolescent girls (married and single); married women of reproductive age; sexually active single women; sex workers; college and university students; pregnant women; and women survivors of sexual abuse and rape. Women constitute 25 per cent of known AIDS cases in the country, and seven of 10 women affected by HIV are from poor rural and poor urban communities (Population Reference Bureau, 2005: wp1)

Women with HIV are subjected to various forms of violence and discrimination based on gender. They could be refused shelter, denied a share of household property, refused access to treatment and care, or blamed for a husband's HIV diagnosis. In cases, where a man has admitted he had sexual relations with sex workers, the burden of blame still falls on the wife for failing to "satisfy" her husband.

(k) Rural and Urban distribution of HIV/AIDS

In India, the epidemic is moved towards rural areas. Increasing number of rural population is getting infected by HIV with the influence of increased migration and unsafe multi-sexual behaviour and low/lack of awareness on HIV/AIDS and safe sex practices.

HIV Sentinel Surveillance data on 2003 revealed that the infection rate is increasing in rural areas. According to the HIV Sentinel Surveillance data on 2003, the total number of infection estimated in urban areas is 20.46 lakhs (40.1%) and among them 12.97 lakhs are male and 7.49 lakhs are female. The estimated number of infection in rural areas is 30.60 lakhs (59.9%) with

19.22 lakhs male and 11.35 lakhs female (NACO – Facts & Figures 2003: 4). The surveillance data on 2004 suggests that 21.27 lakhs (42.43%) people from urban areas and 30.07 lakhs (58.57%) of people from rural areas were infected with HIV (Dhar, 2005: 15).

About 28% of rural people in India and 11% of urban people have never heard of AIDS (Parliamentary Forum of HIV/AIDS, 2004). The Behaviour Surveillance Survey (2001), reveals that the overall per centage of condom use in last sex with non-regular partner is 49.3%. Condom usage among the rural population is considerably low (45%) when compared to urban masses (63%) and it is also found to be low among women (urban-52%, rural-35%) than men (urban - 65%, rural - 48%) (NACO, 2004: 25). The same survey also reveals that the greater per centages (12-13%) of both rural and urban men have non-regular sexual partners than women of rural and urban areas (3-5%).

(l) HIV INFECTION IN HIGH-RISK AND GENERAL POPULATION

Table 4.18. Distribution of HIV Infections in various Sub-population

Group	*STD Patients*	*General population*	*FSWs*	*IDUs*	*Children*	*Total*
No. in lakhs	14.93	34.77	0.103	0.71	0.55	51.06

Source: NACO, Facts and Figures, 2003: 4.

In India, high risk groups are considered as the patient attending STD clinics, MSM (men seeking men) clinics and drug de-addiction centers while mothers attending antenatal clinics are considered as a proxy for the general population. The HIV/AIDS estimate by NACO reveals that the general population is increasingly infected with HIV (34.7 lakhs) followed by patients with STD (14.9 lakhs). Among the STD population two-thirds are females (6.20 lakhs).

(m) SEXUALLY TRANSMITTED INFECTION AND HIV/AIDS IN INDIA

Sexually transmitted infection (STD) and HIV are behaviourally and epidemiologically linked. An individual with sexually transmitted infection is eight to ten times more vulnerable to contracting HIV. Many infected people do not seek treatment due to stigmatization with the diseases. HIV/AIDS intervention programme involved in providing awareness related to increasing treatment seeking behaviour for STD. In India, the STD clinic is increasing year by year. During 2000-2001 it was only 504, but it is raised to 735 in 2003-2004 (NACO, 2004: 41). The annual report of the National AIDS Control Organisation (NACO, 2004: 45) reveals that the STD is increasing in the states of Uttar Pradesh (22.5%), Andhra Pradesh (12.7%), Madhya Pradesh (12.3%), Tamil Nadu (8.1%), Maharashtra (6.5%), Chattisgarh (5.7%), Karnataka (4.3%), Gujarat (4.3%), Orissa (3.1%) and Mumbai (2.8%).

(n) Regionwise distribution of HIV/AIDS in India

(i) Southern Region

Southern regions are called as high prevalent States. Southern regions include Tamil Nadu, Andhra Pradesh, Karnataka, Kerala and Goa. In these regions the epidemic is crossed from high risk population to general population and HIV infection has crossed more than one per cent in antenatal women. Distribution of reported AIDS cases by states cumulative figures till 2003 shows that Tamil Nadu rank first in India in HIV/AIDS with the per centage of 44.7%. HIV infection in Tamil Nadu is increasing year by year. It was reported that 17.30% of HIV infection among patients attending STD clinics (16.30%) and women in antenatal clinics (1.0%) in 1998. But in 2003 higher per centage of infection was recorded among intravenous drug users (63.8%), STD patients (9.20%), and men seeking men (4.40%), female sex workers (8.8%) and women in antenatal clinics (0.75%). It is also recorded that 0.75% of urban and 0.50% of rural women attending antenatal clinics are infected with HIV

The per centage of reported AIDS cases in Andhra Pradesh is 7.9% in 2003. It has higher per centage of HIV infection among patients attending STD clinics. In 1998, HIV infection among STD patients was reported as 24.90% and it has increased to 30.40% in 2002. But during 2003 the infection rate among STD patients was reduced to 19.60% as a result of awareness created by Andhra Pradesh Government. The infection rate among women in antenatal clinics also reduced from 2.25% in 1998 to 1.25% in 2003. The state also observed higher per centage of infection among female sex workers (19.4%) and men seeking men (13.2%) in 2003. In Andhra Pradesh 1.25% of urban and 0.75% of rural women attending antenatal clinics are recorded as HIV positive (NACO, Statewise HIV Prevalence 2004: 1-9).

Karnataka accounted for 3.2% of AIDS cases in 2003 (NACO, July 2004: 24). HIV infection in Karnataka is found to be high among female sex workers (14.4%), men seeking men (10.8%) and patients of STD clinics (10.40%). The State witnessed lower per centage of HIV infection among intravenous drug users (2.8%). HIV infection among women attending antenatal clinics is found to be 1.25% in both rural and urban areas.

In Kerala HIV infection is found to be in increasing trend as a result of large number of its workforce in the Gulf or in other metropolises of India such as Mumbai, Delhi, Kolkata, Chennai etc. HIV infection in 2003 is recorded among female sex workers (2.29%), patients attending STD clinics (4.00%) and women attending antenatal clinics (0.33%) of urban sites.

(ii) Western Region

Western region include Madhya Pradesh, Maharashtra, Rajasthan and Gujarat. In these regions HIV infection is high in Maharashtra and Gujarat. At the end of December 2004, it is estimated that HIV infection in western region is caused by increasing number of STD patients. HIV prevalence among STD patients higher in Maharashtra (10.00%) followed by Gujarat (4.50%) and Rajasthan (3.70%). Low rate of HIV prevalence is estimated among the STD patients in the state of Madhya Pradesh (1.20%). Increasing number of women attending antenatal clinics in the urban sites of Maharashtra (1.25%), Gujarat 0.40%), Madhya Pradesh (1.20%) and Rajasthan (0.13%) are infected with HIV/AIDS (NACO, Statewise HIV Prevalence 2004: 1-9).

In Mumbai, HIV prevalence among female sex worker is estimated as 54.29% in 2003. Higher rate of infection is also estimated among injecting drug users (24.8%), patients attending STD clinics (18.40%) and the clinics of men seeking men (18.8%). It is also estimated that 1.25% of women attending antenatal clinics in Mumbai are infected with HIV (NACO, State wise HIV Prevalence 2004: 1-9).

(iii) Northern Region

In India, the northern region has low rate of infection than southern and western regions. Female sex workers are the primary contributors for the spread of HIV infection in Bihar (4.8%), and West Bengal (6.45%). HIV infection is slowly picking up as a result of increasing number of infection among the patients attending STD clinics in Haryana (1.20%), Himachal Pradesh (0.80%), Jammu and Kashmir (1.86%), Orissa (2.40%), Punjab (1.60%) and Uttar Pradesh (0.55%). The infection rates among women attending antenatal clinics in northern regions are comparatively less and it ranges from 0.13%-0.50% (NACO, State wise HIV Prevalence 2004: 1-9).

(iv) Northeastern region

Injecting drug use is the primary cause for the rapid spread of HIV infection in Northeastern region. Northeastern region include Arunachal Pradesh, Assam, Manipur, Meghalaya, Mizoram, Nagaland and Tripura. HIV infection is less in Arunachal Pradesh, Assam and Tripura and it is high in Manipur, Meghalaya, Mizoram and Nagaland (NACO, State wise HIV Prevalence 2004: 1-9).

The major factors which facilitate for the increase of HIV infection in the State of Manipur is recorded as sex between men (29.2%), injecting drug use (24.8%), STD (13.00%) and female sex works (12.4%). The increasing rate of STD is primary cause for the spread of HIV infection in Assam (1.20%) and Meghalaya (0.40%). Injecting drug use is identified as important contributing factor for rapid spread of HIV infection in Nagaland (12.9%) and Mizoram (6.4%). Sex between men is recorded in Tripura (5.28%) for the spread of infection.

HIV prevalence among women attending antenatal clinics also found to be higher in north eastern regions of Arunachal

Pradesh (0.38% in urban areas), Manipur (1.25% in urban and 0.40% in rural areas), Mizoram (1.38% in urban areas), and Nagaland (1.25% in urban and 1.20% in rural areas).

(v) Union Territories

HIV/AIDS is recorded in Union Territories expect Dadra and Nagar Haveli and Daman and Diu. Among all Union Territories, HIV prevalence is high in Goa. Sex tourism is the unique feature in Goa. Sex tourism causes increased HIV infection among female sex workers (30.1%) in 2003 followed by the patients attending STD clinics (14.30%). The HIV infection among antenatal women in Goa is comparatively less (0.50% in urban and 0.19% in rural areas) in southern regions (NACO, Statewise HIV Prevalence 2004: 1-9).

Increasing rate of STD is identified as major cause for the spread of HIV infection in 2003 in Pondicherry (2.60%) and Andaman and Nicobar Islands (1.60%) and Chhattisgarh (2.27%). HIV infection rate is rapidly increasing in Delhi, the capital of India as a result of increasing number of infection among injecting drug users (14.4%), patients attending sexually transmitted diseases clinics (7.20%), and female sex workers (2.0%). The rates of HIV infection among women attending antenatal clinics are estimated between 0.13% to 0.50% (NACO, State wise HIV Prevalence 2004: 1-9).

HIV Prevalence in Tamil Nadu

The State Tamil Nadu is situated in the extreme south off India with the population of 62.11 million (Census 2001). According to Tamil Nadu State AIDS Control Society, for the year 2004, the projected mid-year population was 64.09 million of which the rural population accounts for 34.86 million (56.12 per cent) while the urban population accounts for 27.25 million (43.88 per cent) Tamil Nadu has 30 districts with 201 Taluks, 385 blocks, 832 towns, 6 corporations, 102 municipalities, two cantonments, 611 Panchayats, 111 census towns and 16,317 villages (Census 2001).

The first HIV positive case was detected in Tamil Nadu in 1986 among the female sex workers. HIV prevalence among the sex workers is also proved in 1990 when the State Government of Tamil Nadu forcibly tested hundreds of sex workers for HIV, and locked up 800 HIV positive women (Dube, 2000: 27). The epidemic today challenges the present social system and safe future of the individual in the State. Earlier, it was believed that the commercial sex workers and truck drivers are at the risk of contracting HIV infection. Today, many other groups have been identified. They are migrant labour, industrial workers, refugees, fisherman, slum-dwellers, hotel and lodge workers, domestic helpers, street children and men seeking men (Tamil Nadu State AIDS Control Society).

According to UNAIDS report, the greater danger for India is the fact that the infection rate in some states, like Tamil Nadu is "three times higher in villages than the cities" (Sinha, 1999: 89). People living with AIDS is high in Tamil Nadu with the per centage of 44.7 and among the 49 HIV high prevalence districts in India, seven are in Tamil Nadu including Madurai, Trichy, Salem, Coimbatore, Namakkal, Tirunelveli and Chennai (NACO: 2004: 15). AIDS cases reported to NACO from Tamil Nadu till March 2005 is 48, 180, the highest in India (NACO, 2005) and the HIV prevalence rate is estimated as 0.75 per cent in 2003 (NACO, 2004).

It is estimated from Sentinel Surveillance data (2003) of the Tamil Nadu State AIDS Control Society, the people living with HIV positive in the State is about 4.32 lakhs. Though the common mode of HIV transmission is heterosexual, the sentinel surveillance between the periods 1993-2004 indicates that intravenous drug users rank first with a HIV prevalence of 39.92 per cent followed by STD patients (8.40 per cent) and antenatal women (0.63 per cent).

HIV rates among antenatal women declined from 1.13 per cent in 2001 to 0.63 per cent in 2004. But, HIV prevalence rate among the antenatal women of 15-24 age groups has increased to 1.25% in 2004 from 0.25% in 2002. The sentinel surveillance also shows that the HIV infection rate is also declined among STD patients from 14.80 per cent in 2002 to 8.40 in 2004. It is also recorded that the infection rate is started decreasing among men seeking men (4.00% in 2000 to 2.40% in 2002) and sex workers 8.8% in 2003 to 4.0% in 2004. But according to NACO 2004 report, the HIV prevalence is increasing among truckers (2.65% in 1994 to 9.43% in 1997), and intravenous drug users (26.70% in 2000 to 39.92% in 2004).

The Department of Health, Government of Tamil Nadu has recorded the highest number of HIV cases in Namakkal and Salem where the lorry movements is high. The HIV cases have been increasing at an alarming rate in Dindigul district. Blood transfusion, pre marital sex, vertical transmission and heterosexual transmission are cited as causes of the infection. The number of cases coming for treatment or preliminary tests at private hospitals and laboratories at Ottanchatram, Palani, Natham, Vedasandur, and Dindigul towns have been steadily growing year after year. Though the officials identify Palani and Kodaikanal vulnerable as both attracted tourists from all over the country, in reality, the number of patients coming to the private laboratories and clinics at Natham, Vedasandur and Ottanchatram and hundreds of peripheral villages is high. A survey conducted by a NGO confirmed that pre marital sex was on the rise among the youth in Dindigul and Ottanchatram towns. About 85% of the cases among the heterosexuals were in the age group of 18-35 years and among them 67% were from rural areas (*The Hindu*, Dec. 5, 2002).

(a) *AIDS Cases in Tamil Nadu*

Table 4.19. District-wise AIDs Cases in Tamil Nadu (Up to June 2003)

Sl. No.	*Name of District*	*Up to 1996*	*1997*	*1998*	*1999*	*2000*	*2001*	*2002*	*2003*
1.	Chennai	96	195	210	497	1237	4128	7012	7656
2.	Thiruvellore	—	—	25	140	216	623	875	933
3.	Kancheepuram	81	46	27	75	106	453	627	650
4.	Vellore	23	51	37	80	205	778	1241	1348
5.	Thiruvannamalai	28	22	39	83	179	547	790	839
6.	Villupuram	40	38	35	109	347	873	1228	1317
7.	Cuddalore	24	30	42	110	223	675	941	1003
8.	Dharmapuri	17	13	19	66	187	527	851	922

Sl. No.	*Name of District*	*Up to 1996*	*1997*	*1998*	*1999*	*2000*	*2001*	*2002*	*2003*
9.	Salem	45	45	75	162	363	1098	1465	1578
10.	Namakkal	—	—	46	201	388	973	1469	1602
11.	Erode	14	13	45	189	259	865	1165	1251
12.	Coimbatore	30	4	21	92	108	364	450	498
13.	Nilgiris	2	4	2	7	9	32	39	29
14.	Perambalur	3	13	31	42	125	309	561	595
15.	Trichy	33	25	44	174	252	885	1267	1340
16.	Ariyalur]	—	—	—	—	1	53	—	—
17.	Karur	1	19	15	48	94	312	547	595
18.	Pudukkottai	5	1	8	16	30	144	214	229
19.	Thanjavur	29	7	14	31	54	227	425	488
20.	Tiruvarur	—	—	1	10	16	55	95	99
21.	Nagapattinam	10	5	10	8	15	71	109	119
22.	Dindigul	19	4	7	66	54	450	1172	1336
23.	Madurai	58	1	7	93	45	932	1576	1682
24.	Theni	—	—	5	41	55	226	299	314
25.	Sivagangai	10	—	1	16	16	97	138	144
26.	Virudhunagar	5	—	5	13	17	90	136	138
27.	Ramanathapuram	—	—	2	9	16	53	62	63
29.	Tirunelveli	5	5	7	17	36	241	335	244
30.	Thoothukudi	2	—	9	24	42	169	212	227
31.	Kanyakumari	2	1	2	6	8	30	41	44
32.	Address not known	297	3	10	—	2	312	312	312
32.	Other States	—	—	—	—	2	83	98	99
	Total	879	545	801	2391	4707	16677	25779	27794

Source: Tamil Nadu AIDS Control Society, June 2003

Table 4.19 reveals that AIDS cases are increasingly reported from all districts of Tamil Nadu from 1998 onwards. Chennai rank first in AIDS cases followed by Madurai, Namakkal, Salem, Vellore, Trichy and Dindigul.

(b) Causes for the spread of HIV in Tamil Nadu

1. Widespread gender inequality coupled with poverty, dependence, exploitation, discrimination are the major cause for the spread of infection among women in particular and people in general (Kannan, 2003).
2. Poverty and illiteracy influences prostitution and encourages bootleggers and drug traffickers. Prostitution in major cities of Tamil Nadu is well organized and networked by mercenary gangs comprised hardened criminals though there are individual operators and streetwalkers, who fetch clients from the roads. Well organized prostitution is brothel dens. At the helm of affairs in these brothels is a 'madam', often a woman who is the in-charge or manager of the brothel house (*The Hindu*, March19, 2002).
3. Irrespective of high awareness on HIV/AIDS, the youth in general and women in particular are lacking access to right information on sexual health issues (Varma, 2004).
4. Tamil Nadu is progressing in industrial, marketing activities and it also invites multinational companies to establish its enterprises in Tamil Nadu. The development on the economic activities increases lorry transport in Tamil Nadu from various parts of the country. The truck transport facilitated the growth of highway prostitution and unsafe sex (Dev, 2005: 59-62).
5. The orthodox Tamil Culture created fear in the minds of women to choose contraception and to discuss safe sex practices with their sexual partners. The only choice before them is sterilization through tubectomies (Sharma, 2005: 3). Once the women get sterilization, they never think about either to use or to suggest condom for safe sex with their husband. The lack of safe sex in the marital life increases women's vulnerability to HIV/AIDS in Tamil Nadu.
6. Poverty and inequality in health care deliveries is a common phenomena in all states of India and especially,

the rural India has poor health care facilities. It prevents women to take treatment for their reproductive health problems (*The Hindu*, Editorial, 2005: 10). Therefore many sexually transmitted infections are unnoticed by women.

7. The prevalence of sexually transmitted infection among general population is high in Tamil Nadu (3.3 million). Asymptomatic infections were high among both sexes and the rate was similar in both rural and urban areas (Krishnamurthy, 2005: 5). The higher rate of sexually transmitted infection in the state is the reflection of unsafe high risk behaviours among the people of Tamil Nadu.
8. Insufficient awareness on HIV/AIDS, its implication and safe sex practices among rural population increases HIV infection in southern parts of Tamil Nadu (Thinamalar, 2005).
9. Atrocities and sexual violence against women and girl children is rapidly increasing in Tamil Nadu. In 2002, 1766 sexual harassment cases were registered in Tamil Nadu and an official analysis of various cases reveals that rape and molestation were most prevalent in Villupuram, Thirunelveli, Chengalpattu, Thanjavur and 557 rape cases were reported in 2003 in Tamil Nadu (Sangameswarm, 2004). Atrocities and violence against women are rampant in homes rather than at public places (Devi, 2004: 4). Violence against women increases women's HIV infection in Tamil Nadu.
10. HIV related stigma is high in Tamil Nadu than any other States of India. The people living with HIV/AIDS are discriminated, harassed and ill treated by medical and para-medical personnel in both the government and private health sectors (Kannan, 2004). Such discrimination prevents people at high risk group to take HIV test to know their HIV status and to adopt sex practices.

11. Due to drought and unemployment in rural areas, the rural people in Tamil Nadu is involved in migration towards urban and sub-urban areas and lives in the environment which provides the ground for multisexual and unsafe sexual behaviour.

(c) HIV/AIDS intervention programmes in Tamil Nadu

Tamil Nadu State AIDS Control Society (TNSACS) - the first in the country, an autonomous organisation, was created in 1994 to implement AIDS intervention programmes more vigorously across the State with non-government organisations (NGOs) partners who conducted intervention programme aimed at various target populations (Singhal *et al.* 2003: 118).

The main components, strategies and intervention under the AIDS Control Programmes includes Blood safety, training and voluntary blood donation activities, Targeted Intervention Programmes through NGOs, Institutional and Infrastructural strengthening, Training and Capacity building activities, Control of Sexually Transmitted Diseases and Reproductive Track Infection care and also Out-reach services, Condom Promotion activities, Information, Education and Communication, Care and Support for AIDS patients, Training, Sentinel Surveillance, Programme Management, and Advocacy, Social mobilization and Sensitization Programmes, Legal and General Counseling and also Help line Services, Voluntary Counseling and Testing Centres to identify HIV affected and to provide counseling and Prevention of Parent to Child Transmission (Finance and Budget, TNSACS, 2004: wp1).

The HIV prevention programme in Tamil Nadu was two-pronged, with a specialized effort, mainly through one-on-one peer communication, aimed at high-risk groups like sex workers, coupled with an intensive mass media campaign aimed at the general population. Sex workers were persuaded to use condoms with their customers by the specialized communication programmes, and their customers were urged to use condoms with sex workers by the general media campaign. Advertising and public relations firms in India were hired to mount the media campaign in Tamil Nadu. As a result, public awareness of AIDS jumped from 23 per cent in 1994 to 98 per cent in 2000 and condom use had increased among sex workers, truck drivers and factory workers (Singhal *et al.*, 2003: 119-20).

TNSACS initiated several measures to strengthen HIV prevention, care and support programmes. The sentinel surveillance survey and behavioural surveillance survey is undertaken among the selected groups in the population known as "sentinel groups" at regular intervals at regular sentinel sites to monitor trends in HIV infection.

(i) Awareness creation Programme

Information, Education and Communication (IEC) interventions have also been launched to reduce the stigma and discrimination associated with HIV/AIDS and also to safeguard and protect the human rights of People Living with HIV/AIDS (PLWHA). The massages of faithfulness and safe are being used as a part of the awareness campaign through the electronic and print media and through outdoor publicity campaigns both in rural and urban areas in Tamil Nadu. Red Ribbon Clubs are formed in colleges to promote awareness about HIV/AIDS, mode of transmission and prevention among adolescent and young adults. (TNSACS, 2004: wp2).

(ii) School AIDS Education Programme

School AIDS Education Programme is conducted with the objectives of creating an awareness of HIV/AIDS among school students and teachers. All the students studying in 9th and 11th standard are covered under the School AIDS Education Programme. During 2003-2004, 5216 Government and Government aided High Schools and Higher Secondary Schools and 3201 Matriculation Schools were covered under the School AIDS Education Programme and 15 lakhs students were benefited out of this programme (Finance & Budget, TNSACS, 2004: wp7).

Tamil Nadu is a pioneering State in introducing HIV/AIDS information in regular school curriculum during the year 2003-2004. All the 8417 High Schools and Higher Secondary Schools including matriculation schools both in the public and private sectors have been brought under this programme with the support of UNICEF and USAID assisted APAC (AIDS Prevention and Control) Project (Health and Family Welfare Department, 2004: wp2).

(iii) Targeted interventions programme

TNSACS is presently implementing 75-targeted interventions, of which 20 are aimed at sex workers, 15 at truckers, 31 at industrial and migrant workers and 2 at men seeking men. The targeted interventions are implemented through non-governmental organisations, which play a crucial role in combating the HIV/AIDS epidemic (TNSACS, 2004: wp2).

(iv) STD Clinics

High burden of sexually transmitted diseases in the society makes it highly vulnerable to HIV/AIDS. The TNSACS extends support, through provision of infrastructure facilities, equipments and drugs to 57 STD clinics in Tamil Nadu in various institutions including Medical College Hospitals (11), District Headquarter Hospitals (26) and Taluk Hospitals (20). Specialist treatment is provided in all the STD clinics free of cost. In addition HIV/AIDS cases are treated as in-patients in Government Hospitals of Thoracic Medicine, Tambaram, and Government General Hospitals and also in Medical College Hospitals for all opportunistic infections at free of cost (TNSAC, 2004: wp1). Measures have also been taken to bring about appropriate attitudinal changes among medical and para-medical staff in the STD clinics to make them patient friendly

(v) Legal Cell

Legal cell is established in Tamil Nadu AIDS Control Society with the objectives of providing counseling for those infected and affected by HIV/AIDS, protecting and promoting Human Rights of those living with HIV/AIDS, mobilizing lawmakers to adopt effective laws and to take legal and establish committees to address legal and ethical issues, establishing effective liaison with People living with HIV/AIDS, NGOs, Academic Institutions, Corporate Sectors and Government Institutions and publishing concept papers on issues and policies.

(vi) Care and Support

Care and support–medical and emotional, can help people living with HIV/AIDS to lead a fulfilled live with free from discrimination. The government accords high priority for making quality medical care and treatments available to the people living with HIV/AIDS in the state. TNSACS extended financial support for the purchase of drugs for opportunistic infections and for Poor Exposure Prophylaxis (PEP) drugs. It also assists the association of People Living with HIV/AIDS towards running day care centers and community care centers. It extended support to 13 private institutional care centers, five community care centers and seven drop-in-centers and seven networks by people living with HIV positive. Further, the government has waived sales tax on ART drugs with a view to help the People Living with HIV/AIDS (TNSACS – Care and Support, 204: 1-wp9). TNSACS employs positive people and it insisted the NGOs working with HIV/AIDS to appoint at least one positive person in their organisations. Special wards have been set up for HIV/AIDS patients for giving treatment for various opportunistic infections in the Government Hospital of Thoracic Medicine in Tambaram, Chennai.

(vii) Family Health Awareness Campaign (FHAC)

The Family Health Awareness Campaign (FHAC) is an important strategy to identify and treat Sexually Transmitted Diseases and Reproductive Track diseases (RTI) and to treat them with syndromic management, basically to eliminate aggravating factors such as STD and RTI which contribute for faster spread of HIV/AIDS. The campaign was concentrated on general public, both in rural and urban areas. FHACs have been conducted in Tamil Nadu from 1999 to 2003 every year and with the support from National AIDS Control Organisation, Government of India. During 2003, FHAC camps were conducted in 14,889 locations across the state with adequate multimedia publicity and as a result, the number of persons with STD identified and treated in these camps went up from 6,63,330 in 2002 to 11,05,047 in 2003, of which 8,31,988 were women (Policy Note - Health and Family Welfare Department, 2005: wp2).

(viii) Condom Promotion

Top priority has been given to promote condom usage among people, both high risk and low risk, to prevent transmission of HIV through sexual route of transmission. NGOs have been involved in social marketing of condoms. At present condoms are available in the fair price shops in the state. Condom at free of cost is distributed to the people through health care institution, STD clinics, outreach camps and also through NGOs. Subsidised or low priced condoms are distributed among the people in targeted intervention areas an non-intervention areas with the support of NGOs.

(ix) Blood Safety

The Tamil Nadu State Blood Transfusion Council closely monitors the activity of the Blood Banks with the association of the Directorate of Drugs Control. Government has taken various efforts to increase the share of voluntary donation and as a result, the share of voluntary donors went up from 59.40% to 64.05% during 2004 and the zero prevalence among the blood donors went down from 0.21% t 0.18% in 2004.

(x) Prevention of Parent to Child Transmission Programme

To prevent the vertical transmission of HIV from the mother to child, Prevention of Parent to Child Transmission of HIV (PPTCT) Programme is being implemented in 65 centers Tamil Nadu including 14 Government medical Colleges, six Private Medical Colleges, 28 District Government Headquarters Hospitals, eight Private hospitals and nine Corporation Mother and Child Health Centers (Finance and Budget, TNSACS, 2004: 6-wp7). The special features of the PPTCT programme are counseling to all the pregnant women and their husbands attending antenatal clinic centers, testing for HIV, administration of ART prophylaxis to the identified positive pregnant women and their children and improvements in general antenatal clinic practices (Policy Note - Health and Family Welfare Department, 2005: wp3).

(xi) Voluntary Confidential Counseling and Testing Centers (VCCTC)

The VCCTC function as a bridge between prevention and care and support intervention. It has the objectives of (i) drawing and counseling the high-risk groups, (ii) bringing about desired changes in their behaviour, (iii) identification of sero positive persons, (iv) extending psychological support to HIV positive persons and (v) referring HIV positive persons for appropriate medical treatment wherever necessary (Policy Note - Health and Family Welfare Department, 2005: 3). There are 43 VCCT Centers established in all government head quarters hospital and government medical colleges. In 2004, 85,801 persons availed testing facilities and among them 20,590 were identified as HIV positive (Finance & Budget, TNSACS, 2004: wp6).

(xii) Anti Retroviral Therapy (ART)

The Government of India has taken a policy decision to make Anti Retroviral drugs available in the public health system in the country. Under this initiative, the ART programme was launched as the first phase in Government hospital for Thoracic Medicine, Tambaram in Chennai with effect from 1st April 2004 (Policy Note - Health and Family Welfare Department, 2005: wp3).

(xiii) Greater involvement of people living with HIV/AIDS (GIPA)

The government is committed to the concept of greater involvement of people living with HIV/AIDS programmes. The positive networks are actively involved in the decision making process of TNSACS at various levels. The government has issued orders to include a women member of Positive Networks in all the Hospital Advisory Committees in the state.

(xiv) Partnership with NGOs to reach high risk groups

The TNSAC had coordinated with NGOs in the implementation of HIV/AIDS prevention Programmes among marginalized and vulnerable population who are at high risk and creating awareness among general public. Now it has shifted its focus towards bringing behavioural changes through Targeted

Interventions involving grass root level NGOs and peer educators/outreach workers/counselors. The TANSAC funds 621 NGOs and currently 107 programmes are implemented in the state for different risk groups such as sex workers, truckers, industrial workers, prisoners, men seeking men, migrant workers, networking with people living with HIV/AIDS, youth and adolescents, tribal and research studies. Awareness, condom promotion and demonstration, STD care, counseling are the important sub-components of these interventions (Finance & Budget, TNSACS, 2004: wp3).

(xiv) Training and Capacity Building

In order to have better service delivery system and to have institutional strengthening in private and public sector, training activities has been given due importance by making adequate provision in Action Plan to impart training on HIV/AIDS to medical, para-medical and personnel of different sectors and departments. During 2003-2004, 930 officials from various medical and para-medical departments were given training on various aspects related to HIV/AIDS.

(xv) Positive net work by the people with HIV positive

TNSACS has provided funds to organize people with HIV positive by establishing positive net work. There are seven net works functioning in Tamil Nadu and recently, the TNSACS has constituted an advisory committee in every Government hospital in the state to monitor and prevent discrimination in treatment and care of persons living with HIV/AIDS and women living with HIV positive are included in all advisory committee (Kannan, 2004: 5).

In spite of all these intervention programmes the rate of HIV infection is increasing among high risk groups in general and women in particular in Tamil Nadu.

5

Analysis and Discussion

This chapter is devoted to analysis and discussion of primary data collected from the study area. It is divided into six sub-sections focusing on a specific aspect of the study.

The first sub-section deals with socio economic status of respondents which includes respondents' personal, family particulars and economic condition of respondents. The second sub-section is directly related to marital status of respondents. The third sub-section deals with circumstances leading to HIV positive both for housewives and sex workers. The fourth sub-section explains about the sexual behaviour of respondents after infection. The fifth sub-section represents the social relationship of respondents with their family members, neighbours, friends and relatives. This section also gives elaborate view about the discrimination faced by the respondents in hospitals and work place. The sixth sub-section evaluates the attitude of respondents towards pregnancy after infection.

Tables are presented logically by merging relevant variables in consonance with the objectives of the study. Percentage and averages are widely used to analyse the available data and accordingly interpretations are made.

SOCIO-ECONOMIC STATUS OF RESPONDENTS

Table 5.1. Age-wise Distribution of Respondents

Sl. No.	*Age (in years)*	*No. of Respondents*	*Percentage*
1.	15 – 19	16	8.0
2.	20 – 24	47	23.5
3.	25 – 29	86	43.0
4.	30 – 34	28	14.0
5.	35 – 39	23	11.5
	Total	200	100

Table 5.1 reveals the age wise distribution of respondents in the study area. It shows that all (100 %) HIV infected respondents fall in the reproductive and economically active age group of 15-39 years. This study also reveals the high (66.5%) concentration of HIV infection in the sexually active age group of 20-29 years.

The inference drawn from the table is that the majority (66.5%) of respondents with infection belong to the hyper sexual active age group of 20-29 years.

Table 5.2. Community-wise Distribution of Respondents

Sl. No.	*Community*	*No. of Respondents*	*Percentage*
1.	S.C	52	26.0
2.	S.T.	3	1.5
3.	M.B.C.	22	11.0
4.	B.C.	93	46.5
5.	F.C.	30	15.0
	Total	200	100.0

The analysis of data on communitywise distribution of respondents indicates that 46.5% respondents belong to backward community (B.C.). The respondents belong to schedule caste (S.C.) is found to be 26%. The respondents belong to forward caste (F.C.) constitute 15%. It is found from the analysis that 11% respondents and 1.5% of respondents belong to most back ward community (M.B.C.) and schedule tribes (S.T.) (Table 5.2).

As regards this study, the higher percentage (57.5%) of respondents belongs to the socially Backward Class (B.Cs) and Most Back Word Class (M.B.Cs) in view of their husbands' involvement in multi sexual behaviour leading to transmission of HIV to their wives (Table 5.2).

Table 5.3. Education-wise Distribution of Respondents

Sl. No.	*Educational Status*	*No. of Respondents*	*Percentage*
1.	Illiterate	28	14.0
2.	Primary	49	24.5
3.	High School	54	27.0
4.	Higher Secondary	35	17.5
5.	Graduation	31	15.5
6.	Technical Education	3	1.5
	Total	200	100

Table 5.3 shows the educational status of the respondents. The analysis of data shows that out of 200 respondents, only 14% were illiterate and the remaining 61.5 per cent were literate. Among the literate groups, 27 per cent respondents have completed high school, 17.5 per cent respondents have studied upto higher secondary, 15.5 per cent have obtained graduate degree and 1.5 per cent were professionally qualified.

The inference drawn from the table is that literate women are highly prone to infection than the illiterate women.

Table 5.4. Religion-wise Distribution of Respondents

Sl. No.	*Religion*	*No. of Respondents*	*Percentage*
1.	Hindu	170	85.0
2.	Muslim	14	7.0
3.	Christian	16	8.0
	Total	200	100

Table 5.4 explains the religion wise distribution of respondents in the study area. It is observed from the table that out of 200 respondents, 85% were Hindus, 8% were Christians and 7% were Muslims.

Since majority (85%) of the respondents were Hindus, the inference drawn from the table is that there is a change in the moral and traditional attitude of younger generation.

Table 5.5. Social Status of the Respondents

Sl. No.	*Social status*	*No. of Respondents*	*Percentage*
1.	Housewives	131	65.5
2.	Sex workers	62	31.0
3.	Students	7	3.5
	Total	200	100

As far as the social status of the respondents is concerned, 65.5% are wives. The sex workers accounted for 31.0%. The remaining 3.5% are students studying in various colleges of Chennai (Table 5.5).

The inference drawn from the table is that wives are highly vulnerable to HIV/AIDS.

Table 5.6. Causes for Migration of Respondents to Chennai

Sl. No.	*Causes*	*No. of Respondents*	*Percentage*
1.	Marriage	54	27.0
2.	Employment	26	13.0
3.	HIV infection	27	13.5
4.	Education	6	3.0
5.	Prostitution	12	6.0
6.	Non-migrants	75	37.5
	Total	200	100

Table 5.6 explains the causes for migration of respondents to Chennai. Of the total, 62.5% of respondents were migrated to Chennai from various parts of Tamil Nadu as well as from various States of India.

Marriage constituted the major (27%) cause of migration to Chennai. HIV infection influenced 13.5% respondents to migrate to Chennai. Employment is the primary cause for 13% respondents' migration. Involvement in prostitution made 6% respondents to migrate to Chennai and education is the important cause for 3% respondents' migration.

It is also identified from Table 5.6 that the higher percentage (61.6%) of respondents migrated to Chennai from different parts of Tamil Nadu. Among outside Tamil Nadu migrants, the women from Andhra Pradesh were dominant (20.8%) followed by Kerala (8.8%), Karnataka (6.4) and Gujarat (2.4%).

The conclusion drawn from the table is that the majority (62.5%) under study is the migrants of different parts of Tamil Nadu for various reasons. The marriage constitutes the major cause for the migration of many women to Chennai. To hide HIV infection from the relatives, friends, neighbours, to avail treatment facilities, etc. also lead many women to migrate to Chennai.

Table 5.7. Family Size of the Respondents

Sl. No.	*Size of the family*	*No. of Respondents*	*Percentage*
1.	Small (> 4 members)	45	22.5
2.	Medium (4 – 6 members)	86	43.0
3.	Large (< 6 members)	69	34.5
	Total	200	100

The analysis of the data on "family particulars of the respondents" have identified that 43% of the respondents have medium size family with the members of 3 to 4. Significant 34.5% of respondents also has large family size with the members above five. The small family of the respondents accounted for 22.5 % with the family members of less than four (Table 5.7).

The inference drawn from the analysis is that the infected women's families have the characteristics of medium and large size families.

Table 5.8. Structure of Family of Respondents

Sl. No.	*Structure of the family*	*No. of Respondents*	*Percentage*
1.	Joint	154	77.0
2.	Nuclear	46	23.0
	Total	200	100

As far as the structure of the family is concerned, the nuclear family is dominant (77%) than the joint family (23%). The conclusion drawn from the table is that HIV infection is high (77%) in the nuclear family than the joint family (Table 5.8).

Table 5.9. Dependent and Non-dependent Family Members of Respondents

Sl. No.	*Family members*	*No. of Respondents*	*Percentage*
1.	Dependent - Children	126	63.0
2.	Dependent - Old age	44	22.0
3.	Non Dependent	30	15.0
	Total	200	100

The study also found that the great proportion (63 per cent) of respondents have dependent children within the age of less than 17 years and also a significant proportion (22 per cent)of respondents have an old age dependents with the age ranging from 58 and above. The respondents who have non-dependent family members constituted only 15 per cent.

The inference drawn from the analysis is that majority (63 per cent) of the respondents have dependent family members that increased the burden of the HIV infected women.

Table 5.10. Educational Status of Respondents' Family Members

Sl. No.	*Education of Family members*	*No. of Respondents*	*Percentage*
1.	Illiterate	34	17.0
2.	School educated	128	64.0
3.	Graduation	38	19.0
	Total	200	100

The educational level of the family members varies from illiterate to graduation. Majority (64%) of the respondents' family members have school education and 19% of the respondents' families have graduates. Besides 17% of respondents family members were illiterate (Table 5.10).

It is explored from the analysis that the majority (82%) of the respondents' family members are literates.

Table 5.11. Employment Status of Family Members

Sl. No.	*Employment status of family members*	*No. of members*	*Percentage*
1.	Government	3	3.9
2.	Private	16	20.5
3.	Business	12	15.4
4.	Casual labours	27	34.6
5.	Hotel workers	5	6.4
6.	Transport workers	3	3.9
7.	Construction workers	11	14.1
8.	Military service	1	1.2
	Total	78	100

It is found from the study that only 15 per cent of respondents have non-dependent family members and they were involved in different kinds of occupation in various sectors such as casual labours (34.6 per cent) in unorganized sectors, employee in private sectors (20.5 per cent), construction work (14.1 per cent), business (15.4 per cent), government (3.9 per cent) hotel industry (6.4) and in military service (1.2 per cent) (Table 5.11).

The inference drawn from the analysis is that majority (59 per cent) of respondents family members are engaged in unorganized sectors which gives less and income and least job security.

Table 5.12. Respondents Status in the Family

Sl. No.	*Respondents status in the family*	*No. of Respondents*	*Percentage*
1.	Earner	49	24.5
2.	Earner dependent	67	33.5
3.	Non-earner dependent	84	42.0
	Total	200	100

Table 5.12 shows the status of the respondents in the family. The table has revealed that 42 per cent respondents were non-

earner dependent, 33.5per cent respondents were earner dependent and 24.5per cent were earners for their families.

The conclusion drawn from the table is that the majority (42per cent) of the HIV infected women were non-earner dependents, who are mostly wives.

Table 5.1.13. Place of Residence of Respondents

Sl. No.	*Place of residence*	*No. of Respondents*	*Percentage*
1.	Urban	84	42.0
2.	Urban slums		
	(a) Housewives	95	47.5
	(b) Sex workers	21	10.5
	Total	200	100

The table on the respondents place of residence has identified that majority (42 per cent) of the respondents reside in urban areas and urban slums (58 per cent).

The inference drawn from the analysis is that the urban slum women are highly vulnerable to HIV infection due to promiscuous relationship of their husbands.

Table 5.14. Occupation of the Respondents

Sl. No.	*Nature of Occupation*	*No. of Respondents*	*Percentage*
1.	Commercial sex work	33	16.5
2.	Casual labour	18	9.0
3.	Self Employed	5	1.5
4.	Government services	7	3.5
5.	Others :		
	(a) Private company	16	8.0
	(b) House maids	12	6.0
	(c) N.G.Os	17	8.5
	(d) Support actors	5	2.5
	(e) Construction work	5	2.5
6.	Unemployed	84	42.0
	Total	200	100

The Table 5.14 explains the occupation of the respondents. It is evident from the analysis that significant percentage (42 per cent) of respondents are unemployed and non-earner dependents. The number of respondents employed in various sectors constituted for 58 per cent.

The analysis of the data further shows that a very few percentage of respondents were employed in organized sectors like Government (3.5 per cent) and private companies (8 per cent). But the majority of the respondents were found to be engaged in unorganized sectors such as casual labour (9 per cent) house maids (6 per cent), construction workers (2.5 per cent), cinema artists (2.5 per cent), self employed (1.5 per cent) and field workers in the N.G.Os (8.5 per cent). The respondents who are working in the N.G.Os joined only after their infection. The women involved in commercial sex work constituted for 16.5 per cent.

The conclusion drawn from the analysis is that the majority (30 per cent) of the respondents were employed in unorganized sectors and in commercial sex work (16.5 per cent).

Table 5.15. Ownership of Property of Respondents

	Immovable Assets				*Movable Assets*		
Sl. No.	*Type of Asset*	*No. of Respondents*	*%*	*Sl. No.*	*Type of Asset*	*No. of Respondents*	*%*
1.	Land	2	1.0	1.	TV Radio	83	41.5
2.	House	6	3.0	2.	Fridge	14	7.0
3.	Shop	1	0.5	3.	Motor cycle	4	2.0
4.	No Assets	191	95.5	4.	Jewels	29	14.5
				5.	No Assets	70	35.0
	Total	200	100		Total	200	100

Table 5.15 explains the ownership of property of the respondents. Of the total, very few percentage of respondents own immovable assets like house (3 per cent), land (1 per cent) and shop (0.5 per cent).

As far as movable assets are concerned, a considerable percentage of respondents owned TV/Radio (41.5 per cent), Jewels (14.5 per cent), Fridge (7 per cent) and Motor cycle (2 per cent).

The inference drawn from the table is that many respondents (95.5 per cent) due to gender biased Indian culture do not enjoy the ownership of immovable property and the women who own movable assets (65 per cent) are due to their earning capacity in various occupations.

Table 5.16. Annual Income and Expenditure of Respondent Families

Sl. No.	*Amount (in Rupees)*	*Income*		*Expenditure*	
		No. of respondents	*Percentage*	*No. of respondents*	*Percentage*
1.	Less than 25,000	96	48.0	62	31.0
2.	25,000 – 50,000	43	21.5	66	33.0
3.	50,000 – 75,000	33	16.5	43	21.5
4.	75,000 – 1,00,000	19	9.5	22	11.0
5.	More than 1,00,000	9	4.5	7	3.5
	Total	200	100.0	200	100

Table 5.16 on annual income and expenditure of the respondent families reveal that the majority (69.5 per cent) of the respondent families fall within the income group of Rs. 50,000 followed by the income group of Rs. 50, 000 – 75,000 (16.5 per cent). The respondent families' income of more than Rs.75, 000 constituted around 14 per cent in this study.

The analysis on respondent families expenditure shows that 64 per cent incurred less than Rs.50,000 and the remaining 36 per cent of respondent families annual expenditure was more than Rs. 75,000. The inference drawn from the above table is that the annual expenditure is more than their annual income.

Table 5.17 on indebtedness of the respondent families reveals that 60 per cent of the respondents were indebted to various sources for different purposes. Of the 120 respondents, 59.2 per cent women were indebted for taking treatment for HIV infection for their husband, children and themselves. The other reasons for the indebtedness of the remaining respondents were identified as education of the children (9.2 per cent), business (6.7 per cent), food, and clothes (10.7 per cent), construction of house (1.7 per cent), marriage (5.0 per cent), and other reasons like recreation, celebrating festivals etc (7.5 per cent).

Table 5.17. Indebtedness of Respondent Families

Sl. No.	Purpose of borrowing	*Sources of borrowing, No. of families (in percentage)*					
		Money Lender	Bank	Relatives	Friends	Others	Total
1.	Treatment	47 (66.2%)	-	15 (21.1%)	9 (12.7%)	-	71 (59.2%)
2.	Children education	1 (9.1%)	-	-	6 (54.5%)	4 (36.4%)	11 (9.2%)
3.	Business	3 (37.5%)	3 (37.5%)	-	2 (25.0%)	-	8 (6.7%)
4.	Food and clothes	8 (61.5%)	-	2 (15.4%)	2 (15.4%)	1 (7.7%)	13 (10.7%)
5.	House construction	-	2 (100.0%)	-	-	-	2 (1.7%)
6.	Marriage	4 (66.7%)	-	-	2 (33.3%)	-	6 (5.0%)
7.	Others	2 (22.2%)	2 (22.2%)	1 (11.1%)	4 (44.5%)	-	9 (7.5%)
	Total	*65 (54.2%)*	*7 (5.8%)*	*18 (15.0%)*	*25 (20.8%)*	*5 (4.2%)*	*120 (100%)*

Among the sources of borrowing, moneylender is found to be a dominant source (54.2 per cent) followed by friends (20.8 per cent) and relatives (15.0 per cent).

The inference drawn from the table is that majority (59.2 per cent) of the respondents borrowed for medical reasons to treat HIV infection and the source of their borrower was moneylenders who charged higher interest.

Table 5.18 on amount borrowed by the respondents reveals that the majority (67.5 per cent) of respondents have borrowed amount ranging from 4,000-10,000. The significant percentage (15.0 per cent) borrowed an amount between 2,000-4,000. About 11.7 per cent is borrowed above 10,000 where as 5.8 per cent borrowed upto 2,000 from various sources.

The inference drawn from the analysis is that the majority (67.5 per cent) have borrowed amount from rupees 4000-10000 due to various reasons which lead to heavy burden for them to repay it in time.

Table 5.18. Amount Borrowed by the Respondents

Sl. No.	*Amount (in Rupees)*	*No. of Respondents*	*Percentage*
1.	Less than 2000	7	5.8
2.	2000-4000	18	15.0
3.	4000- 6000	31	25.8
4.	6000-8000	27	22.5
5.	8000-10000	23	19.2
6.	Above 10000	14	11.7
	Total	120	100

Marital Status of the Respondents

Table 5.19 on marital status of the respondents indicates that out of 200 respondents, 82.5 per cent were married and 17.5 per cent were unmarried. Among the married respondents, 38 per cent were living with their husband, 25.5 per cent were found to be widows, 16.5 per cent are separated from their husbands and 2.5 per cent were identified as divorced.

The inference drawn from the table is that the housewives were at higher risk of getting infection in the study area.

Table 5.19. Marital Status of the Respondents

Sl. No.	*Marital Status*	*No. of Respondents*	*Percentage*
1.	Married	76	38.0
2.	Separated	33	16.5
3.	Divorced	5	2.5
4.	Widow	51	25.5
5.	Unmarried	35	17.5
	Total	200	100

Table 5.20 explains the age at marriage of the respondents and their husbands. Of the total 200 respondents 82.5 per cent were married and remaining 17.5 per cent were unmarried. Among the married respondents, the majority (58.2 per cent) of the respondents have got married in between the age of 19—22 years. Child marriage, i.e. marriage age less than 18 years is found among 32.1 per cent of respondents. The respondents who have married at the age of 23 and above are identified as

9.7 per cent. As far as age at marriage of the respondent's husband is concerned, 92.7 per cent got married at the age above 23 years.

Table 5.20. Age at Marriage of Respondents and their Husbands

Sl. No.	*Age at Marriage, years*	*No. of Respondents*	*No. of Respondents Husband*
1.	Less than 18	53 (32.1 per cent)	0 (0 .0 per cent)
2.	19-22	96 (58.2 per cent)	12 (7.3 per cent)
3.	23-27	15 (9.1 per cent)	54 (32.7 per cent)
4.	28-32	1 (0.6 per cent)	61 (37.0 per cent)
5.	Above 33	0 (0.0 per cent)	38 (23.0 per cent)
	Total	165 (100 per cent)	165 (100 per cent)

The inference drawn from the analysis is that 90.1 per cent of women's' age at marriage is below 22 years. These respondents got married the men who are older than them. Due to the younger age, the women can't either negotiate or suggest reproductive health issues and safe sex to their husbands. Moreover, these young women are highly ignorant about sex and its implication of her body and men have all power to with regard to sex and reproductive health. Therefore, younger the age at marriage, higher the chance for getting sexually transmitted diseases including HIV/AIDS.

Table 5.21. Nature of Kins Relationship between Respondents and their Husbands

Sl. No.	*Nature of relationship*	*No. of Respondents*	*Percentage*
1.	Blood relatives	26	15.8
2.	Distant relatives	46	27.9
3.	Not related	93	56.3
	Total	165	100

Table 5.21 shows the nature of kins relationship between the respondents and their husbands before marriage. The analysis reveals that 56.3 per cent of respondent's husbands were not related to their family before marriage. For 27.9 per

cent of respondents, their husbands were distant relatives and 15.8 per cent of respondents got married within the blood relatives.

The inference drawn from the analysis is that the majority (84.2 per cent) of the marriage taken place outside close kin family relationships. According to the respondents, such kind of marriage would not facilitate them to either to collect or to discuss about the health status of the partners. They also revealed that if the partners are within their close family circle, they can know each other behaviour and characters and if the behaviour of the partner is suspeciable and if they have any doubts on their behaviour on pre marital sex they can avoid the marriage with them.

Therefore, the marriage with unknown person may be resulted in the selection of mate whose character may not be well understood before marriage and if the men have pre marital sex before marriage with multiplex sexual partners, it will increases the chance for HIV infection among the married women with single sexual partners.

Table 5.22 projects the type of marriage of the respondents. It explains that 77.6 per cent of respondent's marriage was arranged by their family members. The marriage that is not arranged by their family members is constituted about 22.4 per cent.

Table 5.22. Type of Marriage of Respondents

Sl. No.	*Type of Marriage*	*No. of Respondents*	*Percentage*
1	Arranged	109	66.1
2.	Love with arranged	19	11.5
3.	Love and married by themselves	34	20.6
4.	Living together without marriage	3	1.8
	Total	165	100

The understanding from the table is that the infection rate is found to be high (66.1 per cent) in arranged marriages and it is comparatively low (32.1 per cent) in the marriage based on love. In the Indian context the marriages are arranged by the elders of the family with the good faith that they have selected a good life partner for their daughters. The elders are very keen to collect information with regard to the matching of horoscope rather than health status and other information related to pre marital sexual behaviour of the bridegroom. In the case of love marriage, the loving girl and boy knows each others behaviour and they always have a chance to discuss about their health condition prior to their marriage.

Therefore, HIV infection is found to be high in arranged marriage and low in love marriage.

Table 5.23. Causes for Respondents Widowhood

Sl.No.	*Causes*	*No. of Respondents*	*Percentage*
1.	Husband died due to AIDS	47	92.1
2.	Other causes	4	7.9
	Total	51	100

Among the 200 respondents selected for study, 25.5 per cent were identified as widows. It is observed from the analysis that HIV/AIDS related diseases is the major cause for the death of 92.1 per cent respondents husbands and among them 9 (17.6 per cent) have committed suicide due to the fear of AIDS related stigma. The remaining 7.9 per cent have become widow even before they are infected by HIV (Table 5.23).

The inference drawn from the table is that the AIDS is the major cause for the majority (92.1 per cent) of the women to become widow at younger age.

All the 51 (100 per cent) women became widow within the age of 30 years. The predominant age at widowhood for 88.2 per cent of respondents is identified as 20-25 year and the remaining became widow between the age of 26-30 years. The table also shows that the majority (72.5) of respondents lived with their husband for 1-5 years and the remaining 27.5 per cent respondents life with their husbands ranges between 6-10 years (Table 5.24).

The inference drawn from the table is that AIDS is the major cause for the majority (88.2 per cent) of women to become widow at the younger age of 20-25 years and many (72.5 per cent) have acquired infection within the 5 years of their marital life. Sexual

Table 5.24 Age at Widowhood and Duration of Life with Husband

Sl. No.	*Age at widowhood (in years) No. of Respondents*			*Duration of life with husband (in years) No. of respondents*		
	20-25	*26-30*		*1-5*	*6-10*	
1.	45 (88.2%)	6 (11.8%)	51 (100%)	37 (72.5%)	14 (27.5%)	51 (100%)

encounter or sexual activity is high among the spouses in the early period of their marital life. The aspirations towards giving birth to child force the young couples to avoid condom and other contraception. Unsafe sex in the early period of marital life increases the chances of infection for the women within the less duration of marital life.

The findings of younger age at widowhood also suggest that the pre marital sex with multiple sexual partners is high among the young men and they might have got infection long before their marriage. The men may or may not be aware of their HIV sero status before marriage and they are the sources of transmitting the virus to their young wives.

Table 5.28. Causes for Separation from Husbands.

Sl. No.	*Causes*	*No. of Respondents*	*Percentage*
1.	Refused to live with the HIV infected husbands	14	36.8
2.	Deserted by infected husbands	11	28.9
3.	Childlessness	1	2.6
4.	Extra marital affairs of husbands	2	5.3
5.	Extra marital affairs of respondents	8	21.1
6.	Family problems	2	5.3
	Total	38	100

In this study, 18.0 per cent women were identified as either separated 33 (86.8 per cent) or divorced 5 (13.2 per cent)) from their husbands. AIDS is identified as major cause for 65.7 per cent women for the separation from their marital life. Among them 36.8 per cent women refused to live with their infected husbands where as 28.9 per cent were deserted by their infected husbands due to avoid the further spread of infection to the child.. Extra marital affair is the cause for 21.1 per cent respondents' separation from their husbands. Family problem accounted for the separation of 5.3 per cent of women. Husband's extra marital affairs made 5.3 per cent women to break their matrimonial bonds and childlessness is the primary cause for the separation of 2.6 per cent women from their husbands (Table 5.5).

The conclusion drawn from the table is that HIV/AIDS of husbands disturbs family life and forces the spouses either to separate or to get divorce (65.7 per cent) from the infected persons. The findings also reveal that the urban life facilitated many young women to develop extra marital affairs (21.1 per cent) not only for satisfying their sexual urge but also to earn money to meet their personal as well as family requirements.

Table 5.26 on the employment status of the respondents' husbands reveals that the majority (35.8 per cent) are casual labourers and industrial workers (25.4 per cent). The transport workers are identified as 16.4 per cent followed by self employment (12.7 per cent). The remaining are engaged in government service (9.7 per cent) and business (5.4 per cent).

Table 5.26. Employment Status of Husband

Sl. No.	*Employment status*	*No. of Respondents*	*Percentage*
1.	Casual labourers	59	35.8
2.	Transport workers	27	16.4
3.	Government service	16	9.7
4.	Self employed	21	12.7
5.	Industrial worker	42	25.4
	Total	165	100

The inference drawn from the analysis is that the casual labourers, industrial workers, transport workers are more prone to HIV/AIDS.

The above table explains the reasons for the unmarried status of 35 respondents. It shows that involvement in sex work prevented 25.7 per cent of respondents to get marriage followed by dowry problem (229 per cent), HIV infection (20 per cent) and lack of interest by the parents (17.1 per cent). The respondents who are not found suitable alliance for marriage accounted for 8.6 per cent. The 5.7 per cent of respondents have no interest in marriage.

Table 5.27 inference drawn from the analysis is that involvement in sex work and dowry prevented majority (48.6 per cent) of respondents to get marriage.

Table 5.27. Reasons for Unmarried Status of Respondents

Sl.No.	*Reasons*	*No. of Respondents*	*Percentage*
1.	Dowry problem	8	22.9
2.	Not found suitable alliance	3	8.6
3.	Not interested	2	5.7
4.	Parents not shown interest	6	17.1
5.	Involvement in sex workers	9	25.7
6.	HIV infection	7	20.0
	Total	35	100

Circumstances Leading to HIV Infection and Related Behaviours

Table 5.28 explains how long the respondents were suffering from HIV infection. The analysis shows that, of the total, 31.5 per cent respondents were living with HIV infection for less than 5 years followed by 25.5 per cent respondents who were suffering with HIV for 5-6 years. The respondents who carry HIV about 6-7 years constituted 24.5 per cent and the women living with HIV for more than 7 years identified as 19 per cent.

The inference drawn from the analysis is that the majority (81.0 per cent) of the respondents tested HIV within seven years and it shows that they are infected within the sexually hyper active younger age.

Table 5.28. Duration of HIV Infection.

Sl. No.	*Duration (in No. of years)*	*No. of Respondents*	*Percentage*
1	Less than 5	62	31.0
2.	5 - 6	51	25.5
3.	6 - 7	49	24.5
4.	7 - 8	32	16.0
5.	Above 8	6	3.0
	Total	200	100

Table 5.29 observed the sources of HIV infection of the respondents. It is evident from the table that 65.0 per cent respondents got HIV through their husband's promiscuous act. For 31.0 per cent respondents, their heterosexual contact is the major cause for their infection. It is also identified from the study that 3.5 per cent respondents have infection through their pre marital sexual contact with their boy friends. The respondents who have infection through an unsterilized needle while injecting drug accounted for 0.5 per cent.

Table 5.29. Sources of Infection for Respondents.

Sl.No.	*Sources of Infection*	*No. of Respondents*	*Percentage*
1.	Husband	130	65.0
2.	Respondents heterosexual conduct	62	31.0
3.	Injected drug use	1	0.5
4.	Pre marital sex	7	3.5
	Total	200	100

The conclusion drawn from the table is that though the majority (66 per cent) of infected women is innocent victims of HIV infection through their husband, significant percentage (31 per cent) of women got infection through their heterosexual contact. It contradicts the general view that most of the women get infection in the marital life through their husbands.

Among the 62 sex workers, 27 (43.5 per cent) sex workers and one (0.5 per cent) injecting drug user are married and they are living with their husbands. These 27 sex workers and injecting drug user have not revealed their infection status to their husbands and they know that their husbands may also infected by HIV (Table 5.30).

Table 5.30. Husbands Infected by Respondents.

Sl.No.	*Wives behaviour*	*No. of husbands infected*	*Percentage*
1.	Sex work	27	96.4
2.	Injecting drug use	1	3.6
	Total	28	100

Of the 158 married respondents living with their husbands, 130 (65.0 per cent) got infection through their husbands where as the remaining 28 (35 per cent) got infection through their behaviours of sex work and injecting drug use. These 35 per cent of respondents' husbands are highly vulnerable to infection.

The inference drawn from the analysis that sex workers husbands are highly vulnerable to HIV infection.

Table 5.31. Sexual Behaviour of Respondents and their Husbands

Sl. No.	*Sexual Behaviour*	*Respondents*		*Respondent's Husbands*	
		Yes	*Percentage*	*Yes*	*Percentage*
1.	Pre-marital sex	35	17.5	79	47.9
2.	Extra marital sex	30	15.0	26	15.7
3.	Both	4	20.0	31	18. 8
4.	No immoral sex	131	65.5	29	17.6
	Total	200	100	165	100

While analyzing the respondents' sexual experiences, it is identified that significant number of respondents were involved in pre marital and extra marital sex. The analysis revealed that 17.5 per cent have experienced pre marital sex including 7 students. Pre marital and extra marital sex is found among 15.5 per cent women in this study. Among the women who have experienced extra marital sex, 6 are housewives with the social status of either widow or deserted and they have sex with their regular partners and 24 are married commercial sex workers. Besides, the women who experienced both pre and extra marital sex accounted for 4 (2.0 per cent). All these four women were commercial sex workers.

The study also explored the respondents' husbands pre and extra marital sex. It is found from the study that 47.9 per cent respondents' husbands experienced pre marital sex, 15.7 per cent respondents' husbands have an experience of extra marital sex. The men who experienced both pre and extra marital sex accounted for 18.8 per cent (Table 5.31).

Among the 165 married couples, 131 (65.5 per cent) women experienced sex only with their husbands whereas only 29 (17.6 per cent) men experienced sex after their marriage only with their wives.

The inference drawn from the analysis is that the pre and extra marital sex is predominant among the men than the women. However, significant number of women involved in such unapproved sexual activities due to the influence of city oriented life and urban culture. The men experience with pre marital sex increases their vulnerability to sexually transmitted diseases including HIV/AIDS. He may or may not be aware of his infection before marriage. The lack of knowledge on the HIV status of men before marriage increases the vulnerability of their spouse infection after marriage.

It is also clear from the analysis that not only the men are responsible for women infection. But also significant number of women themselves is responsible for their own HIV status through their pre and extra marital sex. These women also increase the vulnerability of their spouse infection.

Table 5.32. Pre and Extra Marital Sexual Partners of Respondents and their Husbands.

Sl. No.	*Sexual partners*	*Pre marital*		*Extra marital*	
		No. Respondents	*No. of Husband*	*No. Respondents*	*No. of Husband*
1.	Relatives	5(12.8%)	8 (7.3%)	1(2.9%)	1(1.8%)
2.	Neighbour	8(20.5%)	13(11.8%)	0(0.0%)	2(3.5%)
3.	Friends	11(28.2%)	17(15.4%)	1(2.9%)	0(0.0%)
4.	Co-worker	3(7.7%)	11(10.0%)	0(0.0%)	0(0.0%)
5.	Customers	9(23.1%)	—	32(94.2%)	—
6.	Family Friend	3(7.7%)	7(6.4%)	0(0.0%)	1(1.8%)
7.	Sex worker	—	54(49.1%)	—	53(92.9%)
	Total	39(100%)	110(100%)	34(100%)	57(100%)

Table 5.32 explains the pre and extra marital sexual partners of respondents and their husbands. Among the respondents who have pre marital sexual experiences, the majority (76.9 per cent) have experienced pre marital sex with the people who are known to her which include friends (28.2 per cent), neighbours (20.5 per cent), relatives (12.8 per cent), co-workers (7.7 per cent) and family friends (7.7 per cent) etc. The 23.1 per cent of women experienced their pre marital sex with their sexual customers.

The majority of the respondents' husbands involved in pre marital (49.1 per cent) and extra marital sex (92.9 per cent) with the sex workers.

The inference drawn from the analysis is that the women are sexually abused and induced to have pre marital sex by the men from the close circle of the women and their families. Sex workers are the major sources for majority of the respondents' husbands pre (49.1 per cent) and extra marital sex (92.9 per cent). It shows that the respondents' husbands sexual behaviour with multiple partners are the primary factors for respondents infection.

Table 5.33. Reasons Behind Respondents Pre and Extra Marital Sexual Behaviour.

Sl.No.	*Reasons*	*Pre marital sex*	*Extra marital sex*
1.	Influence of friends	14(36.0%)	8(23.5%)
2.	Love affairs	17(43.5%)	6(17.7%)
3.	Exposure to mass media	8(20.5%)	3(8.8%)
5.	Difference of opinion	—	17(50.0%)
	Total	39(100%)	34(100%)

The major reasons identified for respondents' pre marital sex are love affairs (43.5 per cent), influence of friends (36.0 per cent) and wider exposure to mass media (20.5 per cent).

Table 5.33 also reveals that difference of opinion between the spouses (50.0 per cent) is the major cause for the extra marital affairs of respondents followed by influence of friends

(23.5 per cent) and love affairs (17.7 per cent). The exposure to mass media influenced 8.8 per cent of respondents to experience with extra marital sex.

The inference drawn from the analysis is that love affairs is the major (43.5 per cent) cause for pre marital sex and difference of opinion between the spouses are the significant (50.0 per cent) reason for extra marital sex of the respondents.

Table 5.34. Methods Adopted for Safe Sex

Sl. No.	*Method adopted for safe sex*	*Pre marital sex (No. of respondents)*	*Extra marital sex (No. of respondents*
1.	Condom	6(15.4%)	3(8.8%)
2.	IUDs	(0.0%)	6(17.6%)
3.	Oral pills	21(53.8%)	3(8.8%)
4.	Sterilization.	0(0.0%)	14(41.2%)
5.	Not practiced any methods	12(30.8%)	8(23.6%)
	Total	39(100%)	34(100%)

The analysis on safe sex practices among the women involved in pre marital (19.5 per cent) and extra marital sex (17.0 per cent) has given a new insight to study. It is found that the condom usage is quite less among the women of pre marital (15.4 per cent) and extra marital sex (8.8 per cent). These women were very much bothered about pregnancy rather than contracting sexually transmitted diseases. Therefore, the lack or insufficient awareness on condom forces women to use other safer method that could avoid pregnancy (Table 5.34).

The major percentage (53.8 per cent) of women who experienced pre marital sex revealed that they have prepared oral pills than any other method to prevent pregnancy. It is also identified that 30.7 per cent of pre marital sexual women have not used any method to safeguard themselves from sexually transmitted diseases and pregnancy.

Among the women who have experienced extra marital sex, 41.2 per cent have undergone sterilization to prevent childbirth. Therefore, they were least bothered and not showed any seriousness to use condom to protect them from all sexually transmitted infections. Besides, 26.4 per cent of women were using temporary birth control measures such as copper T (Intra uterus devices) and oral pills. The respondents who have not at all used any safe sex method when they were in extra marital sex are identified as 23.5 per cent.

The conclusion drawn from the analysis is that the respondents who have pre and extra marital sexual contact are more particular about prevention of birth rather than prevention of sexually transmitted diseases, especially HIV/AIDS. In the Indian culture, giving birth out of promiscuous relationship is considered as taboo and women have to face a lot consequence if such birth is taken place. Culture is acting as a stumbling block to use condom for safe sex since the women are very much hesitant to buy condom from the market. Therefore, majority (53.8 per cent) of respondents used oral pills as safer method which prevents child birth. It is also identified that the majority (41.2 per cent) of the respondents who involved in extra marital sex have undergone sterilization. The practices of sterilization prevented the use of condom because the sterilized women have an attitude that they are free from pregnancy.

Table 5.35. Reasons for Respondents' Husbands Extra Marital Sexual Behaviour.

Sl.No.	*Reasons*	*No. of respondents*	*Percentage*
1.	Frequent migration	16	30.2
2.	Alcoholic behaviour	16	22.6
3.	Difference of opinion between spouse	7	13.2
5.	Lack of sexual satisfaction with wife	5	9.5
6.	Poor health condition of wife	4	7.5
7.	Pregnancy of wife	9	17.0
	Total	57	100

Of the total 165 married respondents, 34.6 per cent have extra marital affairs. Among them majority of the respondents' husbands 30.2 per cent are involved in frequent migration due to their occupation. Alcoholic behaviour is the major causes for the extra marital relationship of 22.6 per cent respondent's husbands. Pregnancy of wife is the major factor for 17.0 per cent of respondents' husbands to seek sex with sex workers.

The other important causes are found to be difference of opinion and lack of understanding between the spouses (13.2 per cent), lack of sexual satisfaction with the wife (9.5 per cent), poor health condition of wife (7.5 per cent).

The inference drawn from the analysis is that the migration and alcoholic behaviour has strong influence on the extra marital affairs of the respondents' husbands.

Table 5.36. Reproductive Behaviour of Housewives Lead to Infection.

SL.No.	*Reproductive behaviour*	*No of Respondents*	*Percentage*
1.	Condom	2	1.5
2.	IUDs	21	16.0
3.	Oral pills	14	10.7
4.	Sterilization.	47	35.9
5.	Not practiced any methods	47	35.9
	Total	131	100

Table 5.36 on reproductive health behaviour of housewives reveals that the majority (35.9 per cent) of the respondents have not adopted any safe sex methods either to avoid pregnancy or to avoid sexually transmitted infections. Adoption of sterilization is found to be high (35.9 per cent) among the respondents to avoid pregnancy. The significant percentage (26.7 per cent) of respondents have adopted non-terminal method of birth control, namely IUDs and oral pills. The adoption of condom for safe sex is very meager (1.5 per cent) among the wives.

Table 5.36 shows that the housewives give more importance to avoid pregnancy rather than sexually transmitted infections. Adoption of sterilization, oral pills and IUDs prevented majority (62.6 per cent) of wives to think about condom as safe sex method to safeguard themselves from sexually transmitted infections.

The above table highlights the marital status of sex workers. It is found from the table that out of 200 respondents, 31.0 per cent were commercial sex workers. Of the 62 sex workers, 45.2 per cent were unmarried women, 43.5 per cent were married and have family with husband and children, 6.5 per cent were widows and 4.8 per cent of them were deserted women.

Circumstances Leading to Commercial Sex Work

It is concluded from Table 5.37 that not only the unmarried but also the married women (54.8 per cent) involved in commercial sex work. Socio-economic responsibility of women to take care of the family led them into sex work which resulted in HIV infection.

Table 5.37. Marital Status of Sex Workers.

Sl. No.	*Marital Status*	*No. of Respondents*	*Percentage*
1.	Unmarried	28	45.2
2.	Married	27	43.5
3.	Deserted	3	4.8
4.	Widow	4	6.5
	Total	62	100

Table 5.38. Circumstances Leading to Commercial Sex Work.

Sl.No.	*Circumstances*	*No. of Respondents*	*Percentage*
1.	Poverty	25	40.4
2.	Lavish spending	16	25.7
3.	Sexual harassments	2	3.2
4.	Influence of pimps	3	4.8
5.	Abandoned by lover	4	6.6
6.	Desertion and widowhood	7	11.2
7.	Influence of friends	5	8.1
	Total	62	100

Table 5.38 on circumstances leading to commercial sex works reveals that poverty is the major cause for the women to choose sex work as a means of their livelihood. The financial strain raised out of poverty forced 32.3 per cent of women to involve in commercial sex works. The analysis also revealed that the poverty is the consequences of lack of employment opportunity

in their native place due to lack of skills (6.6 per cent), unemployment of husband (3.2 per cent), crop failure due to failure of rain (11.3 per cent), indebtedness (9.6 per cent) and insufficient income of the husband (9.7 per cent).

Women's attitude towards luxurious life influenced 25.7 per cent of respondents to involve in commercial sex work to earn more money without much effort. These respondents were influenced by the lavish life of other women who are already in commercial sex work.

The absence of male earning members in the family also identified as another motivating factor for 11.3 per cent respondents to take up commercial sex work as their profession to take care of their family. It included desertion (3.2 per cent) and widowhood (8.1 per cent).

Problems in the family are an influencing factor for 8.1 per cent of commercial sex workers. They involved in this work not only to divert their mind from their problems but also to earn for their livelihood. The problems related to the family include lack of care (3.2 per cent), and parents (1.7 per cent) and husbands (3.2 per cent) force to push the women into sex work.

The influence of peer groups including friends brought 8.1 per cent women into commercial sex works. Besides, 6.6 per cent women were abandoned by their lover in the city that forced them to choose commercial sex work to live in the city. Influence of the pimp is the cause for 4.8 per cent women to enter into this work.

Various sexual harassment pushed 3.2 per cent of women into sex work. This sexual harassment includes harassment in the work place 1.6 per cent and the pressure by the owner of the company to have sex with him to retain job 1.6 per cent.

The inference drawn from Table 5.38 is that the poverty is the major (40.4 per cent) factor to forces women into commercial sex work. The problems which are confined to the family are the primary factor for many women to choose commercial sex as an alternative means to earn and solve the problems of the family. The family conditions make them to become innocent victims for the dreaded disease called HIV/AIDS. The deserted and the widows are deprived of income due to lose of their husbands. The lack of economical resources led these deserted and widows to promiscuous sexual behaviour resulting in HIV/AIDS.

Table 5.39. Age at Induction in Commercial Sex Work

Sl.No.	*Age at sex work (in years)*	*No. of Respondents*	*Percentage*
1.	Less than 18	18	29.0
2.	19 – 23	14	22.6
3.	24 – 28	21	33.9
4.	29 – 33	5	8.1
5.	34 and above	4	6.4
	Total	62	100

Table 5.39 illustrates the age of the respondents when they initiated into commercial sex work. Of the 62 respondents, 33.9 per cent entered into this work between the age of 24—28 years followed by the 29.0 per cent respondents who were initiated into commercial sex work at the age of less than 18 years. The 22.6 per cent respondents were started this profession at the age between 19—23 years and the remaining 14.5 have chosen this work at 29 and above 29 years.

The conclusion drawn from Table 5.39 is that the majority (51.6 per cent) of the women are initiated into commercial sex work at the younger age of within 23 years. Due to younger age, the women receive more number of customers and involve in frequent sexual activity. The young age also facilitate them to be submissive in sexual encounters. The less or lack of power over the sexual act of their customers strongly influenced the risk of contracting HIV/AIDS.

A. Details of Clients

The statistical analysis of the study explored that the sex workers are not restricted their service with particular categories of clients. They used to engage all kinds of clients irrespective of their age, profession etc. Money is the only criteria for them.

Labourers (38.7 per cent), business people (37.1 per cent), tourist (33.9 per cent), transport workers, including drivers and cleaners (27.4 per cent), students (21 per cent) and men who are away from home for longer duration (17.7 per cent) are identified as dominant categories of clients who visit commercial sex workers quite often.

The analysis of the study also found that the people who are in business (29.0 per cent) and tourist (25.8 per cent) used to pay more for commercial sex workers. The clients from film industry (12.9 per cent) and the transport workers like drivers (9.7 per cent) are paying considerable amount for paid sex. The labourers (6.5 per cent) and the students (4.8 per cent) are not paying much when compared to others for seeking sex from the sex workers.

As far as the safe sex practices are concerned, significant per cent of business people (30.6 per cent), drivers (25.6 per cent), tourist (14.5 per cent) and students (11.3 per cent) are using condom for safe sex. The safe sex practice is found to be low among labourers (3.2 per cent), man away from home (8.1 per cent) etc.

The analysis on the response (97.3 per cent) of the commercial sex workers reveals that the men who seek sex out side the matrimonial relationship have the character of consuming alcohol or using drugs. Therefore, the addicted behaviour of men towards alcohol and drug increases the chances of unsafe sex with commercial sex workers and to acquire HIV infection.

Table 5.40. Number of Clients Engaged Per Day

Sl. No.	*No. of clients engaged per day*	*No. of Respondents*		
		Part Time Sex worker	*Full Time Sex workers*	*Total*
1.	1 - 2	17 (63.0%)	6 (17.2%)	23 (37.1%)
2.	3 - 4	6 (22.2%)	16 (45.7%)	22 (35.5%)
3.	5 - 6	4 (14.8%)	9 (25.7%)	13 (20.9%)
4.	Above 6	0 (0.0%)	4 (11.4%)	4 (6.5%)
	Total	27 (100%)	35 (100%)	62 (100%)

Table 5.40 explains the number of clients engaged by the sex workers per day. Among the 62 sex workers, 37.1 per cent engaged 1-2 clients per day, 35.5 per cent engaged an on average of 3-4 clients and the remaining 27.4 have more than five clients per day. Most (63 per cent) of the part time sex workers were used to engage less than 3 clients per day whereas most (82.8 per cent) of the full time sex workers have more than 3 clients per day. The inference drawn from the table is that the part time sex workers engage less number of clients (1-2) than the full time sex workers (3-6). Due to frequent sexual encounter, the full time sex workers more prone to HIV/AIDS.

Table 5.41. Earning Per Day by Sex Workers

Sl. No.	*Earning per day (In Rupees)*	*No. of Respondents*		
		Part Time Sex worker	*Full Time Sex workers*	*Total*
1.	Less than 200	13 (48.2%)	7 (20.0%)	20 (32.3%)
2.	200 - 300	11 (40.7%)	9 (25.7%)	20 (32.3%)
3.	300 - 400	3 (11.1%)	13 (37.1%)	16 (25.8%)
4.	Above 400	0 (0.0%)	6 (17.2%)	6 (9.6%)
	Total	27 (100%)	35 (100%)	62 (100%)

Table 5.41 reveals the earnings of the commercial sex workers per day. It shows that the majority (48.2 per cent) of the family based sex workers earn less than Rs. 200 per day. Among the part time sex workers, 51.8 per cent earns Rs. 200-400 per day. Among full time sex workers, majority (54.3 per cent) of women earns more than Rs. 300 per day and the remaining 45.7 per cent of full time sex workers per day earning is found to be less than Rs.300 per day.

The conclusion drawn from the table is that the sex workers are taking risk of contracting HIV/AIDS by exchanging their sex service to the customers for meager amount.

B. Sources of Contact with the Clients

The analysis of the data on various sources used by the sex workers to have a contact with the clients reveals that the majority (33.9 per cent) of the sex workers are picking up men by themselves from the crowded place like bus stand, railway station, market, beach, cinema theater, busy areas of city, tourist attractive places etc. The brokers are the important source for 17.7 per cent of sex workers to meet customers. The modern communication media - phone (12.9 per cent) and cell phone (6.5 per cent) are used to contact the customers. The other sources are found to be the contact person (6.5 per cent), regular clients (6.5 per cent), family members including mother (9.2 per cent), friends including boy friends (4.8 per cent) and the sex workers who are already in services (1.6 per cent).

C. Place of Resident of Sex Workers

The majority (37.1 per cent) of the sex workers in Chennai are found in the slums and urban centers of the city. The significant percentage (27.4 per cent) is coming from near by rural areas of Chennai for their business.

D. Nature of Sex Work

The study also reveals that 50 per cent of the sex workers under the study are involved in sex work individually. The 27.5 per cent of sex workers are doing this sex trade along with the brokers, the 12.9 per cent are engaged in sex work with their friends, and the 9.6 per cent have support from their other family members to meet and catch men who need sex with commercial sex workers. The sex workers who are under the control of brokers are getting their wage either daily or on contract basis.

The sex workers under this study have reported that they have a strong network, which is invisible to the public and police. Their network will help them to develop contact with the brokers, experienced sex workers, clients etc. However, they have no commercial sex workers organisation to protect their interests.

Number of Sex Workers not Asking their Clients to use Condom

The analysis of the study revealed that after knowing HIV infection only 25 (40.3 per cent) sex workers started insisting their clients to use condom and the remaining 37 (59.7 per cent) have not showed any interest to ask their clients to use condom to prevent them from HIV infection. Among them, lack of awareness (45.9 per cent) among sex workers on HIV/AIDS is the major cause for neglecting condom use. The other causes identified in this study for not insisting condom use to the clients by the sex workers are fear of loosing clients (24.3 per cent), lack of faith on the impact of HIV/AIDS (8.1 per cent), restriction imposed by the brokers (16.2 per cent) and stigma attached to the diseases (5.5 per cent). This study also explored that none of the infected sex workers under this study have revealed their HIV status to their clients due to fear of rejection (35.5 per cent), lack of awareness on AIDS (43.5 per cent), vengeance on men (9.7 per cent) and stigma associated with HIV/AIDS (11.3 per cent).

Table 5.42. Reasons for not using Condoms by Clients

Sl. No.	*Causes*	*No. of Sex workers*	*Percentage*
1.	No sexual satisfaction	18	29.0
2.	Fear of asking condoms	8	12.9
3.	Alcoholism hinter usage of condom	24	38.7
4.	Lack of awareness on safe sex	15	19.4
	Total	62	100

Table 5.42 indicates responses of the sex workers with regard to the various causes for not using condom by the clients. It is found from the table that the behaviour of taking alcohol (38.7 per cent) and its associated intoxicated mood prevent the clients to think and use condom while they have sex with the sex workers. The inherent faith on lack of sexual satisfaction owing to condom use prevents 29 per cent of clients to use condoms. The clients also reported that the fears of asking condom (12.9 per cent) from the shops and lack of awareness on safe sex (19.4 per cent) as important causes for not using condom. The finding from the table is that the behaviour of taking alcohol before sex prevents men to take rational decision to use condom whenever they have paid sex. The above table represents the present status of the infected commercial sex workers under this study. The Non-governmental organisations with the sex workers have taken efforts to influence the sex workers to withdraw their

involvement in sex industry. As a consequences many have came out of their profession and started looking for alternative jobs for their survival. Therefore, it is found from the table that after knowing HIV infection, 46.7 per cent has withdrawn their involvement in sex work. Among them (12.9 per cent) were staying in short stay home run by the non-governmental organisations, 11.3 per cent were working as a causal labourers, each 6.5 per cent were employed in non-governmental organisations and as casual labour and 4.8 per cent were found to be housemaid.

Table 5.43. Present Status of the Sex Workers after Knowing HIV Infection

Sl.No.	*Present Status*	*No. of Respondents*	*Percentage*
1.	Unemployed	3	4.8
2.	Employed in N.G.O.	4	6.5
3.	Staying in short stay home	8	12.9
4.	House maid	3	4.8
5.	Self employed	4	6.5
6.	Causal labour	7	11.3
7.	Sex worker	33	53.2
	Total	62	100

The inference drawn from the analysis (Table 5.43) is that the sex workers who came out of sex work engaged in various occupations for their survival.

Table 5.44. Causes for Remaining in Sex Work After Knowing HIV Infection

Sl.No.	*Causes*	*No. of sex workers*	*Percentage*
1.	No alternative jobs	2	6.1
2.	Lack of skill to change the job	5	15.2
3.	Less income in other jobs	17	51.5
4.	People are not willing to give job	9	27.2
	Total	33	100

Table 5.44 explains the number of sex workers who continue the sex work even after knowing their HIV infection. The major causes mentioned by these sex workers are identified as less income in other jobs (51.5 per cent), difficulties in getting alternative jobs (27.2 per cent), lack of skill to change jobs (15.2 per cent) and non availability of alternative jobs (6.1 per cent). The conclusion drawn from the table is that the less income in other jobs prevent majority of the sex workers to find alternative job to come out of the sex work.

F. Sex Workers Awareness on their Role in Spreading HIV/Aids andtheir Willingness to be Lodged in Special Home

The analysis of the data revealed that all the infected sex workers were aware of their role in transmitting the virus to the clients.

Among the 62 infected sex workers, 61.3 per cent have opposed the idea of accommodating infected sex workers in the special home and only 38.7 per cent extended their willingness to be lodged in special home.

It is evident from the analysis, though the sex workers are aware of their role in transmitting the virus, they were not willing to stay in the special home if it is run for the infected people.

HIV Testing

Table 5.45. Places of HIV Testing

Sl.No.	*No. Place of HIV testing*	*No. of Respondents*	*Percentage*
1.	Private labs	41	20.5
2.	Government Hospitals	123	61.5
3.	Voluntary organisations	1	0.5
4.	Private Hospitals	35	17.5
	Total	200	100

Table 5.45 indicates the places where the respondents have undergone HIV positive test. Of the total 200 respondents, 61.5 per cent have undergone HIV positive test in Government hospitals, the 20.5 per cent have tested in private labs, the 17.5 per cent were tested their HIV positive status in private hospital and 0.5 per cent has known her HIV status by testing it in voluntary organisations. It is also evident from the table that the government hospitals played a vital role in providing facilities for HIV test. Therefore, the majority (61.5 per cent) of the respondents under this study have undergone HIV positive test in Government hospitals.

Table 5.46. Factors Influenced for HIV Test.

Sl. No.	*Factors*	*No. of Respondents*	*Percentage*
1.	S.T.D. infections	29	14.5
2.	Continuous illness	21	10.5
3.	Pregnancy	14	7.0
4.	Husband's HIV infection	117	58.5
5.	Others	19	9.5
	Total	200	100

Table 5.46 reflects the factors which influence to take HIV positive test by the respondents. It shows that 58.5 per cent have undergone HIV test after knowing their husband's HIV status. The infection of sexually transmitted diseases (S.T.D.) influenced 14.5 per cent of respondents to take up HIV test. Continuous illness made 10.5 per cent of respondents to undergo HIV test. HIV test is compulsory for the pregnant women in Tamil Nadu. Therefore, the pregnancy forced 7.0 per cent women to go for HIV test. The 9.5 per cent respondents have under went HIV test for various reasons including awareness created by the media (2.0 per cent), influence of N.G.Os. (1.5 per cent), heterosexual contact of the respondents (1.5 per cent), blood donation by the respondents (1.0 per cent), regular health check up (1.0 per cent), blood donated by the husband (1.0 per cent), illness of the child (0.5 per cent), brother in law HIV status (0.5 per cent), partner's HIV status (0.5 per cent).

The inference drawn from the table is that the HIV status of the respondent's husband is the important factor for majority of the women to take up HIV test in Tamil Nadu.

Table 5.47. Sources of Pre and Post Test Counseling to Respondents and their Family Members.

Sl. No.	*Sources of counseling*	*Respondents*		*Respondent's Parents*	
		Pre Test	*Post Test*	*Pre Test*	*Post Test*
1.	Doctors	17 (8.5%)	24 (12.0%)	6 (3.0%)	18 (9.0%)
2.	Counselors	20 (10.0%)	12 (6.0%)	11 (5.5%)	20 (10.0%)
3.	N.G.Os	13 (6.5%)	14 (7.0%)	18 (9.0%)	9 (4.5%)
4.	Others	1 (0.5%)	6 (3.0%)	4 (2.0%)	3 (1.5%)
5.	Counseling not given	149 (74.5%)	144 (72.0%)	161 (80.5%)	150 (75.0%)
	Total	200 (100%)	200 (100%)	200 (100%)	200 (100%)

Table 5.47 explains the pre test and post test counseling given to the respondents and their family members to cope up and living with HIV. The analysis shows that on an average of 75 per cent of respondents and their family members have not given both pre and post test counseling to know and live with HIV.

It is identified that only 25.5 per cent have got pre test counseling from doctors (8.5 per cent), counselors (10.0 per cent), Non Governmental Organisations (N.G.Os) (6.5 per cent) and others including friends (0.5 per cent). The respondents who have post test counseling accounted for 28 per cent. The sources of post test counseling are identified as doctors (12.0 per cent), counselors (6.0 per cent), N.G.Os (7.0 per cent) and others such as friends etc (3.0 per cent).

As far as respondent's parents are concerned, only 19.5 per cent are given pre test counseling and 25 per cent are exposed to post test counseling through the doctors, counselors, N.G.Os and others.

The conclusion derived from the table is that the majority of the respondents and their family members were not exposed to pre and post test counseling to under stand fully about the HIV, its social impact and living with HIV peacefully by coping with social stigma.

Table 5.48. Respondents Knowledge on HIV/Aids At the Time of Testing

Sl. No.	*Knowledge on HIV/AIDS*	*No. of Respondents*	*Percentage*
1.	Killer disease	31	15.5
2.	No Medicine	14	7.0
3.	Spread through sex and blood	7	3.5
4.	No Knowledge	148	74.0
	Total	200	100

The analysis indicates in Table 5.48 that the respondent's knowledge on HIV/AIDS at the time of testing. It shows that out of 200 respondents, 74 per cent have no knowledge on HIV/AIDS and its implication in their socio-economic life. The respondents who have little knowledge on HIV/AIDS accounted for 26 per cent. Among them 15.5 per cent were aware that the HIV/AIDS is a killer disease, the 7.0 per cent were known that the HIV/AIDS have no medicine and no cure and only 3.5 per cent respondents were well aware that the HIV spread through sex and blood.

The inference drawn from the table is that the majority (74 per cent) of respondents were unaware of HIV/AIDS when they have undergone HIV testing in various centers.

Sexual Behaviour of Respondents After Infection

Table 5.49 on the sexual behaviour of the sex workers after knowing their HIV status shows that 53.3 per cent of sex workers were still remaining in prostitution and only 46.8 per cent have withdrawn their involvement in sex work after knowing their HIV status

Among the women who are continuing prostitution, 19.5 per cent were practicing safe sex, 12.9 per cent have not adopted any changes in their sexual behaviour, 11.2 per cent have avoided students, 6.5 per cent have avoided youth and 3.2 per cent have avoided unmarried men.

Table 5.49. Changes in Sexual Behaviour of Sex Workers After Knowing HIV Infection

Sl. No.	*Nature of changes*	*No. of sex workers*	*Percentage*
1.	Avoided youth	4	6.5
2.	Avoided students	7	11.2
3.	Avoided unmarried men	2	3.2
4.	Withdrawn from sex work	29	46.7
5.	Practicing safe sex	12	19.5
6.	No change	8	12.9
	Total	62	100

It is clear from the table that majority (53.2 per cent) of the women continues sex work even after knowing their HIV status but significant change in the sexual behaviour of the sex workers is observed after HIV infection.

Table 5.50 reveals the changes in the sexual behaviour of housewives after knowing their HIV infection. In this study 130 respondents are identified as innocent housewives and the remaining are sex workers, students and drug user. Among the wives, the majority (80.9 per cent) have not changed their sexual behaviour after their infection. The respondents who are practicing safe sex to avoid pregnancy are accounted for 14.5 per cent. The practice of abstinence is found to be only 4.6 per cent.

The conclusion drawn from the analysis is that there is no significant change in the sexual behaviour of majority (80.9 per cent) of respondents.

Table 5.50 on the revelation of HIV by the respondents shows that 55.5 per cent of respondents revealed their HIV status to their family members where as 44.5 per cent have not revealed their HIV status to their family members. It also reveals that the majority (68.6 per cent) of the full time sex workers (which include 28 unmarried women, 4 widows and 3 deserted) and housewives (66.9 per cent) revealed their HIV status to their family members and the remaining respondents including students. Part time sex workers and injecting drug user deliberately hided their HIV status from their family members.

Table 5.50. Changes in Sexual Behaviour of Housewives After Knowing HIV Infection.

Sl. No.	*Nature of changes*	*No. of sex workers*	*Percentage*
1.	No change	106	80.9
2.	Practicing safe sex	19	14.5
3.	Practicing abstinence	6	4.6
	Total	131	100

Impact of HIV/Aids on the Social Relationship of Respondents

Social Relationship in the Familiy

Table 5.5.1. Revelation of HIV/Aids By Respondents

Sl.No.	*Revelation*	*Revealed (No. of Respondents)*	*Not revealed (No. of Respondents)*	*Total*
1.	Students	0 (0.0%)	7 (100%)	7 (3.5%)
2.	Housewives	87 (66.9%)	43 (33.1%)	130 (65.0%)
3.	Sex workers –Part time	0 (0.0%)	27 (100.0%)	27 (13.5%)
4.	Sex workers-Full time	24 (68.6%)	11 (31.4%)	35 (17.5%)
5.	Injecting drug us	0 (0.0%)	1 (100.0%)	1 (0.5%)
	Total	111 (55.5%)	89 (44.5%)	200 (100%)

The inference drawn from Table 5.51 is that the revelation of HIV infection is high (66.9 per cent) among the housewives and high secrecy is maintained among the women who got HIV through their heterosexual contact and injecting drug use.

Table 5.51 reveal that the majority (90.8 per cent) of the respondents HIV status was known to their family members through their hospital staff where they undergone HIV test.

For respondents' husbands, 64.4 per cent respondents involved in the revelation of HIV status followed by the hospital staff 25.3 per cent and respondents' husbands 10.3 per cent. The inference drawn from the table is that the hospital staff are the major sources of revelation of respondents HIV status where as the respondents are the primary sources of revelation of her husbands HIV status to their family members.

Table 5.51. Person Involved in the Revelation of HIV Status

Sl. No.	*Revelation on*	*Respon-dent*	*Husband*	*In-laws*	*Friends*	*Hospital Staff*	*Total*
1.	Husband	56 (64.4%)	9 (10.3%)	0	0	22 25.3%)	87 (100%)
2.	Housewife	6 (6.9%)	2 (2.3%)	0	0	79 (90.8%)	87 (100%)

Table 5.52. Respondents' Husbands Awareness About HIV Infection Before Marriage

Sl. No.	*Nature of Knowledge*	*No. of Husbands*		*Total*
		Yes	*No*	
1.	Aware before marriage	12 (9.2%)	118 (90.8%)	130 (100%)
2.	Disclosed to his parents	0(0.0%)	12 (100%)	12 (100%)
3.	Disclosed to respondents	0(0.0%)	12 (100%)	12 (100%)

Table 5.52 on the respondents' husbands knowledge on his HIV infection reveals that only 9.2 per cent were aware of their infection before marriage. All these 12 also not revealed their HIV status either to his parents or to the bride proposed for him.

The analysis highlighted that the majority (90.8 per cent) of the men were undergoing HIV test only after their marriage. This is mainly because of absence of compulsory blood test for couples before marriage. As a result, even if the men have infection before their marriage, they can easily blame their innocent wife and escape from the social criticism.

Table 5.53 on husband reaction towards his wife after knowing his HIV infection highlights the husbands reaction towards his wife after knowing his HIV infection. Of the 130 couples, 39.2 per cent men showed sympathetic attitude towards their wives due to their guilty over sex outside the marriage. The 35.4 per cent involved in harassing their wives in various forms including physical harassment, 8.5 per cent forcibly deserted their wives and the remaining 16.9 per cent involved in isolating their wives in the home. It is clear from the table that the infected husbands harassed majority (60.6 per cent) the respondents though they are aware their wives are not responsible for their infection.

Table 5.53. Husbands Reaction Towards his Wife After Knowing his Infection

Sl.No.	*Husband's Reaction*	*No. of Respondents*	*Percentage*
1.	Sympathetic	51	39.2
2.	Physical Harassment	46	35.4
3.	Divorced/deserted	11	8.5
4.	Others	22	16.9
	Total	130	100

Table 5.54 on housewife's reaction towards her husband after knowing her husband infection shows that except 42.3 per cent the other 57.7 per cent showed indifferent attitude towards her infected husband by way of not providing care (46.9 per cent) and leaving him (10.8 per cent) with out any considerations. The inference drawn from the table is that the infected men get least support and care from their wives. Generally, the wives neglect most (57.7 per cent) of their infected husbands.

Table 5.54. Housewifes' Reaction Towards Infected Husband

Sl. No.	*Reaction*	*No. of Respondents*	*Percentage*
1.	Supporting	55	42.3
2.	Not provided care	61	46.9
3.	Left the husband	14	10.8
	Total	130	100

The analysis on the relationship between respondents and their husbands reveals that out of 130 couples, except 17.7 per cent the majority samples (82.3 per cent) have indifferent relationships with their husbands like frequent quarrel (43.8 per cent), neglecting each other (33.1 per cent) and other problems like blaming each other (5.4 per cent) etc.

Table 5.55. The Relationship Between Respondents and their Husbands After Knowing HIV Infection

Sl.No.	*Nature of relationship*	*No. of Respondents*	*Percentage*
1.	Compassionate	23	17.7
2.	Frequent quarrel	57	43.8
3.	Neglecting each other	43	33.1
4.	Others	7	5.4
	Total	130	100

It is evident from the analysis (Table 5.55) that the relationship between husband and wife after knowing HIV infection is not compassionate in many cases.

Table 5.56. Reaction of In-laws on Respondents and their Husbands before and After Knowing HIV Infection

Sl. No.	*Nature of Reaction*	*Before Infection*		*After Infection*	
		Husband	*wife*	*Husband*	*wife*
1.	Supporting	118 (90.8%)	110 (84.6%)	45 (51.7%)	12 (13.7%)
2.	Verbal abuse	12 (9.2%)	16 (12.3%)	17 (19.5%)	28 (32.2%)
3.	Physical abuse	0 (0.0%)	4 (3.1%)	5 (5.8%)	19 (21.9%)
4.	Social Isolation	0 (0.0%)	0 (0.0%)	20 (23.0%)	28 (32.2%)
	Total	130 (100%)	130 (100%)	87 (100%)	87 (100%)

The study has identified the responses of the in-laws towards the respondents and their husbands before and after knowing HIV infection. The analysis reveals that among the 130 couples the greater percentage of respondents (84.6 per cent) and her husbands (90.8 per cent) got support from their in-laws before knowing their infection. Among the 130 couple, 87 couple infection is known to their in-laws (Tabnle 5.56).

But after knowing HIV infection, the infected spouses have received verbal abuse, physical abuse, and social isolation from their in-laws in different magnitudes. The data explored that the women get less support (13.7 per cent) from their in-laws than her husband (51.7 per cent). Social isolation by the in-laws is also comparatively high among the respondents (32.2 per cent) than their husbands (23.0 per cent). The verbal (32.1 per cent) and physical abuses (21.8 per cent) are high towards the women by the in-laws whereas men receive less verbal (19.5 per cent) and physical abuses (5.8 per cent) from their parents.

We can infer from the analysis that the discrimination towards the infected women by the in-laws is comparatively high than their husbands.

Table 5.57. Reaction of Parents Towards Respondents and their Husbands

Sl. No.	*Nature of Reaction*	*Before Infection (for 130 couples)*		*After Infection (for 87 couples)*	
		Husband	*wife*	*Husband*	*wife*
1.	Supporting	124 (95.4%)	127 (97.7%)	18 (20.7%)	61 (70.1%)
2.	Verbal abuse	6 (4.6%)	3 (2.3%)	53 (60.9%)	13 (14.9%)
3.	Physical abuse	0 (0.0%)	0 (0.0%)	4 (4.6%)	5 (5.8%)
4.	Social Isolation	0 (0.0%)	0 (0.0%)	12 (13.8%)	8 (9.2%)
	Total	130 (100%)	130 (100%)	87 (100%)	87 (100%)

Table 5.57 on the reaction of parents towards respondents and their husband shows that the significant percentage of respondents (97.7 per cent) and their husbands (95.4 per cent) got all social and economic support from the parents of the respondents before knowing their HIV status.

After disclosing the infection, generally the respondents and their husbands lost importance among their parents and family circles. While compare to the respondents husbands, the majority (70.1 per cent) of respondents got support from their parents than their husbands (20.7 per cent). The respondents husbands are comparatively more abused verbally (60.9 per cent) than their wives. The social isolation by the respondents' parents is also found to be high among respondents' husbands (13.8 per cent) than respondents (9.2 per cent).

The inference drawn from the analysis is that the respondents get more support from their parents rather than their husbands. This is mainly because all the respondents are the innocent victims of HIV and they acquired HIV through their husbands. Therefore, the respondents' parents are against their son in-laws sexual behaviour and they ill-treated them in various forms including verbal and physical abuse and social isolation.

A. Treatment of Parents Towards their Infected Daughters Who are Deserted and Widows Even Before Infection

Furthermore, the study also reveals that 4 women were widow and 3 were deserted even before infection. All these 7 women got full support from their parents before infection. However, after infection all these 7 (100 per cent) lost support and totally isolated by their parents.

B. Treatment of Parents Towards their Unmarried Infected Daughters

Among the 35 unmarried women which include 28 sex workers and 7 students, 88.6 per cent got full support from their parents and 11.4 per cent were socially isolated by their parents before infection due to their unapproved social behaviour. The analysis found that 48.5 per cent sex workers have disclosed their HIV status to their parents whereas 51.4 per cent including 7 students concealed their HIV status from their parents. After disclosing the HIV status to their parents, the majority (64.7 per cent) got support form their parents and the remaining (35.3 per cent) verbally abused and socially isolated from their parents.

The above table represents the nature of restriction imposed by the family members on respondents and their husbands whose infection is revealed to them. It is already stated that among the 130 couple, 33.1 per cent have not revealed their HIV status to their family members. As a result they have not experienced any discrimination from their family members. Like that among 62 sex workers, only 38.7 per cent have revealed their HIV status to their family members where as 61.3 per cent have not revealed their HIV status to their family members. The respondents who hided their HIV status from their family members have no problem with regard to socio-cultural restriction.

Table 5.5.1.9. Nature of Restriction Imposed on People Infected With HIV by their Family Members

Sl. No.	*Nature of Restirction*	*No. of Respondents*			
		Husband	*Housewife*	*Sex worker*	*Children*
1.	No restrictions	18 (20.7%)	13 (14.9%)	11 (45.8%)	6 (42.8%)
2.	Separate place is given	4 (4.6%)	5 (5.8%)	—	0
3.	Restriction on inter dining	9 (10.3%)	2 (2.3%)	—	0
4.	Participation on socio cultural functions	5 (5.8%)	9 (10.3%)	—	0
5.	On sharing articles	16 (18.4%)	7 (8.1%)	—	2 (14.3%)
6.	On touching	23 (26.4%)	17 (19.5%)	—	4 (28.6%)
7.	All above restrictions	12 (13.8%)	34 (39.1%)	13 (54.2%)	2 (14.3%)
	Total	87 (100%)	87 (100%)	24 (100%)	14 (100%)

Among the 87 (66.9 per cent) couple who revealed their HIV status to their family members, only 20.7 per cent men and 14.9 per cent women have not èxperienced any discrimination from the family. The remaining couple (79.3 per cent men and 85.1 per cent women) (Table 5.58) have experienced various forms of discrimination in the form of separate place in the home, restriction on inter dining, participation on socio-cultural functions, sharing articles and touching.

Majority of the sex workers (54.2 per cent) and children (57.2 per cent), whose infection is revealed out also experienced same discrimination from the family members.

It is found from the analysis (Table 5.58) that the difference in gender discrimination is not significant between men and women. Irrespective of sex, the people living with HIV are generally restricted in socio and cultural activities of the family in day today life.

Table 5.59. Decision taken in the Family Before and After Infection

Sl. No.	*Person involved in taking decisions*	*Before infection*	*After infection*
1.	Husband	81(40.5%)	43(21.5%)
2.	Respondent	19(9.5%)	8(4.0%)
3.	Both	49(24.5%)	16(8.0%)
4.	Others	51(25.5%)	133(66.5%)
	Total	200(100%)	200(100%)

The analysis (table 5.55) on the decision-making process in the family before infection shows that the respondent's husbands (40.5 per cent), respondents (9.5 per cent) and both by consultations (24.5 per cent) are involved more in taking decision in the family. The involvement of parents (16.5 per cent) and in-laws (9.0 per cent) in taking decision is seems to be less before knowing the infection of the samples under the study.

But after infection, the participation of the infected people [respondent's husbands (21.5 per cent), respondents (4.0 per cent) and both (8.0 per cent)] in making decision to their own family have gone down to the per cent of (33.5 per cent) while compare to before infection (74.5 per cent). The parents (29.0 per cent) and in-laws (27.5) became a dominant figure in taking decision for respondents and their families. Considerable percentage of respondents family members like brothers (6.0 per cent), son (2.0 per cent) and uncles (2.0 per cent) also entered into the decision making process of the families of people living with HIV positive.

As far as gender role in decision-making process is concerned, men dominated more in taking decision related to family affairs before (40.5 per cent) and after (21.5 per cent) knowing infection. Women role in decision making process is considerably reduced after their infection.

Therefore, it is evident from the study the role of people living with HIV positive in decision-making process has affected due to their infection.

Table 5.60. Participation in the Socio-cultural Activities in the Family

Sl.No.	*Participants*	*Before infection*	*After infection*
1	Husband	27 (13.5%)	9 (4.5%)
2.	Respondent	12 (6.0%)	7 (3.5%)
3.	Both	102 (51.0%)	36 (18.0%)
4.	In-laws	15 (7.5%)	62 (31.0%)
5.	Parents	41 (20.5%)	53 (26.5%)
6.	Others	3 (1.5%)	33 (16.5%)
	Total	200 (100%)	200 (100%)

The analysis (Table 5.60) also explored the participation of the respondents in socio-cultural activities of the family before and after infection.

It is found from the study that the majority (51.0 per cent) of the married couples have participated in all socio-cultural functions of the family before knowing their HIV infection. In 20.5 per cent of cases including 17.5 per cent unmarried women, the respondent's parents were taken part followed by respondents' husbands (13.5 per cent) and in-laws (7.5 per cent). The respondents who participated in socio-cultural activities are accounted for 6.0 per cent. In few cases, (1.5 per cent) respondent's siblings are participated in the family functions.

However, after knowing HIV infection, 157 (78.5 per cent) respondents have withdrawn their participation in all functions of their families. The participation of the infected people has gone down to 18 per cent from 51 per cent before infection. In-laws (31.0 per cent), parents (26.5 per cent) and other members in the family (16.5 per cent) are taking part in socio-cultural activities of the families. The respondents (3.5 per cent) and their husbands (4.5 per cent) have reduced their participation due to infection.

The inference drawn from the analysis is that the participation of respondents in social and cultural ceremonies of their family have adversely affected due infection.

Table 5.61. Reasons for Non-participation in Socio-cultural Ceremonies

Sl.No.	*Reasons*	*No. of respondents*	*Percentage*
1.	Not getting invitation	33	21.0
2.	Reluctant to participate in ceremonies	88	56.1
3.	Fear on discrimination	36	22.9
	Total	157	100

Majority (56.1 per cent) of the respondents are reluctant to participate in ceremonies and functions. They imposed self restriction in the participation of social and cultural ceremonies of families. The significant percentage (22.9 per cent) avoided their participation due to the fear of facing discrimination followed by not getting invitation (21.0 per cent) from their family members to take part in the family functions (Table 5.61).

The analysis highlighted that the majority of the respondents have self imposed restriction in participating socio-cultural activities due to shame and guilty though most of their HIV status is not known to others.

It can be understood from the analysis that the infected people are not participating much in the family functions in general and women in particular due to guilt and shame.

Table 5.62. Maintenance and Property Given to Deserted and Widows

Sl. No.	*Maintenance and property*	*No. of respondents*		*Total*
		Yes	*No*	
1.	Deserted	2 (8.0%)	23 (92.0%)	25 (100%)
2.	Widows	12 (25. 5%)	35 (74.5%)	47 (100%)

It is already stated that four women became widow and three became deserted even before infection. However, it is observed from the study that 25 women became deserted and 47 became widows due to AIDS. Among the 25 deserted women only 8.0 per cent have given maintenance from their husbands and the others (92.0 per cent) have denied maintenance from their husbands. With regard to property for the widows, only 25.5 per cent got property of their husbands share and the remaining 74.5 per cent have not got share from the property of their husbands from their in-laws (Table 5.62).

The analysis reflected that the infected women were deprived of either getting property or maintenance from their husband's side due to the perception that the infected people will have short life.

Table 5.63. Place of Present Stay of Respondents

Sl. No.	*Places of present stay*	*No. of Respondents*	*Percentage*
1.	Parents	39	19.5
2.	In-laws	16	8.0
3.	Husband	69	34.5
4.	Children	48	24.0
5.	Alone	4	2.0
6.	N.G.Os	24	12.0
	Total	200	100

Table 5.63 on the present stay of the respondents reveals that 34.5 per cent of respondents live with their husbands. The 24.0 per cent found to be along with their children followed by parents (19.5 per cent). The 12.0 per cent respondents stayed in the short stay home run by the N.G.Os. The 8.0 per cent of respondents are under the care of their in-laws and the remaining 2.0 per cent staying alone without their family members support.

The analysis indicates that the majority of the infected women living either with their husbands (34.5 per cent) or with their children (24.0 per cent). The abundant sex workers are staying with the N.G.O. in the short stay home at Chennai.

Social Relationship in Neighbourhood

Neighbourhood relationship is indispensable for any individual to sustain in the society. The study has attempted to bring out the social relationship of infected women with their neighbours.

Table 5.61. Infection Known to the Neighbours

Sl. No.	*Infection known to neighbours*	*No of Respondents*		
		Yes	*No*	*Total*
1	Wives	3 (2.3%)	127 (97.7%)	130 (100%)
2	Sex workers	0 (0.0%)	62 (100%)	62 (100%)
3	Students	0 (0.0%)	7 (100%)	7 (100%)
4.	Drug user	0 (0.0%)	1 (100%)	1 (100%)
5.	Children	0 (0.0%)	14 (100%)	14 (100%)
6.	Respondents' Husbands	3 (2.3%)	127 (97.7%)	130 (100%)

Table 5.64 has identified that the infected men and women have adopted the strict principles of hiding the infection from their neighbours. Therefore, the neighbours were not aware of the majority of the respondents (97.7 per cent) and respondent's husbands (97.7 per cent) infection.

Table 5.65. Social Relationship of Respondents and their Husbands with Neighbours Before Infection

Sl. No.	*Nature of Interaction*	*No. of Respondents*	*Percentage*
1.	No Interaction	4	2
2.	Discuss and participate in all activities	184	92
3.	Just based on needs	12	6
	Total	200	100

The inference drawn from the table is that the people living with HIV positive are maintaining secrecy of their infection from their neighbours due to the problem of stigma and discrimination.

The respondents have very good social relationships (92.0 per cent) with neighbours before knowing their infections. They have participated in the social functions of marriage, childbirth, death, community festivals and other rituals and ceremonies organized by the neighbours. Majority of the married respondents (86.7 per cent) have participated in these functions along with their husbands and children.

It is found from the analysis that the respondents have established very good social relationship with their neighbours before infection.

Table 5.66. Social Relationship of Respondents and their Husbands with Neighbours After Infection

Sl. No.	*Nature of relationship*	*No. of Respondents*	*Percentage*
1.	Withdrawn relationship	144	72.0
2.	Discuss and participate in all activities	23	11.5
3.	Just based on needs	33	16.5
	Total	200	100

However, after knowing infection many respondents have felt guilt and shame to interact with the neighbour as like before infection. It is found from the analysis that the majority (72 per cent) of the respondents have themselves withdrawn their relationship from their neighbours and they hesitated to participate in the social functions freely due to the fear of facing social stigma attached to the HIV/AIDS though their infection in not known to their neighbours. The responses of the married respondents revealed that their husbands were more reluctant to participate in the functions outside the family because of shame and guilt. It is found from the analysis that only 11.5 per cent of respondents maintained good relationship with their neighbours and 16.5 per cent respondents relationship with their neighbour is just based on needs.

The conclusion drawn from Table 5.66 is that the people living with HIV positive withdrawn themselves from the socio-cultural activities with their neighbours due to the impact of stigma and discrimination.

A. Neighbour's Interaction Towards People Living with HIV Positive whose Infection is Known to Them

Of the 200 respondents, the 3 (1.5 per cent) of respondents infection was known to their neighbours. All the three respondents are not getting support from their neighbours. They are all socially distanced from their neighbours.

It is clear from the analysis that social distance is the common response from the neighbour towards the people living with HIV positive.

Table 5.67. Reasons for Discrimination by the Neighbours

Sl. No.	*Reasons for discrimination*	*No. of Respondents*	*Percentage*
1.	Lack of knowledge on HIV/AIDS	47	23.5
2.	Fear of infection	134	67.0
3.	Fear about other's comments	11	5.5
4.	Respondent's deviant behaviour	5	2.5
5.	Husband's deviant behaviour	3	1.5
	Total	200	100

It is evident from the above said analysis that the misconception about the spread of HIV is the major cause for discrimination as the fear of infection was reported by 67 per cent of respondents.

The understanding from the table is that the fear of contracting infection is the major cause for stigmatizing and discriminating the infected people.

B. Person Blamed for Respondents Infection by the Neighbours

Among the 200 respondents, only three respondents infection was known to their neighbours. All the three are blamed for their infection by the neighours for their ignorance and inability to control their husband from having extra marital affairs.

C. Effects of Discrimination on the Respondents

The discrimination by the neighbour produced certain negative impact on the socio-economic life of the people living with HIV positive. Because of discrimination, the 3 respondents have changed their residence and moved to the place where no one is aware of their infection. All the 200 (100 per cent) respondents have developed fear towards social isolation, and complex of inferiority and guilt and they restricted their social mobility.

Social Relationship with Friends

Every individual life is in one or other way linked with friendship settings. The friends are called as peer groups or reference groups. Many individual have close tie-up with the friends than their family members and relatives. They share all their happiness and sorrows with them. Each and every event of individual life is closely associated with their friends. If the individual is affected by any chronic illness, the friends are the first person in providing courage, moral, psychological and financial support, care and other needs expected by the sick persons. But in the case of HIV/AIDS, stigma makes certain difference between the infected persons and their friends. The study also made an attempt to find out the discrimination in friendship settings.

The above table reflects the respondents and the husbands of married respondent's involvement with their friendship circle before and after infection. It shows that the majority of both the respondents (53 per cent) and their husbands (59.5 per cent) were often with their friends before knowing their HIV-status.

Their associations with their friends have drastically changed after knowing their infection. The infected men and women were themselves reluctant to meet their friends and share their feeling. When compared to infected men, the majority (42.5 per cent) of infected respondents were completely out of their friendship circle and many (41.5 per cent) have developed the attitude of rarely meeting their friends instead of often (13.5 per cent) or very often (2.5 per cent) meeting them.

Table 5.68. Frequency of Respondents and their Husbands with their Friends before and after Infection

Sl. No.	Frequency of involvement with friends	Before Infection Respondents	Before Infection Husbands	After Infection Respondents	After Infection Husbands
1.	Not at all	9 (4.5%)	1 (0.6%)	85 (42.5%)	17 (10.7%)
2.	Rarely	56 (28.0%)	35 (22.2%)	83 (41.5%)	53 (33.5%)
3.	Often	106 (53.0%)	94 (59.5%)	27 (13.5%)	79 (50.0%)
4.	Very Often	29 (14.5%)	28 (17.7%)	5 (2.5%)	9 (5.8%)
	Total	200 (100%)	158 (100%)	200 (100%)	158 (100%)

As in the case of infected men, though they are gradually coming out of their friendship circle, more than 50 per cent have still maintaining their close relationship with their friends.

The analysis of data given in Table 5.68 also identified that the unmarried women, sex workers and separated/divorced are more particular in hiding themselves from their friends as a result of their guilt and fear on stigma with their behaviour and infections.

Out of 35 unmarried women, 28 (80.0 per cent) are sex workers and 7 (20.0 per cent) are students. All the 7 (20.0 per cent) students are completely out of their friendship circle after knowing their infection. As far as the unmarried sex worker is concerned, they have developed the attitude of meeting their friends very rarely after infection. Among the 27 family based sex workers, majority (77.8 per cent) have rarely meeting their friends after infection.

It is evident from Table 5.68 that the infection has brought significant changes in the respondents' relationship with their friends than the infected men. The infected women were more reluctant to meet their friends as before their infection.

Table 5.69. Revelation of HIV Status to the Friends

Sl. No.	*Revelation of HIV status*	*No. of Respondents*		*Total*
		Yes	*No*	
1.	Housewives	4 (3.1%)	126 (96.9%)	130 (100%)
2.	Part time sex workers	19 (70.4%)	8 (29.6%)	27 (100%)
3.	Full time sex workers	13 (46.4%)	15 (53.6%)	28 (100%)
4.	Students	0 (0.0%)	7 (100%)	7 (100%)
5.	Drug user	0 (0.0%)	1 (100%)	1 (100%)
6.	Respondents' Husbands	23 (17.6%)	107 (82.3%)	130 (100%)

The analysis explored that only 3.1 per cent respondents and 17.6 per cent husbands of respondents were disclosed their HIV status to their friends. Among the 200 respondents, majority (82.3 per cent) have not revealed their HIV status to their friends. Among the 158 husbands of married respondents, 27 part time sex workers husbands and 1 injecting drug user husbands are ignorant about their of their infection which they got through their wives. These husbands were not undergone HIV test. Among the remaining 130 husbands, majority (82.3 per cent) not revealed their HIV status with their friends. The hiding of infection is mainly due to the negative impact of HIV on the affected people (Table 5.69).

Part-time sex workers (70.4 per cent) followed by full time sex workers (46.4 per cent) are predominant among the respondents who have revealed their HIV status to their friends. Majority of the housewives (96.9 per cent), students (100 per cent) and drug user (100 per cent) are deliberately hiding their HIV status from their friends.

The finding drawn from the table is that the majority of the respondents (82.0 per cent) and their husbands (82.3 per cent) have not disclosed their. HIV status to their friends. The revelation of HIV status is found high among the sex workers (51.6 per cent) than the housewives, students and drug users.

Table 5.70. Reaction of Friends Towards Respondents and their Husbands After Infection

Sl. No.	*Reaction of the friends*	*No. of Respondents Respondents'*	*No. of Husbands*
1.	Sympathetic	4 (11.1%)	3 (13.0%)
2.	Withdrawn friendship	3 (8.3%)	0 (0.0%)
3.	Disclosed HIV status to others	8 (22.2)	3 (13.0%)
4.	Supporting – moral/financial	21 (58.4%)	17 (74.0%)
	Total	36 (100%)	23 (100%)

Table 5.70 on the reaction of the friends towards the respondents shows that among the 36 (18 per cent) respondents whose infection is revealed to their friends, 58.4 per cent got moral and financial support from their friends. All these 21 respondents are sex workers. The friends have disclosed 22.2 per cent respondents HIV status to others including their family members and relatives. The 11.1 per cent respondents got sympathy from their friends. All these four respondents are housewives and innocent victims of HIV. The 8.3 per cent respondents' friends have withdrawn their friendship from the infected respondents.

Except eight friends, others have not disclosed the infection of the respondents to their family members.

Out of 23 men who have disclosed their HIV status to their friends, 74 per cent have got moral and financial support and 13 per cent have got sympathy from their friends. The remaining 13 per cent respondents were discriminated from their friends by disclosing their HIV status to others.

The inference drawn from the analysis is that majority (58.4 per cent) of the respondents and their husbands (74.0 per cent) are getting moral and financial support from their friends. But when compared to men, less number of infected women is getting support from their friends.

Social Relationship with Relatives

Relatives are part and parcel of every individual's life. Individual is not only very close to their family members, but also with their relatives and they used to take part in all social events of their relatives. Sharing of emotional feelings with the close kin and kith used to bring psychological support for the individual. Everyone normally *get al.*l supports including moral, financial, physical etc. during crisis. This part of the analysis will highlight the discrimination and support experienced by the women living with HIV positive from their relatives.

Table 5.71. Respondents and their Husbands Infection Known to the Relatives

Sl. No.	*The person's infection known to relatives*	*No. of respondents*	*Percentage*
1.	Respondents	27	37.0
2.	Respondent's Husband	6	8.2
3.	Both	40	54.8
	Total	73	100

Table 5.71 shows that 127 (63.5 per cent) respondents have not revealed their HIV status to their relatives and only 73 (36.5 per cent) respondent's infection was known to their relatives. Among them, 37.0 per cent respondent's infection alone known to their relatives of whom 70.4 per cent are housewives and 29.6 per cent are sex workers. In the cases of respondents living with husbands, 54.8 per cent couples infection is known to their relatives and only 8.2 per cent respondent's husband's infection alone revealed to their relatives.

The inference drawn from the analysis is that the majority of the infected housewives and their husbands' infection is known to their relatives. The infection of sex workers and students infection is not known to their relatives.

Table 5.72. Reaction of Relatives Towards People Infected with HIV

Sl. No.	*Nature of Reaction*	*No. of Respondents*	*No. of Respondents' Husbands*
1	Isolated	24 (32.9%)	13 (28.3%)
2	Verbal abuse	13 (17.8%)	6 (13.0%)
3.	Physical abuse	1 (1.4%)	0 (0.0%)
4.	Withdraw their visit of coming	16 (21.9%)	3 (6.5%)
5.	Supporting-moral, financial	12 (16.4%)	23 (50.0%)
6.	Others.	7 (9.6%)	1 (2.2%)
	Total	73 (100%)	46 (100%)

Tanle 5.7 reveals that among the respondent's infection known to their relatives, only 16.4 per cent of respondents have got financial and moral support from their relatives. All these 12 respondents are housewives who got infection through their husbands. The remaining respondents are discriminated by their relatives in the form of social isolation (32.9 per cent), withdraw their visit to respondents house (21.9 per cent), verbal abuse (17.8 per cent), other form of discriminations like not inviting the respondents to take part in the social events of relatives house (9.6 per cent) and physical isolation (1.4 per cent).

Among the respondents HIV status known to relatives, eight are sex workers and the remaining are housewives. All these eight sex workers are socially isolated by their relatives.

Of the 46 men's infection known to their relatives, 23 (50.0 per cent) have got both moral and financial support from their relatives and the remaining 50.0 per cent are discriminated by their relatives.

The inference drawn from the table is, irrespective of sex if the infection is known to relatives, they are discriminated by them as a result of fear of contagious and stigma associated with the mode of infection. While comparing the discrimination experienced by infected respondents and their husbands, the infected women are subjected to severe discrimination and criticism by the relatives.

Table No. 5.73. Frequency of Visit to Relatives House Before and after Infection by Respondents

Sl.No.	*Frequency of visit*	*Before Infection*	*After Infection*
1	Not al all	6 (3.0%)	107 (53.5%)
2	Rarely	15 (7.5%)	72 (36.0%)
3.	Often	74 (37.0%)	19 (9.5%)
4.	Very often	105 (52.5%)	2 (1.0%)
	Total	200 (100%)	200 (100%)

The analysis of the data on the social participation of respondents before knowing their infection status showed that the majority of the respondents visited their relatives house for various social functions either very often (52.5 per cent) or often (37.0 per cent). Very few respondents rarely visited their relative's house (7.5 per cent). Only 3.0 per cent of women have not at all participated in any social events of their relative's house due to certain dispute and misunderstanding between them.

After knowing the infection, the analysis observed drastic changes in the social participation of respondents with their relatives. It is identified that 54.5 per cent of respondents have stopped their social participation in their relatives house due to guilty and fear about stigma and discrimination. Among them the 16.5 per cent unmarried girls are more reluctant to take part in the social events of their relatives house. The 36.0 per cent respondents have rarely taking part in the social gathering of their relative house. Very few respondents either often (9.5 per cent) or very often (1.5 per cent) participated in the social events of their relatives house.

The inference drawn from the analysis is that the majority (53.5 per cent) of respondents are not visiting their relatives' house after knowing their infection.

Table 5.74. Reason for not Visiting Relatives House After Infection by Respondents

Sl.No.	*Reasons*	*No. of Respondents*	*Percentage*
1.	Self imposed restriction	127	63.5
2.	Fear on discrimination	56	28.0
3.	Due to guilt and shame	17	8.5
	Total	200	100

The analysis identified that, though the majority of the infected women not disclosed their HIV status to their relatives, they themselves developed self imposed restriction (63.5 per cent) to visit their relatives house. Fear on discrimination restricted 28.0 per cent of respondents to restrict their visit to relatives house followed by guilty and shame (8.5 per cent).

Table 5.75. Participation in Socio-cultural Activities of Relatives House Before and After Infection

Sl.No.	*Participants*	*Before infection*	*After infection*
1.	Parents	35 (17.5%)	78 (39.0%)
2.	In-laws	24 (12.0%)	59 (29.5%)
3.	Respondents	44 (22.0%)	16 (8.0%)
4.	Respondent's husbands	41 (20.5%)	13 (6.5%)
5.	Respondents and her husbands	56 (28.0%)	7 (3.5%)
6.	Others : Brothers	0	21(10.5%)
	Son	(0.0%)	6(3.0%)
	Total	200 (100%)	200 (100%)

Fear owing to stigma associated with AIDS majority (63.5 per cent) of the respondents developed self imposed restriction to visit their relatives house.

Table 5.75 reveals the people who have participated in the socio-cultural activities of relative's house before and after the infection of respondents.

Before infection the majority of the respondents were participated along with their husbands (28 per cent) in the socio cultural activities of relatives. Majority of the respondents, especially married respondents (22.0 per cent) were empowered to take part with their relative's social events followed by their husbands (20.5 per cent). In the case of unmarried 35 (17.5 per cent) girls the parents are participated where as in the case of widows and deserted/divorced majority of the in-laws (12.0 per cent) are participated in the socio-cultural activities of relatives.

After infection, significant changes have taken place in the participation of respondents in the socio-cultural activities of relatives house. The table showed that only 36 (18 per cent) of respondents including their husbands were willingly participated after infection as against 70.5 per cent in before infection. The respondents participation is replaced by their parents (39.0 per cent) followed by their in-laws (29.5 per cent), brothers (10.5 per cent) and son (3.0 per cent).

The inference drawn from the table is that the respondents have themselves isolated from the socio-cultural activities of relative's house after infection due to various reasons.

Table 5.76. Person Blamed for Respondents and their Husbands Infection by Relatives

Sl. No.	*Person Blamed for Infection*	*No. of Respondents*	*Percentage*
1.	Respondents	49	67.1
2.	Respondents' Husbands	24	32.9
	Total	73	100

The analysis revealed that only 36.5 per cent respondent's infection was known to their relatives. Among them except eight respondents (sex workers), the remaining were housewives.

In majority of the cases (67.1 per cent) the women were blamed for her as well as her husband's infection. In the remaining cases (32.9 per cent) the respondent's husbands are blamed for respondent's infection.

Table 5.77. Reasons for Blaming the Respondents By Relatives

Sl. No.	*Reasons*	*No. of Respondents*	*Percentage*
1.	Promiscuous behaviour	8	16.3
2.	Ignorance and inability to control husbands promiscuous behaviour	16	32.7
3.	Frequent stay with parents	11	22.4
4.	Fidelity is suspected	14	28.6
	Total	49	100

In the case of majority (32.7 per cent) of respondents are blamed due to their inability and ignorance to control their husbands promiscuous behaviour. Fidelity and morality is suspected for 28.6 per cent of respondents by their relatives. Besides, 22.4 per cent of respondents blamed for their frequent stay with their parents and 16.3 per cent of respondents blamed due to their promiscuous behaviour.

The inference drawn from the analysis is that the majority (32.7 per cent) of respondents are blamed for their infection by the relatives due to their ignorance and inability to control their husbands' promiscuous behaviour.

Table 5.78. Impact of Relatives Discrimination on Respondents

Sl. No.	*Impacts*	*No. of Respondents*	*Percentage*
1.	Changed the place of residence	19	26.0
2.	Developed the complex of inferiority	47	64.4
3.	Restricted the activities in the public	7	9.6
	Total	73	100

As a result of discrimination, the majority of the respondents (64.4 per cent) have developed the complex of inferiority followed by changing the place of residence (26.0 per cent) and restriction of activities in and out side home (9.6 per cent) (Table 5.78).

The conclusion drawn from the analysis is that the majority of the respondents were blamed not only for her infection but also for her husband's infection though they got infection through their husbands. The gender biased and baseless discrimination created inferiority complex among the infected women.

Discrimination in Treatment

The study has made an attempt to identify the gender discrimination existed between men and women in taking treatment for opportunistic infections.

Table 5.79 on treatment seeking behaviour of the people living with HIV positive reveals that the infected men are regularly taking treatment than the infected women. Among the housewife the majority (59.3 per cent) takes treatment whenever they fall sick and 31.5 per cent have not taken any treatment for their infection.

As far as sex worker is concerned, the full time sex workers are non family based sex workers which includes unmarried girls, deserted and widows are taking treatment either whenever they fall sick (77.1 per cent) or in monthly once (22.9 per cent) than the family based sex workers Table 5.79. The 27 part time sex workers are family based sex workers and have husbands and children. The part time sex workers infection was not known to their husbands. These men might also get infected by HIV by their infected wives. To hide their HIV status these part time sex workers are not taking treatment for their illness.

The seven students and one injecting drug user are not taking treatment for their infection.

The inference drawn from the table is that the treatment seeing behaviour for the infection is found to be high among the full time sex workers and housewives. While comparing the treatment seeking behaviour with infected husband, the women give less priority than men.

Table 5.79. Treatment Seeking Behaviour of Infected People

Sl. No.	*Frequency of Treatment*	*No. of Respondents*					
		House wife	*Part Time Sex worker*	*Full time Sex worker*	*Student*	*Drug user*	*Husbands*
1.	Weekly	0 (0.0%)	0 (0.0%)	0 (0.0%)	0 (0.0%)	0 (0.0%)	12 (9.2%)
2.	Monthly	12 (9.2%)	0 (0.0%)	8 (22.9%)	0 (0.0%)	0 (0.0%)	68 (52.3%)
3.	When ever fall sick	77 (59.3%)	0 (0.0%)	27 (77.1%)	0 (0.0%)	0 (0.0%)	43 (33.1%)
4.	No Treatment	41 (31.5%)	27 (100%)	0 (0.0%)	7 (100%)	1 (100%)	7 (5.4%)
	Total	130 (100%)	27 (100%)	35 (100%)	7 (100%)	1 (100%)	130 (100%)

Table 5.80. Place of Treatment

Sl. No.	Place of Treatment (Hospital)	No. of Respondents					
		House wife	Part Time Sex worker	Full time Sex worker	Student	Drug user	Husbands
1.	Government	29 (22.3%)	0 (0.0%)	9 (25.7%)	0 (0.0%)	0 (0.0%)	19 (14.6%)
2.	Private	6 (4.6%)	0 (0.0%)	0 (0.0%)	0 (0.0%)	0 (0.0%)	87 (66.9%)
3.	N.G.O	54 (41.5%)	0 (0.0%)	26 (74.3%)	0 (0.0%)	0 (0.0%)	17 (13.1%)
4.	No treatment	41 (31.6%)	27 (100%)	0 (0.0%)	7 (100%)	1 (100%)	7 (5.4%)
	Total	130 (100%)	27 (100%)	35 (100%)	7 (100%)	1 (100%)	130 (100%)

Table 5.80 show that the treatment taken by the respondents and their husbands reveals that majority of the housewives (41.5 per cent) take treatment in the N.G.Os followed by government hospitals (22.3 per cent) and very few housewives (4.6 per cent) are taken treatment in the private hospitals.

Majority of the full time (74.3 per cent) of sex workers are taking treatment in the N.G.Os. Significant number of full time sex workers (25.7 per cent) also seeks treatment in Government hospitals.

The students and drug user are not taking treatment for their illness in order to maintain secrecy with regard to their infection.

As far as respondents husbands is concerned, majority (66.9 per cent) are taking treatment in the private hospitals followed by Government hospitals (14.6 per cent) (Table 5.80).

The inference drawn from the table is that the N.G.Os played a vital role in providing treatment to the respondents either at free of cost or by charging very less amount. In the same time men take treatment in the private hospital by paying huge amount for treatment. This is the clear indication of gender discrimination prevailing in the treatment for HIV/AIDS related illness.

Table 5.80 explains the expenditure incurred by the person towards the medical treatment of respondents and their husbands. Of the 130 housewives, 31.6 per cent is not taking treatment for their HIV/AIDS related illness. In the remaining 89 housewives, majority of their medical expenditure is met by their parents (39.2 per cent) followed by respondents' husbands (14.6 per cent).

All the 100 part time sex workers not taking treatment in order to hide their inflectional status from their family members. All the 35 full time sex workers and one injecting drug user incurred their medical expenditure by themselves.

Table 5.80 shows that as far as respondents' husbands are concerned, 32.3 per cent of respondents' husbands met their own medical expenditure. Significant percentage (26.9 per cent) of respondents' husbands' expenditure is incurred by their wives. Respondents' in-laws incurred 20.8 per cent of respondents'

Table 5.81. Expenditure Met by the Person for Respondents' Treatment

Sl. No.	*Expenditure met by*	*No. of Respondents*				
		Housewife	*Drug User*	*Part Time Sexworker*	*Full time Sex worker*	*Respondents Husbands*
1.	In-laws	6 (4.6%)	0 (0.0%)	0 (0.0%)	0 (0.0%)	27 (20.8%)
2.	Parents	51 (39.2%)	0 (0.0%)	0 (0.0%)	0 (0.0%)	19 (14.6%)
3.	Respondents	13 (10.0%)	0 (0.0%)	0 (0.0%)	35 (100%)	35 (26.9%)
4.	Respondents' Husbands	19 (14.6%)	0 (0.0%)	0 (0.0%)	0 (0.0%)	42 (32.3%)
5.	No Treatment	41 (31.6%)	1 (100%)	27 (100%)	0 (0.0%)	7 (5.4%)
	Total	130 (100%)	1 (100)	27 (100%)	35 (100%)	130 (100%)

husbands medical treatment. Respondents' parents met the expenditure of 14.6 per cent of respondents' husbands.

The inference drawn from the analysis is that significant percentage (26.9 per cent) of housewives gives preference to their husbands for treatment and they spent amount for the treatment of their husbands. It is also evident from the analysis that the majority of the housewives medical expenditure is met by their parents rather than their husbands and in-laws. Besides, among the sex workers the full time sex workers are giving importance for their treatment and they themselves incurred the medical expenditure for the treatment. In the same time the full time sex workers, students and injecting drug user are not taking treatment due to the fear of exposure of their infection to others.

Table 5.82. Problems Faced by the Respondents in Hospitals

Sl. No.	*Nature of problems*	*No. of Respondents*	*Percentage*
1.	Hospital admission	42	21.0
2.	Care in the wards	39	19.5
3.	Confidentiality of report	33	16.5
4.	All	78	39.9
5.	No discrimination	8	4.0
	Total	200	100

The analysis on the problems faced by the people living with HIV positive reveals that except few (4.0 per cent) respondents the others (96.0 per cent) have experienced various discriminations in the hospitals with regard to hospital admission, care in the wards, confidentiality of report etc. As far as the magnitude of the problems is concerned, the women were comparatively facing more (96.0 per cent) problems than men (91.1 per cent) (Table 5.82). According to the respondents, the people in the health care sectors are thinking that all the infected women are sex workers and they are responsible for transmitting the virus to the innocent men. Therefore, every infected woman is treated as a sex worker in the hospitals though they got infection through their husbands. The medical personnel, though aware of HIV/AIDS, show reluctance over the affected persons. As like common populace, they also fired them with wounding words. While treating these people, they denied touching them and diagnosing the HIV/AIDS related illness. Majority of the women (58.0 per cent) also reported that they have not find much difference in discrimination between men and women in the hospitals.

The inference drawn from the analysis is that the practice of discrimination on HIV/AIDS is high in health care institutions.

Discriminatiion in the Place of Work

Many studies have revealed that the discrimination experienced by the people living with HIV positive in the place where they are working. Majority of the people living with HIV positive have lost their job and faced various discriminations and humiliations in the work place after revealing their HIV status to their employer and colleagues. The present study also made on attempt to explore the discrimination faced by the respondents in the place of their working.

Table 5.83. Employment Status Of Respondents

Sl.No.	*Employment Status*	*No. of Respondents*
1.	Working from before infection	48(41.4 per cent)
2.	Working after infection	68(58.6 per cent)
	Total	116(100 per cent)

In this study, of the total 200 respondents, 58 per cent were employed in various sectors. Among the employed women, the 58.6 per cent have started working only after knowing their HIV infection.

The inference drawn from the analysis is that the majority (58.6 per cent) of the respondents were taken up job only after knowing their HIV status (Table 5.83).

Table 5.84 shows that the causes for taking up jobs by the respondents after knowing their HIV status is identified as widowhood (26.5 per cent), to meet medical expenses (23.5 per cent), to get free from mental torture and tension (20.6 per cent), separation or desertion from husband (16.2 per cent) and husband's unemployment and his inability to do work (13.2 per cent) due to sickness.

Table 5.84. Reasons for Taking Job after Knowing HIV Status

Sl. No.	*Reasons*	*No. of Respondents*	*Percentage*
1.	Widowhood	18	26.5
2.	To meet medical expenses	16	23.5
3.	To get rid of mental torture and tension	14	20.6
4.	Separation or desertion from husband	11	16.2
5.	Husband's unemployment and his inability to do work due to sickness.	9	13.2
	Total	68	100

The conclusion drawn from Table 5.84 it is that the widowhood due to AIDS and heavy medical expenses to treat opportunistic infection are the major cause for the women to go for employment after knowing their HIV status.

A. Discrimination Experienced by the Respondents and their Husbands in the Place Of Work

As for the analysis, 158 respondents were with their husbands. Among these husbands, 93.0 per cent were employed in various sectors. Their employers known about 6.1 per cent respondent's husband's infection and they discriminated all these men by throwing them out of jobs.

Among the 116 (58.0 per cent) employed respondents, only 20.7 per cent have revealed their HIV status in their working places under the circumstances of getting sympathy and jobs in Tamil Nadu State AIDS Control Society and in voluntary organisations working in AIDS prevention and control. The revelation of HIV status brought employment opportunity for all these 24 respondents in voluntary organisations (17 (70.8

per cent)) and Tamil Nadu State AIDS Control Society (7 (29.2 per cent)). By knowing the HIV status of these respondents, the employer showed sympathy and immediately agreed to observe them for their organisations.

However, these respondents reported that they have experienced different kinds of discrimination both from their employer and colleagues. According to them, whenever visitors come to their organisations, their employers used to introduce them as a HIV infected person to get name and fame. They revealed that such kind of introduction to unknown persons make them to think about their HIV status with fear of guilt and death. Besides, their colleagues are also maintaining social distance in the work due to lack of knowledge and the fear of contracting infection through causal contacts.

The discrimination produced certain psychological impact on their personality development. They felt that their working condition was not favorable for them to forget their infection and get relief from tension and fear. Therefore, in the beginning many have thought of resigning their jobs and find some other organisations where no one is aware of their infection. Nevertheless, the reasonable income and other facilities for their treatment made them to continue their work in the NGOs and Tamil Nadu State AIDS Control society. Now, they are all adjusted with the present circumstances and mould their mind to work for the people living with HIV positive and to create awareness to the general population and high risk groups on HIV/AIDS and its impact.

B. Organisation to Fight for Women Living with HIV Positive Against Stigma and Discrimination

The infected women have an organisation in Chennai under the name of "Positive Women Net Work". It fights against the discrimination of AIDS and involved in providing counseling, support and care to the women living with HIV positive. It is functioning under the financial support of Tamil Nadu AIDS Control Society.

The analysis clearly revealed that the infected women were maintaining secrecy with regard to their HIV infection in the place where they are working. The infected women were very much scared about the impact of stigma associated with AIDS if they revealed their infection with their employer and colleagues. Therefore, stigma and discrimination played a vital role to prevent the infected people to share their infection with others.

Respondents Attitude Towards Pregnancy and Childbirth after Infection

The status of women in India is determined by her fertility status. Motherhood is glorified in all religion and the children are essential to perform all religious rituals and last rites of the parents. The infertility of women is stigmatized and it discriminate women throughout her life and it may end with divorce, separation or desertion. Therefore, the women in particular and family in general give more importance for pregnancy and childbirth.

Pregnancy and child birth is purely personal. But in the context of HIV/AIDS, it is proved that the infected women can transmit the virus to the infant if she is not taking antiretroviral treatment and adopt breast feeding to the infants. Once the child is infected by HIV, its survival is questionable and the child also has to face all discrimination like adult without knowing anything about HIV/AIDS.

The analysis makes an attempt to understand the women's attitude towards pregnancy and child birth, sexual behaviour after infection etc.

Table 5.85. Number of children born before and after infection to respondents

Sl. No.	*No. of Children*	*No. of Respondents*			*Total*
		1-2	*3-4*	*4-5*	
1.	Before infection	74 (46.5%)	82 (51.6%)	3 (1.9)	159 (100%)
2.	After infection	27 (93.1)	2 (6.9%)	0	29 (100%)
3.	Children infected	14	0	0	14 (48.3)
4.	Children died due to infection	2	0	0	2 (14.3%)

Table 5.85 shows that among 165 married respondents 96.4 per cent have children even before knowing infection and 14.5 per cent of respondents delivered babies after infection. Among the babies born to infected mother, 48.3 per cent were infected with HIV and among 14.3 per cent children have died due to HIV/AIDS. All these children living with HIV are under the age group of 1-5 years.

The conclusion drawn from Table 5.85 is that the majority of the children (48.3 per cent) born to the respondents after infection are infected by HIV.

Table 5.86. Causes for Pregnancy after Infection

Sl.No.	*Causes for Pregnancy*	*No. of Respondents*	*Percentage*
1.	Not practiced birth control	13	44.8
2.	To fulfil the role as mother	6	20.7
3.	Not aware of infecting the child	10	34.5
	Total	29	100

Of the 29 respondents who have given birth to child after infection, 44.8 per cent have not practiced any birth control measures to prevent child birth, 20.7 per cent have decided to have children to fulfill the role as motherhood and the remaining 34.5 per cent aware not aware that the infection of mother will infect the child.

Lack of awareness on mother to child transmission (34.5 per cent) and lack of practices of birth control measures (44.8 per cent) are the major causative factor for the pregnancy of women after infection.

A. Reaction of Respondents and her Husbands about Pregnancy after Infection

Of the 29 respondents who have conceived after infection, the majority of the respondents 89.7 per cent were decided to terminate the pregnancy, but it couldn't possible for them due to their advanced stage of pregnancy and the remaining 10.3 per cent prepared to have children with the support of their husbands (Table 5.87).

Of the 29 respondents who have given birth to child after HIV infection were stated that they are all consulted the doctors by knowing their HIV status. Among them 48.3 per cent of respondents (Table 5.87) are asked by the doctors to terminate the pregnancy and 41.4 per cent have reported that they were discriminated and denied treatment in the hospital. Only 10.3 per cent respondents have been advised by the doctors to take antiretroviral treatment.

Table 5.87. Reaction of Doctors Towards Infected Pregnant Respondents

Sl.No.	*Reaction of Doctors*	*No. of Respondents*	*Percentage*
1.	Asked to take treatment regularly	3	10.3
2.	Asked to terminate the pregnancy	14	48.3
3.	Refused tr give treatment	12	41.4
	Total	29	100

The inference drawn from the table is that the HIV infected women are highly discriminated in the hospitals by doctors.

B. Preventive Method Adopted by the Respondents to Avoid Mother to Child Infection

The high cost of antiretroviral drugs prevented all the respondents from taking antiretroviral treatment to prevent mother to child transmission.

Table 5.88. Strategy Adopted by the Respondents for Delivery

Sl. No.	*Strategy adopted for delivery*	*No. of Respondents*	*Percentage*
1.	Getting admission in the hospital at the time of labour pain without informing HIV status	17	58.6
2.	Delivered at home with the support of local midwives without informing HIV status	12	41.4
	Total	29	100

The discrimination experienced by the respondents in the hospital made 58.6 per cent respondents to get admission in the hospital only at the time of labour pain without informing their HIV status. The remaining 41.4 per cent were scared to face the discrimination in the hospital and therefore they have delivered baby in the home with the support of local midwives.

The findings suggested that the discrimination in the healthcare settings made many infected pregnant women either to get admitted into the hospital at the time of emergency by hiding their HIV status or to prepare to deliver at home with the help of midwives by hiding their HIV status. The tendency of hiding the infection status further facilitates the spread of infection among the innocent people who have attended delivery.

Table 5.89. Reproductive Sexual Behaviour After Infection to Avoid Pregnancy

Sl.No.	*Reproductive sexual behaviour*	*No. of Respondents*	*Percentage*
1.	Sterilization	34	17.0
2.	Oral pills	21	10.5
3	Condom	28	14.0
4.	IUD (Intra Uterine Device)	32	16.0
5.	Abstinence	3	1.5
6.	Avoided Marriage	35	17.5
7.	Sterilized before infection	47	23.5
	Total	200	100.0

Table 5.89 represents the reproductive behaviour of the respondents to avoid pregnancy in order to prevent mother to child transmission.

The table shows that 23.5 per cent respondents have undergone female sterilization even before knowing infection. These respondents have reported that there is no need of using any other preventive method to avoid pregnancy as well as transmission.

All 35 (17.5 per cent) of unmarried respondents have decided to avoid marriage due to the fear of infecting their husbands as well as the child. Among the married women 17.0 per cent have undergone sterilization 16.0 per cent have adopted the temporary method of contraception or non-terminal measures called IUDs (Intra Uterus Devices). The 14.0 per cent were using condom to avoid pregnancy and among them majority (25 respondents) were female sex workers who were motivated by the non-governmental organisations to use condom to prevent transmission to their male sexual partners. Oral pills is used by 10.5 per cent of respondents to avoid pregnancy and only 1.5 per cent of respondents were adopted the concept of abstinence to prevent their child from infection.

The conclusion drawn from the table is that the unmarried women were well aware of the passing of infection to their husbands if they get married. So they have all avoided marriage. Among the married respondents, the majority have prepared terminal method followed by non terminal method called IUDs. Condom usage is not popular among the married women rather than the women in sex work.

Table 5.90. Attitude of Respondents Towards Pregnancy and Child Birth

Sl.No.	*Respondents Attitude*	*Yes*	*No*	*Total*
1.	Infected women must have pregnancy	48 (24.0%)	152 (76.0%	200 (100%)
2.	Pregnancy of infected women is unadvisable	128 (64.0%)	72 (36.0%)	200 (100%)
3.	Infected women can have pregnancy to experience motherhood	56 (28.0%)	144 (72.0%)	200 (100%)
4.	Pregnancy right should not be denied to infected women	45 (22.5%)	155 (77.5%)	200 (100%)
5.	Child will get infection from infected mother	105 (52.5%)	95 (47.5%)	200 (100%)
6.	Infected child will have less survival	100 (50.0%)	100 (50.0%)	200 (100%)
7.	Regular Antiretroviral treatment prevent child from infection	57 (28.5%)	143 (71.5%)	200 (100%)
8.	Government can ban the pregnancy of HIV positive women	156 (78.0%)	44 (22.0%)	200 (100%)

Table 5.90 reveals the respondent's attitude towards pregnancy and child birth by the women living with HIV positive.

The table reflects that though the majority of the women were against the pregnancy of HIV infected women, they were not supported the denial of pregnancy right to the HIV infected women either by the public or by the Government. At the same time almost 50 per cent of the respondents were unaware of mother to child transmission and the less survival chance for the infected child. The table also shows that the majority (71.5 per cent) of the respondents were unaware of the antiretroviral treatment and its administration to prevent child from infection.

The inference drawn from the table is that the infected women were against the denial of pregnancy right to the infected women and most of them were ignorant about mother to child transmission and the antiretroviral treatment to safeguard the child from infection.

Table 5.91. Facilities Expceted by the Respondents to Take Care of Infected Child and Positive Parents

Sl.No.	*Facilities Expected by the Respondents*	*No. of Respondents*	*Percentage*
1.	Treatment along with other patients	193	96.5
2.	Free antiretroviral drugs	200	100.0
3.	Financial assistance to take up self employment	164	82.0
4.	Insurance for people with HIV positive	157	78.5
5.	Admission in the school for the infected children	200	100.0
6.	Special care home for the abundant people	189	94.5
7.	Reservation in the employment	83	41.5
8.	Alternative avenue to the infected sex workers	163	81.5

Table 5.91 represents the facilities expected by the respondents to take care of infected child and positive parents. All the respondents (100.0 per cent) were expected free

antiretroviral drugs for both the child and infected parents and all the respondents (100.0 per cent) were demanded admission for the infected child in the schools. Besides, majority (96.5 per cent) of the respondents were expected the facilities of treatment which is free from stigma along with other patients instead of treatment in special isolated ward and the larger proportion of respondents were suggested special care home for the abundant people with HIV positive. Greater percentage (82.0 per cent) of respondents were in need of financial assistance from the government to take self-employment to compensate the loss of income due to unemployment as result of their infection status.

The 81.5 per cent of respondents were in favour of creating alternative employment avenue for the sex workers to prevent them to continue their sex work after infection. The facilities of insurance for the people living with HIV positive are suggested by 78.5 per cent of people followed by reservation in the employment (41.5 per cent).

It is found from the table that all the infected people were expected the facilities of antiretroviral treatment, treatment along with other patients and financial assistance to cope up with the loss of employment due to HIV/AIDS.

CASE STUDIES

Case : 1

Vennila (name changed) is aged 31, studied upto 12th standard and working as a clerk in garment industry in Chennai. She got married at the age of 21 and her husband is a taxi driver working in a travel agency in Chennai. His frequent tour to various parts of the country influenced him to enjoy sex with various sex workers of different states and got infection even before his marriage. He confirmed his HIV positive status by blood test before getting marriage but he has not revealed it to any one including his parents. When his parents arranged marriage for him, he happily agreed without any guilt and he has not disclosed his HIV status to his wife and her family members not only before marriage but also after marriage. When Vennila became pregnant, her doctor suggested her to take HIV test which is mandatory test for pregnant women in

Tamil Nadu. The blood test confirmed that she is HIV positive. By knowing her HIV status she was shocked and made a lot of quarrel with her husband, her mother in-law and parents. She blamed her husband for passing HIV virus to her and refused to continue living with him. But her parents and in-laws forced her to live with him due to the fear of social criticism on the family as a result her desertion from her husband. She delivered a male baby with HIV negative status and now she is living with her husband and continue her work in garment industries in Chennai.

It is clear from this case that the women are the victims of HIV infection in the male dominated society. It is a social crime committed by men for transmitting the virus to his loyal and innocent wife

Case : 2

Gangammal (name changed) is aged 24, studied upto 10th standard and belong to poor agricultural family in Thirupathi, Andra Pradesh. She has aged parents and 3 adolescent sisters and 2 brothers. Her family is perennially marked by poverty, unemployment and inadequate income as a result of large family size and crop failure. Since her old parents are unable to involve in any productive activity, the family commitment has fallen on her shoulder. In view of her family's economic distress, taking advantage of possibility of getting employment in Tamil Nadu she moved out of her native place and entered into Chennai city with a view to seek decent gainful employment to take care of her family. Her hopes shattered when she understood that Chennai is not providing decent opportunity for her livelihood as against her previous understanding about Chennai.

Due to family compulsion and her disinterest to get back home forced her to come under the influence of women pimps in Chennai. Her involvement in prostitution is not informed to her family members. She visits to her family once in a month and provides money and gifts to parents and sisters and brothers. Her sexual engagement with a number of clients brought sexually transmitted diseases. She went for treatment in the sexually transmitted diseases clinics and she tested HIV positive. When she was told about her HIV/AIDS, she was unable to understand the infection. Later she understood that the infection carries severe stigma and discrimination and it affects not only her but also her family. Therefore, she has decided to keep it secretly unto herself. She continued her commercial sex work even after knowing her infection as there is no option left for her.

The inference is that there are a number of Gangammas living in our society. The social health of society would be affected severely if more number of Gangammas continue to involve in commercial sex even after knowing their infection status. Hence the social implication is severe. The strong taboo and stigma prevented Gangamma to reveal her HIV status and the economic necessity forced her to continue her sex work. She is infecting her clients every day, as she is young. Her clients may be young and unmarried; their future life is uncertain and dangerous

It is evident from this case that social and economic problems forced women to take to prostitution as an option for their survival without recognizing their social responsibility to prevent others from infection. Social taboo and stigma compelled sex workers to hide HIV status, if they are infected

Case : 3

Savithiri (name changed) is aged 23, illiterate and belong to a poor agricultural labour family in the remote village of Villupuram in Tamil Nadu. She has lost her parents during her childhood (at the age of 6) and was brought up under the care of her maternal grandmother. Being the agricultural labour family, her grand parents also lived under the condition of poverty and they harassed her and forced her to go for any work which generates income. Therefore, she ran way from her grand parents and went to Villupuram as a stranger. She was helped by a woman-a hotel owner. While she is working in the hotel she met another woman and believing her words she went along with her at the age of 8 with a view to get better job and income. Actually, the woman is the pimp and she has close contact with the brokers of child trafficking. The woman pimp sold Savithiri to the brokers at Villupuram. Then she is taken to Bangalore and from there to Mumbai.

The 8 year old Savithiri was harassed and severally beaten up and raped by the gang in the Bombay red light area. At this tender age she was forced to have sex with the older men with superstitious belief that sex with a child will cure all sexually transmitted infections. With no other option to escape, she started living with similar girls. During her routine check up for sexually transmitted diseases she was identified as HIV positive at the age of 17. She was not given any counselling. She knew nothing about AIDS except that it is a killer disease. The brothel keeper took her to Thambaram Thoracic Sanatorium, at Chennai and disappeared without informing her. The World Vision of India – an N.G.O. working for care and support for the people living with HIV positive helped her and shifted her to the short stay home.

In this case, it is clear that child racketing took place and violated the rights of the child and abused her, which is an incident of violence against childhood. The myth associated with sex with child and the cure of sexually transmitted disease increases child rape and child prostitution. Here also the girl child succumbs to innocent victim.

Case : 4

Nirmala (name changed) is a 21-year old woman, studied upto 10th standard and belong to an agricultural family in Ottanchatram in Dindigul District, Tamil Nadu. She got married at the age of 19 to her maternal uncle who is a lorry driver aged 27. From the third month of her marriage her husband fell sick frequently and took treatment in a private hospital at Coimbatore where he tested HIV positive. The medical advice forced Nirmala to take HIV test and her positive status was confirmed and revealed to her and family members. She was shocked to know her HIV status because she knew some thing related to AIDS, its route of transmission and its implication through various media. Since then she vehemently neglected her husband and refused to provide care and support to him. Her husband was given treatment by her parents and he died eight months after the marriage. She lived with him only for three months and got infected as a result of her marriage and she became widow at the younger age for none of her fault. She is now under the care and support of her parents and in-laws.

It is evident from this case that the innocent women are getting infected mostly through their marital partner.

Case : 5

Rathakrishnan (name changed) is a casual labour, aged 39, and studied upto higher secondary. He has two wives and 2 children aged 3 and 1. His nature of work necessitated him to move frequently to many places. During his mobility he had a contact with the sex worker and got infected and it was transmitted to his wives. When he tested HIV positive as a result of his continuous illness in the private hospital at Palani he was mentally shocked and fearful of his immature death. His mental shock made him to behave like an insane person and he unconsciously revealed his HIV status publicly in the village. He died within 6 months of his HIV test and none participated in his funeral except his family members. As a result of this revelation, the whole family is subjected to social boycott and social sanctions by the community. Their uninfected children are also facing the same discrimination and stigma. They are also not allowed to play with the children in the neighborhood. The widowed women are denied cooly work and all economic avenues outside their family are closed to them.

In this case the women again became the innocent victim of HIV infection in marital life. It is also evident that the stigma and discrimination are very strong in HIV/AIDS.

6

Summary of Major Findings, Suggestions and Conclusion

The study has been undertaken among the women living with HIV positive in Chennai City, Tamil Nadu. The major findings derived from the analysis and interpretations of primary data are summarized in this chapter.

MAJOR FINDINGS

The Social and Economic Status of Women Living with HIV Positive

Age of Respondents

The study revealed that a large number of respondents living with HIV positive fall in the age group of 20-29 years (66.5 per cent). The women in this age group are hyper active in reproduction as well as in social and economic activities. The increasing infection among women in sexually active age group will lead to great damage to human resources, national economy and social fabric of the society.

Community of Respondents

HIV/AIDS epidemic is not restricted to particular community. Though the infection is found among all the communities, women from the backward (46.6 per cent) and schedule caste (26 per cent) communities are worst affected by this dreaded disease. Limited or lack of access to information, lower social and economic status always force women to be sexually submissive to their sexual partner which prevent them to adopt safe sex mechanism.

Religion of Respondents

HIV/AIDS is not confined to particular religion. The people from all religions including Hindu, Muslim and Christian are vulnerable to HIV/AIDS. In this study, an overwhelming majority of respondents (85 per cent) belong to Hindu religion which is well known for its high moral and social values. The rapid spread of HIV among Hindus might be due to the changes occurring in the religious attitude of the youth in the contemporary society.

Education ofRespondents

A vast majority of the women (81.6 per cent) in the study are literate. Therefore, it is a myth that illiterate women are more vulnerable to HIV infection.

Social status of Respondents

Social status of the respondents is concerned, the majority (65.5 per cent) are housewives. The sex workers (31.0 per cent.) and students (3.5) are considerably less in this study. Housewives are more vulnerable to HIV/AIDS due to their husbands promiscuous behaviour.

Family Structure

As far as the structure of the family is concerned, the nuclear family (77 per cent) is predominant among the respondents. The joint family system can act as informal social control agent to check and control the behaviour of the individual. But in the contemporary society the elders have less control over the youth which led to the rapid spread of HIV infection in the nuclear families.

Dependent Family Members

Majority (63 per cent) of the respondents have dependent family members that increased the burden of the HIV infected women.

Educational Status of the Family Members

Literacy rate is high (81 per cent) among the members of respondents family.

Employment Status of Family Members

Overwhelming majority (59 per cent) of respondents family

members are engaged in unorganized sectors which give less income. The transport workers are found to be less (3.9 per cent) in the families of respondents.

Causes for Migration of Respondents to Chennai

Majority (62.5 per cent) of the respondents migrated to Chennai due to two major reasons namely marriage, and HIV infection. Marriage necessitated 27 per cent of women to migrate to Chennai whereas 13.5 per cent of respondents migrated to Chennai in order to hide their HIV status from their family members, relatives and friends as well as for treatment in the Tambaram Sanitarium nearby Chennai.

Economic Status of Respondents

Non-earner dependent (42.3) and earner dependents (33.5 per cent) are predominant in this study. The dependent women have either less or no power over their reproductive health which led to the contract of HIV/AIDS through their husbands.

Place of Residence

The study has identified that majority (42 per cent) of the respondents reside in urban areas and urban slums (58 per cent).

Occupation

The overwhelming majority (42 per cent) of respondents are unemployed. At the same time 30 per cent of women are engaged in unorganized sectors. The women in commercial sex work are also found in significant per centage (16.5 per cent). The power of negotiation about safe sex is strongly influenced by the economic empowerment of women. The unemployed and the women in unorganized sectors are economically deprived and they have less control over their reproductive health. The less or lack of power on reproductive health makes women more vulnerable to HIV/AIDS.

Ownership of Property

The majority (95.5 per cent) of women do not own any immovable assets. Women property right is not encouraged in the Indian society. In the patriarchal society, men dominate in all resources and the women are subordinate to men and hence lack ownership.

Annual Income and Expenditure

More than 65.5 per cent of respondents family incurred annual expenditure more than their annual income. The significant per centage (60 per cent) of respondents have borrowed amount ranging from Rs. 2,000-10,000 from various sources. Majority (59.2 per cent) of respondents borrowed money for medical treatment for HIV related illness of their husbands and children. Money lender is found to be the dominant sources of (54.2 per cent) lending money to the respondents. The medical treatment for HIV/AIDS made respondents to become indebted.

Marital Status of the Respondents

Marital Status

Married women are predominant (82.5 per cent) in this study. The unmarried women account for only 17.5 per cent. It is revealed that the married women are at the higher risk of contracting HIV infection.

Age at Marriage

The overwhelming majority (90.1 per cent) of the respondents got married when they were below 22 years. All the respondents married men who are 3-8 years older than them. The women have either no or less negotiation power with regard to their reproductive health choice due to their younger age. The age at marriage is an important factor for women in the Indian context to accept the male domination over their reproductive health. Therefore younger the age at marriage, higher the chance for getting infection through their husbands who experienced pre marital sex with multiple sexual partners.

Nature of Relationship between Respondents and their Husbands

Majority (84.2 per cent) of the respondents' marriage have taken place out side the close kin family relationship. Marriage with unfamiliar persons has high risk of contracting HIV. In this study, majority of husbands are not familiar with the respondents at the time of marriage. The sexual behaviour of the bride or bridegroom can be observed among the known person rather than the unknown person. Marriage among the familiar person has least chance for contracting HIV.

Type of Marriage

The infection rate is found to be high (66.1) in arranged marriages than the marriage based on mutual love (32.1 per cent). Arranged marriage with unknown persons has the high risk of contracting HIV rather than the marriage based on mutual love. In arranged marriages consideration is given only for horoscope and related matters of match making instead of personal background of individual proposed for marriage.

Causes for Respondents Widowhood

One-fourth (25.5 per cent) of the respondents are widows. Majority (92.1 per cent) of the respondents became widows due to the death of their HIV infected husbands. It revealed that their husbands got infected long back and even before marriage. Therefore, mortality rate is high among the infected men.

Age at Widowhood and Duration of Married Life

The majority (88.2 per cent) of the women age at widowhood is identified as 20-25 years and majority (72.5 per cent) of respondents lived with their husbands only for 1-5 years. Therefore, younger the age at marriage higher the chance for becoming widow at younger age due to HIV/AIDS.

Causes for Separation

Nearly one-fifth of the respondents (19.0 per cent) are separated women. HIV/AIDS is identified as major cause for the separation of majority (65.8 per cent) of respondents. The infection of HIV among any one of the spouse disturb the family life and it challenge the sacramental nature of marital bonds.

Employment Status of the Husbands

Of the 165 married respondents, the majority (35.8 per cent) of their husbands are casual labourers and industrial workers (20.0 per cent). The transport workers are comparatively less (16.4 per cent). Due to the migratory nature work the casual labourers are more prone to HIV infection

Reasons for Unmarried Status of Respondents

Involvement in sex work and dowry prevented majority (48.6 per cent) of respondents to get marriage.

Circumstances Leading to HIV Infection and Related Behaviours

Duration of HIV Infection

Majority (81.0 per cent) of the respondents understood their HIV status since seven years during their young and sexually hyper active age.

Sources of Infection

The overwhelming majority (65.0 per cent) of the women were infected through their husbands. At the same time significant per centage (34.5 per cent) of women got infection through their multi sexual behaviour which includes married women (31.0 per cent) and students (3.5 per cent). It revealed that the promiscuous sexual behaviour of women not only led her to acquire HIV/AIDS but it also increases the vulnerability of infection to their husbands and it is identified that 17.6 per cent of respondents husbands might be infected with HIV/AIDS due to the promiscuous behaviour of women.

Husbands Infected by Respondents

Of the 158 married respondents, 130 (65.0 per cent) got infection through their husbands whereas the remaining 35 per cent got infection through their behaviours of sex work and injecting drug use. Their husbands are highly prone to HIV infection. These 35 per cent of respondents' husbands are highly ignorant about their infection and they are also not aware of their wives HIV infection.

Pre and Extra Marital Sexual Behaviour

The majority (76.9 per cent) of women experienced pre marital sex with the men who are known to her, for example, relatives, family friend, friends, neighbour and co-workers. It revealed that the women pre marital sex is confined with the people who are close to them. Significant per centage (15.0 per cent) of respondents experienced extra marital sex with those who are regularly patronising them. It increases not only their vulnerability towards HIV but also their innocent husbands.

Majority (82.4 per cent) respondents husbands are promiscuous and among them the significant per centage (66.7 per cent) have experienced pre marital sex mostly (49.1 per cent) with sex workers. Pre marital sex of the men increases the vulnerability of infection of innocent wives.

Reasons for Respondents Husbands Extra Marital Sexual Behaviour

Majority (51.8 per cent) of the respondents husbands also involved in extra marital sex with sex workers (92.9 per cent). Their sexual involvement with commercial sex workers resulted in HIV/AIDS. Migration (30.2 per cent) and alcoholic behaviour (22.6 per cent) appears to be important factors for the development of extra marital affairs of the respondents husbands. Since they satisfy their sexual urge with sex workers they have increased chance of contracting infection and spreading it to their wives.

Reasons for Respondents Pre and Extra Marital Relationships

Love affair is the major (43.5 per cent) cause for pre marital sex and difference of opinion between the spouses are the significant (50.0 per cent) reason for extra marital sex of the respondents.

Safe Sex Practices in the Pre and Extra Marital Relationship

Condom usage is found to be low among the respondents who have experienced pre (15.4 per cent) and extra marital (8.8 per cent) sex. The practice of oral pills is higher among the women experienced pre marital sex (53.8 per cent) and adoption of sterilization is high among the respondents experienced extra marital sex (41.2 per cent). These respondents are very much bothered about avoiding pregnancy due to cultural implications of giving birth out side wedlock. The culture surrounding around the notion of pregnancy increases the vulnerability of women towards HIV/AIDS.

Significant per centage of respondents engaged in pre (30.8) and extra marital (23.6 per cent) sex are not practicing any method of safe sex to prevent sexually transmitted infection as well as child birth. The culture of silence around sex and the fear to ask or to buy condom increases the vulnerability of women's HIV infection. The sterilization also led women not to use condom since they are already safe in avoiding pregnancy.

Reproductive Behaviour among Housewives

Housewives give more importance to avoid pregnancy rather than sexually transmitted infections. Adoption of sterilization, oral pills and IUDs prevented majority (62.6 per cent) of housewives to think about condom as safe sex method to safeguard themselves from sexually transmitted infections.

Circumstances Leading to Commercial Sex Work

Marital Status of Sex Workers

The majority (54.8 per cent) of sex workers are married women and among them 43.5 per cent have husbands and children. The unmarried respondents in sex work are accounted for 45.2 per cent. The responsibilities on catering the needs of the family members force the women, especially the married women to involve in exchanging sex for money. Their engagement in multiple sex is considered as potential sources of contracting HIV/AIDS. The husbands of these sex workers also have greater possibility of contracting HIV/AIDS through them.

Reasons for the Involvement in Commercial Sex Work

Poverty and related economic deprivation of the family is the central factor for the involvement of 77.3 per cent respondents in commercial sex. The economical necessities force the commercial sex workers to be less empowered with regard to demanding condom use with their customers. Unsafe sex is the major contributing factor for contracting HIV.

Age at Induction in Commercial Sex Work

The significant per centage (51.6 per cent) of sex workers inducted in sex at the young age of within 23 years. It indicate that early involvement in sex involve longer duration of sexual participation which has strong influence on the risk of contracting HIV/AIDS. Due to younger age the sex workers have less negotiation power with regard to safe sex which has strong influence both for contracting and spread of HIV/AIDS.

Clients of Commercial Sex Workers

Labourers (38.7 per cent), business people (37.1 per cent), tourist (33.9 per cent), transport workers, including drivers and cleaners (27.4 per cent), students (21 per cent) and men who are away from home for longer duration (17.7 per cent) are identified as dominant categories of clients who visit commercial sex workers quite often.

Safe Sex Practices of Clients

Safe sex practice is significant among business (30.6 per cent) people and transport workers (25.6 per cent). The safe sex practice is found to be less among labourers (3.2 per cent). Unsafe sex practice and use of alcohol is closely related HIV/AIDS. The overwhelming majority (97.3 per cent) of respondents customers have the habit of drinking alcohol and due to the influence of alcohol the customers are not in a mental state to use condom as safe sex. The unsafe sex between the sex workers and their customers increases the vulnerability of infection for sex workers and their customers.

Number of Clients Engaged Per Day

All the 27 part time sex workers are married and they have husband and children. The part time sex workers engage less number of clients (1-2) per day rather than the full time sex workers (3-6). The full time sex workers include 28 unmarried girls, four widows and three deserted. As a result of frequent sexual encounter with multiple partners the full time sex workers are more prone to HIV/AIDS.

Earning Per Day

The majority (88.9 per cent) of part time sex workers earn less Rs. 300 per day where as the majority (62.8 per cent) of the full time sex workers earn upto Rs. 400 per day. The sex workers are taking risk of contracting HIV/AIDS by involving in multiple sex for earning considerable amount for their survival.

Sources of Contact with the Clients

Most of the full time sex workers (33.9 per cent) contact and pick their clients directly from the crowded places like bus stand, railway station, market, beach, tourist centres etc. The majority (19.4 per cent) of the part time sex workers use modern communication technology including mobile phone, e-mail to contact the customers who are regular to them. The 17.7 per cent of part time sex workers also have a close link with the brokers to meet their customers. The part time sex workers choose particular place for their sex work and they returned home like other employed women.

Network and Place of Residence

The sex workers have strong invisible net work to contact fellow sex workers as well as customers in Chennai and most (37.1 per cent) of the sex workers are residing in slums which is known for many illegal activities. The poor social and economic background of the sex workers residing in slum will not acquire power of negation of safe sex with their customers.

Nature of Sex Work

The majority (50 per cent) of the respondents involved in sex work independently and 27.5 per cent are under the influence of brokers. The economic necessity resulted many impoverished women to choose prostitution as a means for their survival.

Reason for not Insisting the Clients to use Condom

Lack of awareness on the implication of HIV/AIDS is the major factor for 59.7 per cent of sex workers who do not insist their clients to use condom. The lack of safe sex practices has spread effect for both the sex workers and their customers.

Reason for not Using Condoms by the Clients

Drinking of alcohol prevents majority (38.7 per cent) of customers to use condom during paid sex. The intoxicative mental state has direct influence on unsafe sex and behavioural change with regard to sex and sexuality.

Changes in the Sexual Behaviour of the Sex Workers after Knowing their HIV Infection

Majority (53.2 per cent) of women continues sex work even after knowing their HIV status but significant change in the sexual behaviour of the sex workers with regard to safe sex is observed after HIV infection. At the same time significant per centage (46.7 per cent) of sex workers are withdrawn their involvement from sex work after knowing their HIV infection. It revealed that these sex workers have realized their role in transmitting the virus to the innocent clients.

Present Status of the Sex Workers after Knowing their HIV Infection

After the withdrawal from the sex work due to infection, the 42 per cent of sex workers found alternative avenues for their survival with the support of non-governmental and governmental organisations.

Causes for Remaining in Sex Work after Knowing HIV Infection

Lack of alternative job and less income in other job made 53.2 per cent of sex workers to remain in the same work even after knowing their HIV status. The spread effect of HIV is higher due to the involvement of women in sex work with HIV status.

Awareness on HIV/AIDS and Willingness to be in Special Home

After knowing the infection all the sex workers are aware of their role in transmitting the virus to their clients. At the same time they are not willing to stay in the special home if it is run for the infected people. The stigma and discrimination prevent the infected sex workers to be lodged in special home since it has the label which carries HIV positive.

HIV Test

Places of HIV Test

Majority (61.5 per cent) of the respondents tested their HIV status in government hospitals. The government hospitals have the facilities for HIV test at free of cost. It facilitated the respondents to take HIV test in government hospitals.

Factors Influencing HIV Test

HIV status of the respondents husband influenced more than 50 per cent of respondents to take HIV test. The Sexually

Transmitted Diseases (STD) and its related illness in other important factors which forced the women to take HIV test.

Pre and Post Test Counseling to the Respondents and their Family Members

More than 75 per cent of the respondents and their family members are not exposed to pre and post test counseling to understand fully about the HIV, its social impact, care and support and living with HIV peacefully by coping with social stigma. The absence of pre and post test counseling for the respondents and their family members led to discrimination, personality disorder and lack of confidence to live with HIV status.

Knowledge on HIV/AIDS at the Time of Testing

The majority (74 per cent) of respondents have no knowledge on HIV/AIDS when they have undergone HIV test in various hospitals. Lack of awareness on HIV/AIDS at the time of testing created fear and lost confidence and courage to share their infection with their family members.

Impact of HIV Status in the Social Relationship in Family

Revelation of HIV/AIDS of the Respondents

The revelation of HIV infection is high (66.9 per cent) among the housewives and high secrecy is maintained among the women who got HIV through their heterosexual contact and injecting drug use. The cultural taboo on promiscuous relationship not allowed the multisexual women to share their infection with their family members.

Sources of Revelation of HIV

Majority (90.8 per cent) of respondents HIV status is revealed to their family members through the hospital where they underwent HIV test. Respondents husbands HIV status revealed to the family members mostly (64.4 per cent) through the respondents. HIV revelation to any individual is insisted only after proper guidance and counseling. More than 90 per cent of the respondents HIV status is revealed without counseling.

Guidance and counseling have direct influence on the social relationship of infected persons.

Respondents Husbands Awareness about his HIV Infection before Marriage

The vast majority (90.8 per cent) of respondents husbands are not aware of their infection before their marriage. They married with the ignorance of their HIV status and they infected their innocent wives unknowingly. The absence of mandatory HIV test before marriage increases the vulnerability of infection for the women after their marriage.

Husbands' Reaction Towards Wives after Knowing Infection

Majority (60.6 per cent) of respondents infected husbands harassed their wives after knowing their HIV status. Though the men fully aware that their wives got infection through them and they are the innocent victims of infection, they involved in harassing their wives due to guilt and shame.

Respondents Reaction Towards Husbands Infection

Majority (57.7 per cent) of respondents have not provided care and support for their infected husbands. At the same time 42.3 per cent of respondents supported their husbands due to the cultural bound existed between husband and wife in the Indian Society. The culture of marriage and family made majority (42.3 per cent) women to remain with their infected husbands.

The Relationship between Respondents and Husbands after Knowing HIV Infection

The relationship between husband and wife after knowing HIV infection is not compassionate and majority (49.2 per cent) have involved in frequent quarrel with each other. The stigma associated with promiscuous relationship and HIV/AIDS led to family dispute resulting in family disintegration.

Reaction of in-laws

Discrimination towards the infected women by the in-laws is comparatively higher (86.3 per cent) than their husbands (48.3

per cent). The significant per centage (32.2 per cent) of respondents are socially isolated by their in-laws. The Indian culture is always favourable to men and his promiscuous relationship is tolerated by their family members. Due to the tolerance based on cultural influence the infected men is comparatively experience less discrimination than infected women.

Reaction of Parents

The majority (70.1 per cent) of respondents parents give support to the respondents rather than the respondents husbands (20.7 per cent). Very less number of respondents and their husbands are socially isolated by the parents of respondents. In view of the fact that the housewives get infection through their husbands they get more support from their parents. At the same time the widowed and deserted (3.5 per cent) women have not got support from their parents due to the infection as a result of promiscuous relationship. The majority (64.7 per cent) of the unmarried sex workers got support from their parents after sharing their HIV status with them. It revealed that they are involved in sex work with the knowledge of their parents.

Nature of Restriction Imposed by Family Members on HIV Infected Persons

Majority of the housewives (85.1 per cent), their husbands (79.3 per cent), sex workers (57.2 per cent) and infected children (57.2 per cent) are restricted to casual contact, for example, touching and sharing articles and to take part in the socio cultural ceremonies of the family. The stigma associated with HIV/AIDS is the primary factor for such restriction imposed on people living with HIV positive.

Decision taken in the Family before and after Infection

The role of people living with HIV positive in decision-making process has affected due to their infection. Before knowing HIV status, the respondents husbands (40.5 per cent) played a dominant role in taking decision with regard to their family affairs. At the same time significant per centage (24.5 per cent) of respondents are consulted by their husbands while taking decision. The parents and in-laws played insignificant role in taking decision related to respondents families. But after infection majority (33.5 per cent) of the respondents and their husbands have not participated in decision making and it indicated a way to their parents and in-laws to take decision with regard to their family affairs.

Participation in the Socio-cultural Ceremonies in the Family

More than 70 per cent of the respondents are not participating in the socio cultural ceremonies of the family due to the fear of discrimination. They voluntarily restricted their participation in such functions. The status of HIV resulted in self imposed restriction and lack of courage to associate with the family members.

Maintenance and Property given to the Deserted and Widows

The majority of the widows (74.5 per cent) and separated women (92 per cent) have not been given property or maintenance support for their survival. The infected women are deprived of getting property or maintenance from their husbands side due to the perception that the infected people will have short life.

The Place of Present Stay of the Respondents

The significant per centage (58.5 per cent) of infected women are living along with husband or children. The abundant infected sex workers (12 per cent) got accommodation in short stay home run by the NGOs.

Social Relationship with Neighbourhood

Infection Known to the Neighbours

The people living with HIV positive are maintaining secrecy of their infection from their neighbours due to the problem of stigma and discrimination. The overwhelming majority (97.7 per cent) of respondents and their husbands infection is not known to their neighbours.

Social Relationship of Respondents and their Husbands with Neighbourhood

The majority (92.0 per cent) of respondents and their husbands have good relationship with their neighbours before they know their HIV positive status. They participated in all socio cultural functions of their neighbours. But after knowing their infection, 72 per cent have voluntarily withdrawn their participation in socio cultural ceremonies of their neighbours due to guilt and shame. The fear of stigma associated with the diseases resulted in self imposed restriction among the people living with HIV positive.

Neighbours Interaction Towards People with HIV Status

Very least per centage (1.5 per cent) of respondents infection is known to their neighbours. All these respondents were socially distanced by their neighbours. Therefore, social distance is the common response from the neighbours towards the people living with HIV positive.

Reasons for the Discrimination by the Neighbours

Fear of contracting infection is the major (67.0 per cent) cause for stigmatizing and discriminating the infected people. The general population still has a belief that they get infected if they have a causal relationship with the infected persons. The poor awareness on the mode of spread of infection created such kind of fear among the general population

Person Blamed for Respondents Infection by the Neighbours

Only three (1.5 per cent) respondents infection was known to their neighbours. All the three are blamed for their infection by the neighbours for their ignorance and inability to control their husband from extra-marital affairs.

Effects of Discrimination on theEespondents

The three respondents migrated to other areas as they were fear of facing the isolation by the neighbours. The discrimination by the neighbours led to migration of infected people.

Social Relationship with Friends

Frequency of Respondents, their Husbands with their Friends before and After Infection

The majority (64.5 per cent) of the respondents and their husbands (77.2 per cent) have frequent contact with their friends before knowing their HIV status. Their relationship with the friends has drastically changed after knowing their HIV status. The majority (42.5 per cent) of infected respondents were completely out of their friendship circle and at the same time 50 per cent of their husbands have frequent contact with their friends. The infected women were more reluctant to meet their friends than their husbands. The myth that the immoral people or the multisexual alone get HIV made women to restrict their contact with their friends.

Disclosure of HIV Status by Respondents to the Friends

The majority of the respondents (82.0 per cent) and their husbands (82.3 per cent) have not disclosed their HIV status to their friends. The revelation of HIV status is found to be high among the sex workers (51.6 per cent) than the housewives (3.1 per cent), students (0.0 per cent) and drug users (0.0 per cent). The stigma and discrimination associated with AIDS made the respondents to maintain high confidentiality about their infection.

Reaction of the Friends Towards the Respondents Infection

Majority (58.4 per cent) of the respondents and their husbands (74.0 per cent) are getting moral and financial support from their friends. But when compared to men less number of infected women are getting support from their friends.

Social Relationship with Relatives

Respondents, Husbands Infection Status known to the Relatives

Very few (36.5 per cent) respondents and their husbands have revealed their HIV status to their relatives. The revelation is high among the housewives (70.4 per cent) than the sex workers (29.6 per cent). The housewives innocent victims and they got infection through their husbands. Therefore, they are comparatively comfortable to share their infection to their relatives. The cultural restriction towards promiscuous contact prevents sex workers in sharing their infection with their relatives.

Reaction of the Relatives Towards Respondents and their Husbands

One-third of the respondents are isolated by their relatives after revelation of their HIV status. Social isolation by the relatives is high among the sex workers than the housewives. One fifth of the relatives have restricted their visit to the respondents house. Very few (16.4 per cent) respondents got moral and financial support from their relatives. While comparing the discrimination experienced by infected respondents and their husbands, the infected women are subjected to severe discrimination and criticism by the relatives than their husbands. The 50 per cent Of respondents husbands got moral and financial support from their relatives. It revealed that due to the influence of culture, men's extra marital sex is tolerated by the society.

Frequency of Visit by Respondents and their Husbands to the Relatives House

Before knowing their infection status more than 50 per cent of the respondents and their husbands visited their relatives house regularly for various social functions. After knowing the infection status around 55 per cent of respondents and their husbands have stopped their visit to their relatives house due to the fear of criticism and discrimination. Though the majority of the infected women and men were not disclosed their HIV status to their relatives, they themselves felt guilty and developed fear owing to stigma associated with AIDS and withdrawn their social participation with their relatives.

Participation in the Socio-cultural Ceremonies by Respondents

Before infection, 70.5 per cent of married respondents participated in the socio-cultural ceremonies of relatives house along with their husbands. In the case of unmarried respondents, deserted and widows their parents have participated in the socio cultural ceremonies of their relatives house. After infection, significant changes have taken place in the participation of respondents in the socio-cultural ceremonies of relatives house. As against 70.5 per cent of participation, only 18 per cent have taken part in the socio-cultural ceremonies after infection. The fear of discrimination resulted in self imposed restriction by the respondents in participating all functions in the relatives house.

Persons Blamed for Respondents and their Husbands Infection

The majority (83.7 per cent) of the respondents are blamed not only for their infection but also for their husbands infection though they got infection through their husbands. The gender biased and baseless discrimination created inferiority complex among the infected women resulting in self imposed isolation from the society.

Discrimintion in Medical Treatment

Medical Treatment Seeking Behaviour of the Infected People

Treatment seeing behaviour for the infection is found to be high (100 per cent) among the full time sex workers and housewives (68.5 per cent), part time sex workers (0.0 per cent), students (0.0 per cent) and drug user (0.0 per cent). The respondents who maintain high confidentiality with regard to their infection is not taking treatment for their HIV related illness. While comparing the treatment seeking behaviour with infected husband, the women get less priority than men. The majority (94.6 per cent) of respondents husbands avail treatment for their illness. The gender discrimination in medical treatment prevents many women from availing treatment for their illness.

Place of Treatment

The N.G.Os played a vital role in providing treatment to the respondents either at free of cost or by charging very less amount. Majority of the housewives (41.5 per cent) and sex workers (74.3 per cent) availed treatment in the N.G.Os which is working in AIDS intervention programmes. While comparing the place of treatment by the respondents and their husbands, 66.9 per cent of respondents' husbands got treatment in the private hospital by paying considerable amount. The economic power vested with the men facilitated them to avail treatment in private hospitals. Taking treatment in the private hospitals also helped them to hide their infection status from others. Lack of control over economic resources increased gender discrimination in treatment.

Person Met the Expenditure of Medical Treatment

Significant per centage (26.9 per cent) of housewives gave preference for their husbands treatment rather than their treatment. They are also involved in incurring the expenditure of their husbands treatment. The sex workers spent amount by themselves for their treatment. Besides, 39.2 per cent of housewives medical expenses had been met by their parents rather than their in-laws and husbands.

Problem Faced by the Respondents in the Hospitals

The overwhelming majority (96 per cent) of women faced discrimination in the hospitals. The health care personnel have an opinion that the women get infection through their promiscuous contact. Though the health care personnel are aware of the means of the spread of HIV, they are more reluctant to treat the infected patients and they discriminated them by denying admission in the hospitals, maintaining confidentiality of infection, calling them with the label of AIDS patient etc. The discrimination in the health care sector is mainly due to irresponsibility of medical personnel.

Discrimination in the Place of Work

Employment Status of the Respondents

The majority (58.6 per cent) of the respondents have taken up job only after knowing their HIV status. The widowhood and separation due to AIDS and heavy medical expenses to treat opportunistic infection are the major causes for the women to go for employment after knowing their HIV status.

Discrimination Experienced by the Respondents and their Husbands

The 20.7 per cent of respondents employed in Tamil Nadu State AIDS Control Society and N.G.Os working in AIDS intervention and Control Project have revealed their HIV status to their employer and colleagues. Though the revelation of HIV status brought them certain monetary benefit, they faced discrimination in different forms. Whenever the visitors come to these organisations, the employee with HIV status is introduced by them as HIV infected people. Such kind of introduction resulted in certain psychological problem which always made them to think about early death due to AIDS.

Attitude Towards Pregnancy and Childbirth after Infection

Number of Children Born before and after Infection of Respondents

The majority (96.4 per cent) of respondents gave birth to children before infection. The respondents who gave birth after infection account for14.5 per cent and the majority of the children (48.3 per cent) born to the respondents after infection are infected by HIV.

Causes for Pregnancy after Infection

The respondents who have given birth after infection is accounted for 17.5 per cent from the 165 married respondents. Lack of awareness on mother to child transmission (34.5 per cent) and lack of practices of birth control measures (44.8 per cent) are the major causative factor for the pregnancy of women after infection.

Reaction of Respondents and her Husbands about Pregnancy after Infection

The majority (89.7 per cent) of respondents and their husbands have decided to terminate the pregnancy after knowing the impact of infection on their children. The high cost in antiretroviral treatment to prevent mother to child transmission force the respondents and their husbands to think about the termination of pregnancy.

Reaction of the Doctors Towards the Infected Pregnant Respondents

The majority (82.8 per cent) of respondents have asked to terminate the pregnancy by the doctors and they denied admission and treatment in the hospitals. Due to the fear of facing discrimination, 41.4 per cent of respondents delivered their baby in the home with the support of local midwives without informing their HIV status. At the same time 58.6 per cent of pregnant respondents went to the hospital only at the time of labour pain and got admission without revealing their

HIV status. The existing discrimination towards people living with HIV positive increased the possibility of taking treatment by the infected people by hiding their infection status. It may increase the risk of infection for the people working in the health care sectors.

Reproductive Sexual Behaviour of Respondents

The majority (40.5 per cent) of respondents have adopted non-terminal method of contraception including oral pills (10.5 per cent), IUDs (14.0 per cent) and condom (16.0 per cent) to avoid pregnancy. Significant per centage (17 per cent) has undergone sterilization to avoid pregnancy after knowing their infection. Condom usage is not popular among married women rather than the women in sex work. The unmarried women have taken the decision to avoid marriage in order to further spread of infection to others.

Attitude of Respondents towards Pregnancy and Child birth

The infected women are in favour of pregnancy right and many (47.5 per cent) respondents are unaware of mother to child transmission and the availability of antiretroviral treatment (50.0 per cent) to prevent child from getting infection from mothers.

Respondents Expectation for Child Care and Positive Parenthood

Majority of respondents expected the facilities of antiretroviral treatment (100 per cent), treatment along with other patients (96.5 per cent), financial assistance (82.0 per cent) to cope up with lose of employment due to HIV/AIDS and life insurance (78.5 per cent) for the people living with HIV positive. They also expected the provision of admission of children in schools (100 per cent), special care home for the abundant women and children with HIV/AIDS (94.5 per cent) and rehabilitation of sex workers by providing alternative employment opportunities (81.5 per cent). They have all suggested that the Government should ensure these facilities for the people living with HIV positive.

SUGGESTIONS

1. Since most of the women are getting infection only after their marriage from their infected husband. Therefore, both the women and men should be motivated to voluntary testing of HIV before marriage for both bride and groom. In order to ensure HIV test, all marriage should be registered under the Marriage Act and a certificate of HIV positive test should be produced at the time of registration.
2. Poverty plays a vital role in the existence of prostitution. The women who are in sex work should be rehabilitated or they should be provided alternative avenues for their survival. This can be possible by associating the sex workers with the women self help group for micro credit. The Department of Social Welfare and Corporation for Women's Development could play a significant role in this regard.
3. Defective socialization is the primary cause for sex outside the marriage. Family and schools are the primary agencies to socialize the individual in accordance with the expectation of the societal norm. Counseling centres should be established in all schools and colleges with the involvement of Sociologist. Community counseling centres should also be established in all villages and towns in co-ordination with local N.G.Os to provide counseling and education to the parents and youths.
4. Exposure to multi media due to the implication of globalization, peer group pressure, modern communication facilities and easy availability of paid sex directly influence the youth to experience pre marital sex. The youth should be advocated the implication of pre marital sex and the importance of having sex after marriage. The youth forum should be formulated in all schools, colleges, villages, towns and cities with the support of N.G.Os , academicians and local government leaders to sensitize the implication of pre marital sex in the context of HIV/AIDS.

5. HIV/AIDS information, its implication and preventive mechanism should reach to the door step of each and every house. This is only possible through mass media, especially through television. The information related to AIDS should be telecasted in all channels frequently between the serials or programmes like other advertisements. The same may also help to overcome stigma and discrimination associated with HIV/AIDS.
6. HIV/AIDS Care Centre should be established in every district with financial support of Government to provide shelter to the abandoned people living with HIV positive.
7. Migration, especially rural to urban migration has direct influence on contracting HIV by youth and transmitting the virus to the housewives. Rural migration owing to economic necessity should be controlled by creating employment opportunities by using locally available resources in the villages and extending financial support to the youth to establish their own enterprises in the village.
8. Gender inequalities should be addressed in all possible ways to empower the women to control over their reproductive health. Women should be educated to negotiate safe sex with their husbands without any hesitation. Gender Sensitization through mass media is a step in the right direction.
9. Culture and tradition of Indian society acting as stumbling block for the implementation of AIDS intervention programmes. The culture prevents people to negotiate issues on reproductive health. Therefore, the culture and tradition of each and every society should be taken into consideration while planning AIDS intervention programmes.
10. Sex education should be incorporated in school and college curriculum in order to influence the students to share their feelings and doubts with regard to their general health and reproductive health without any inhibitions.

11. Government should enact strict law to prevent cross border and internal trafficking of women and girls for sexual exploitation.
12. The reproductive health programme should be incorporated with the programmes of family planning in order to educate the women not only on the methods of fertility control but also the AIDS, route of spread, its implication, safe sex and prevention and control.
13. People living with HIV positive are experiencing various kinds of discrimination in the hospitals. The health care personnel should have the commitment to treat all the patients equally irrespective of their diseases. The discrimination in the hospitals resulted in strengthening the discrimination in the society. Therefore, the health care personnel should be given regular orientation with regard to the treatment of people living with HIV positive.
14. Every Government hospital should have exclusive ward for HIV/AIDS patients with specialized doctors and other medical personnel. It will promote treatment seeking behaviour among the people living with HIV positive.
15. All red light areas in India should be abolished in order to arrest sale of illegal sex, trafficking of girls and the spread of HIV to the general population.
16. Under existing law the sex workers are punished rather than the men who seek sex from them. Therefore, effective law should be enacted to give severe punishment to the women who involve in prostitution as well as to the men who seek sex from prostitutes.
17. The Members of Parliament and Legislative Assemblies should be given target to ensure AIDS free status to their respective constituency.
18. In India, especially in Tamil Nadu, women self help groups are emerging as powerful agents in the social transformation of villages as well as empowering the women in family and community. Therefore, women

self help group should be encouraged to participate in implementing AIDS intervention programmes in their respective areas. Their participation in AIDS intervention programmes will help to eliminate stigma and discrimination associated with AIDS and to bring family and community care to the people living with HIV positive.

19. The local panchayat members should be trained to take up AIDS intervention programmes in their panchayat. The participation of panchayat members in the AIDS intervention programmes will help to prevent and control HIV/AIDS in rural areas.
20. Financial support should be strengthened to the N.G.Os by the Government to ensure regular intervention programmes in all sections of the community.

CONCLUSION

In the span of just two decade, AIDS has turned into an epidemic affecting millions of men, women and children in all countries. It becomes a serious public health problem and expresses the intensity of seriousness the popular term 'Pandemic' is associated with AIDS. The continued spread of HIV is not only threatening millions of lives, but is also either slowing or reversing the progress made in the social and economic development of the countries. The epidemic continues to develop in the atmosphere of fear, prejudice, stigma, silence and discrimination. In spite of serious AIDS intervention programmes to create awareness and advocacy, denial still exists in all sections of society. India is rapidly becoming the epicenter of the AIDS epidemic. Its mobile population and their families, women and children living under hazardous or exploitative conditions and women and children under trafficking are highly vulnerable to HIV/AIDS. Effective law is the urgent requirement to create internal employment opportunities and to check migration, criminal net work of prostitution and trafficking.

Social inequalities, gender discrimination and cultural prejudice made women and children to become the worst victims of HIV/AIDS. The low social and economic status of women and dependence on men limit their control over their sexual and reproductive lives. The power imbalance, violence, and abuse in the family and society increase the chances for women to get exposure to HIV and other sexually transmitted diseases.

Women in sex work are most defenseless and they have no power to insist their customers to use condom. They have not taken this profession on their own choice. Abject poverty, domestic abuse and violence, destitution and abduction and trafficking have pushed these women into this profession. Appalling living condition, entertaining many clients in a day, lack of power to negotiate condom use make them most vulnerable to HIV infection.

Economic uncertainty and growing rural unemployment and underemployment resulted in rural migration. Separation from the family and the hazardous nature of work forces the migrant to seek pleasure with sex workers. The poor access to reproductive health information and AIDS increased not only their vulnerability to HIV but also to their wives. In the context of HIV/AIDS, housewives are adversely affected and they are prone to get infection through their husbands in the marital life which is described as sacrament. Gender insensitivity, discrimination, lack of social and economic status and basic rights reduce the access of women to gain knowledge on HIV/AIDS and its prevention. Economic dependence, social expectations of wives and fear of disrupting family life are powerful disincentives for wives to insist on the use of condoms, especially in environments in which sexual issues are not an acceptable topic for discussion even between husbands and wives. Marriage has given right to men to have unprotected sex with their wives and it also expected wives that accepting unprotected sex of their husband is their responsibility. Moreover, where conception is the desired outcome of marital sexual relations, the use of a condom for protection is unavailable and it is considered as taboo in India. Advocating condom usage in the marital life will not help to promote safe sex and preventing HIV among the innocent wives. Alternative strategy is needed with the consideration of cultural implication and traditional attitude towards sex and sexuality in the marital life.

As consequences of HIV/AIDS, women has to shoulder triple burden – facing stigma and discrimination and caring sick and bearing loss of income in the family. The study has revealed that women experienced more discrimination in the society rather than men. The discrimination is higher in the family due to lack of counseling to the family members and poor knowledge and misconception of HIV/AIDS.

The study further highlighted that the care and support system to the people living with HIV positive in the society is non-existent. Family and community care is essential not only to provide moral support to the infected people but also to control further spread of HIV to the innocent women and to the larger society.

The awareness and knowledge in the practice of safe sex is not correlated in the marital life due to certain cultural importance given to sex and procreation. The notion of sex and sexuality in the Indian context is acting as an obstacle to create safe ground for women to protect themselves from the dreaded infection HIV/AIDS. The power imbalance in interpersonal relationships and in society which create women's subordination must change if women are to be able to protect themselves from HIV/AIDS infection and its consequences. This can be possible through empowerment of women with regard to their reproductive health and it should be given high priority in all matters related to HIV/AIDS. The empowerment of women alone help to realize the dream of AIDS free society.

Commitment from all sections – political, religion, academic, family, health care sector, Government, Non-governmental organisation, public, mass media – is essential to mobilize the people to join together to fight against AIDS to create AIDS free India. Social transformation through Millennium Development Goals in Indian context involves this coordination to realize the vision of HIV/AIDS free world with a missionary zeal. The success depends through value education, morality and social ethics based life among people. The task in this regard is voluminous, l*et al.*l people living in the 21st century take a collective pledge to root out this Global killer as a challenge. IF THERE IS WILL DEFINIELY THERE IS A WAY.

7

Implication of the Research

Based upon the issues highlighted in this study, an attempt is made here to suggest a suitable plan of action towards prevention and control of HIV/AIDS. The major aspects considered under the plan are stated below along with relevant details.

AIDS is not only a medical problem but it is also a social problem. Social responsibility or collective responsibility is the prerequisite for tackling any social problems. With this perspective the model suggested for action is an Integrated Model. This model integrates social and medical aspects with due consideration of cultural values in the society.

Integrated Approach to Provide Care and Support to Women Infected with HIV Positive

Integrated approach is needed to ensure commitment from all sections of population in India to provide care and support to women infected with HIV positive and to establish AIDS free society. The social institution of family, community, hospitals, N.G.Os, women self-help groups and government can be integrated to fight against AIDS and to provide care and support and relief and rehabilitation to the infected and affected people.

Creation of Mechanism for Collection of DATA

Collection of relevant primary data with regard to number of women infected by HIV and circumstances leading to HIV is highly important to formulate policy and plan appropriate intervention programmes for the care and support and relief and rehabilitation of women infected with HIV positive. At present, the Government of India is estimating the number of women with HIV positive based on the sentinel surveillance cases from different government hospitals. The present method provides no accurate information about the number of women infected with HIV and causes and consequences of HIV on women. Therefore, alternative mechanism can be evolved to get the reliable data and information about women infected with HIV positive.

The data on women infected with HIV can be collected not only from Government hospitals and its voluntary testing and counselling centres butlllllll also from private hospitals and private labs. It will help to know the actual rate of infection among women and to plan policy and programmes for prevention and control of HIV among women, care and support and relief and rehabilitation of infected women.

Sensitization of Women with HIV Positive to Take Self Care

Women with HIV positive are either ignorant or lack of knowledge about HIV/AIDS and positive living. The insufficient knowledge on HIV/AIDS made many women to get more depression and lack of hope in life soon after they were told that they are HIV positive. It leads to family disintegration and separation of spouses. Therefore, the infected women must be sensitized with correct information. It will help them to accept the infection and lead a positive life without infecting others. The infected women can also be sensitized on safe sex to protect themselves from reproductive tract infection, safe pregnancy and delivery, breast feeding and non-transmission of infection to their babies.

Family and Community Sensitization

To promote family and community care and support, the basic social institution of family and community can be sensitized in all possible ways with the support of mass media. The integration of infected women into social life is only possible when the family and community accept the reality of HIV/AIDS infected people. The social health of the infected women can be protected by integrating them into family and community life in the society.

Review of Law

The law can be reviewed to protect the civil and human rights of women infected with HIV positive. The review of law is highly essential due to following reasons :

(*a*) **Monitoring of atrocities** : The infected women are subjected to various abuse and violence both in the family and in the society. The HIV infection is feminized in India and all infected women are looked down as immoral women. As a consequence of this notion the infected women are experiencing trauma which affects their total personality. Therefore, law can be reviewed to monitor the atrocities against women infected with HIV positive in order to guarantee a decent and dignified life for them.

(*b*) **Inheritance of property right** : The infected women finds very difficult to inherit the property of her husband after his death. Therefore, the newly formulated property inheritance right of the women can be strengthened to help the infected women get their share like any other women in India.

(*c*) **Job of deceased husband** : The infected women are subjected to severe economic hardships after the death of their husbands. To ensure economic security, law can be enacted to support the infected women to get the job from their husbands' employers.

(*d*) **Life Insurance** : At present the people with HIV positive are denied life insurance scheme by the insurance companies of India. Therefore, law can be formulated to cover the people infected with HIV positive in insurance schemes to enable them to ensure for the benefit of their children and family.

(*e*) **Legalisation of marriage between infected man and woman** : To get mutual care and support, the marriage between infected people can be encouraged by enacting appropriate legalisation. This will also help to control the spread of infection to the larger society. There is no provision in the existing marriage Act of India for legalising the marriage between the HIV infected people. Therefore, the Marriage Act should be reviewed to give provision for legalising the marriage between people living with HIV positives.

(*f*) **Law against HIV/AIDS discrimination** : At present severe stigma is associated with HIV/AIDS. The stigma resulted in social discrimination in which the infected people are subjected to social boycott and social distancing. The elimination of discrimination is only possible by taking the issue under the influence of law. The person or any organisation which involved in discriminating the infected people in general and women in particular can be punished as per legal provisions. The formulation of law against HIV/AIDS discrimination will ensure a decent and dignified life for the people infected with HIV positive.

Formulation of Social Policy and Planning

Social policy and its related planning and implementation are important to secure the right to life of women infected with HIV positive. Formulation of social policy for the welfare of people infected with HIV positive will help to build movements for social justice, economic equality, and participation of infected people in AIDS prevention and control programmes. Social policy can be formulated to ensure the following activities for the care and support and relief and rehabilitation of women infected with HIV positive :

(*a*) **Involving women infected with HIV positive in formulation of policy** : Women infected with HIV can be given representation in the formulation of policy. By involving the infected women in the formulation of policy, the policy-makers will receive first hand information about the urgent needs of the infected women to survive in the society in a dignified manner.

(*b*) **Benefits to infected women under poverty alleviation programme :** The women infected by HIV positive are suffering due to economic deprivations. Economic support from government is essential to empower them and motivation towards self care and participation in AIDS prevention and control activities. The government can consider the women infected with HIV positive as economically deprived and marginalized segments and they are to be included in poverty alleviation programmes so as to avail the benefits to sustain their livelihood.

(*c*) **Integration of positive women net work with Women Development Corporation :** The State AIDS Control Societies are encouraging emergence of positive women net work in all districts to provide platform for the infected women to get peer support to share their feelings and problems, information and counseling, and to get economic and medical support in coordination with State AIDS Control Societies and various national and international funding agencies. Women Development Corporation is functioning in Tamil Nadu for the empowerment of women through the concept of women self-help groups. The positive women net work can be integrated with Women Development Corporation to get the status of self help groups and avail financial assistance with subsidy from banks to generate assets and employments. Support for generation of assets and employment will empower the infected women to control their reproductive health as well as to improve their socio-economic status in the society.

(*d*) **Integration of positive women with Women Self-Help Groups :** Women self-help groups in Tamil Nadu are emerging as movement for the empowerment of women. They must be sensitized to participate in AIDS intervention activities as well as in providing care and support to women infected with HIV positive in their respective areas. The integration of positive women with women self-help groups will promote de-stigmatization of diseases, empowerment of infected women and social support system for the women infected with HIV positive.

(*e*) **Integration of Panchayat Raj Institution with State AIDS Control Societies in AIDS prevention and control and care and support programmes for infected people :** Panchayat Raj Institution play an important role in various aspects of Indian social life. It has contributed a lot for the socio-economic transformation in India. Evolving people's participation from identification of problems to evaluation of development programmes implemented for them are the principal areas of Panchayat Raj Institutions. Panchayat Raj Institution can easily mobilize public commitment towards AIDS intervention programmes. Therefore, they can be integrated with State AIDS Control Societies to mobilize public commitment towards AIDS prevention and control, care and support and relief and rehabilitation. It will help for creation of awareness, de-stigmatization of disease and promotion of community care and support for the people infected with HIV positive in general and women in particular.

(*f*) **Creation of free legal cell** : Free legal cell can be created in all State AIDS Control Societies in order to provide legal support to the infected women to fight against atrocities, to avail social security measures and inherit property from their parents and in-laws. Creation of free legal cell also help to protect the women infected with HIV positive from social discrimination and boycott.

(*g*) **Creation of HIV/AIDS information Cell in all hospitals** : HIV/AIDS information cell can be created in all hospitals of rural and urban areas. The HIV/AIDS information cell can have all updated information with regard to medicine, availability of treatment, counselling, availability of provision and benefits and the mechanism of availing these benefits etc. It will help the infected women to sensitize themselves to lead a life with HIV positive without fear and confusion.

(*h*) **Creation of short stay home for women with HIV positive :** Short stay home can be established in all district head quarters in co-ordination with N.G.Os to provide care and support to infected women who are abandoned by their family members. These homes can be provided financial and technical assistance to built infrastructure for the capacity building of inmates. Relief and rehabilitation of infected women can be ensured through these short stay homes.

(*i*) **Integration of media in mobilizing public commitment to create awareness on HIV/AIDS** : Public commitment is essential both for creating awareness on HIV/AIDS without myth and promoting care and support and relief and rehabilitation of people infected with HIV positive. The media can play a vital role as change agents in the society. The regular dissemination of message of HIV/AIDS and the problems experienced by the infected people can bring attitudinal change among the public. The positive attitudinal change among the public will help to build social support system and community care and support for the women infected with HIV positive.

(*j*) **Capacity building** : Capacity building means to equip the people to do things by their own based on 'what they know', 'what they have', 'what they are capable of', and 'what they can do'. The women infected with HIV positive can be helped to identify their innate capacities and accordingly the capacity building programmes are formulated to improve their knowledge, competencies, and vocational, managerial and marketing skills.

Holistic and Non-judgemental Medical Care

Comprehensive medical care and support is the immediate need of women infected with HIV positive. The widespread discrimination in the health-care system created guilt and fear in the minds of infected women to take treatment in the hospitals. In general, treatment seeking behaviour is less among the Indian women. The stigma and discrimination associated with AIDS prevents women to take early treatment for their ailment in the hospital. When compared to other diseases, the cost for the treatment of HIV/AIDS related illness is high and most of the Indian women are not in a position to spend large amounts for availing treatment. The infected women can be given care and support without considering the root cause of infection. There is no need of separate ward for HIV/AIDS patients. They can be given equal treatment like any other patient. The infected women can have easy access to Anti-Retro Viral (ARV) drugs. Therefore, the Government can plan to distribute ARV to the AIDS patients in all Government hospitals including Primary Health Centre. All Primary Health Centre can be equipped with all necessary medical equipments and it can be upgraded to provide treatment for HIV related illness. The upgrading of Primary Health Centre will help to promote treatment seeking behaviour among infected women in India.

Operation of Action Plan

The plan can be operated with the strategy of integration of the social institution of family, community, hospitals, organisations such as N.G.Os, women self help groups and the Government. The role of N.G.Os is very important to sensitize family, community and women self help group to extend their support to the infected women to lead a normal life in the society. Government is the powerful institution to mobilize political commitment towards AIDS intervention by formulating appropriate policy, programmes and reviewing the laws for the welfare of people infected with HIV positive in India.

Institutional Approach for Creating AIDS Free Society

The network of invisible rules and institutional arrangements which guide the behaviour of individual are the base for Indian social structure. By interacting with each other, people are governed by cultural patterns of norms, values, beliefs and symbols. It defines the behaviour of individual towards the fulfillment of social goals. All social institutions are interrelated and interdependent to accomplish basic social tasks. Institutions provide established answers to recurring problems of living. Each institution is a sort of societal master plan – a kind of "grand design" – whereby essential activities are organised, directed, and executed. Because of institutions, every one in the society feels that there is some measure of regularity, efficiency and certainty in daily activities. In the context of HIV/AIDS, every institution can contribute by taking up certain specific social function to realise the goal of AIDS free society.

The institutions of family, marriage, community, religion, social organisations, government, academic institution, hospitals, industries, media, N.G.Os and women self help groups can be motivated and mobilized towards the activities of AIDS prevention and control, care and support and relief and rehabilitation of people infected by HIV/AIDS.

Family

Family is the primary agent of socialization of individual. If there is any defect in socialization it will lead to the unapproved social behaviour of individual resulting in pre or extra marital sex and using drugs for enjoyment. Therefore, the family can be made aware of its important role in socializing the individual according to the expectation of the society with regard to moral values and ethics. Throughout the world, the family has been assigned the responsibility for shielding, protecting, sustaining and otherwise maintaining children, the infirm and other dependent members of the community. Healthy family relationships afford companionship, love, security, a sense of worth and a general feeling of well being.

Each and every family can be integrated in the AIDS intervention programmes to sensitize the family members to take active part in prevention and control of HIV/AIDS in the family and providing care and support to the infected and affected members of the family. By sensitizing the family with regard to care and support of people infected with HIV positive and destigmatization of disease, it is possible to mobilize the family to take the role of advocacy to provide the community care and support to the infected people.

To prevent and control the spread of HIV in the society, the family can be motivated to socialize the individual on the line of values of society to avoid sex out side marriage and to integrate the infected people within the family. Family harmony is important to prevent extra marital sex which leads to acquiring

HIV infection. Gender equality with regard to reproductive health and women empowerment can be promoted in the family to prevent HIV infection. The family can be motivated to create friendly atmosphere to the adolescents to share their doubts on sex and sexuality with their parents. Sharing and getting information related to sex and sexuality from the parents will prevent the adolescents from sexually transmitted infections including HIV/AIDS. The family can also be made aware of taking early treatment for their sexually transmitted diseases to avoid the possibility of acquiring HIV infection.

To promote care and support in the family, the HIV infected people can be advocated to stay within the family instead of absconding from the family. All family members can be advocated to take care of infected people like any other sick persons and to provide financial and moral support for treatment. Destigmatization of disease can start from the family by considering HIV/AIDS like any other disease. The infected people, especially the women can get their property share of husbands and parents to lead a decent life and they can be encouraged self employment by the parents to sustain in the society.

The N.G.Os and mass media can take a leading role to sensitize the family about HIV/AIDS and integration of infected people within the family.

Marriage

The rate of HIV infection is high among married women who are in monogamous relationship. In many cases the men who experienced pre marital sex with multisexual partners and got infected by HIV are not aware of their infection before marriage. They are married with out being aware of their HIV status. The women are also socialized to be a passive partner in sexual life with their husband. Woman's assertive role in sexual life is condemned by the society in general and husband in particular. This rigid notion on sex and sexuality in marital life is the major cause for the rapid spread of HIV among married women in India. Therefore, changes can be made in the Institution of marriage with regard to sex and sexuality of women in order to empower women over their reproductive health.

Voluntary HIV testing can be advocated among youth before marriage to prevent HIV infection through marriage. Pre-marriage counseling on sex related issues, mutual trust and marital harmony and creation of awareness on sex and reproductive health can be imparted to prevent HIV infection in marital life. Awareness on safe sex, early treatment for STD and parent to child transmission can be imparted to infected couples to control HIV infection in society. Mutual care giving can be promoted among the infected couples in order to prevent separation of spouses due to HIV/AIDS. Marriage between infected male and female can be encouraged as a part of providing relief and rehabilitation for the people infected with HIV positive.

Community

Community sensitization is the urgent need today to control the spread of HIV/AIDS and to provide care and support and relief and rehabilitation of people infected with HIV positive. Since HIV/AIDS is considered as social problem, it is the responsibility of the community to provide care, support, relief and rehabilitation to the infected and affected people. If the community is sensitized, people can be easily mobilized to achieve AIDS free society and to promote care and support and relief and rehabilitation to the people infected with HIV positive.

The HIV/AIDS sensitized community can prevent and control the spread of HIV infection through social mobilization with community participation to promote gender equality in reproductive health and empowerment of women to control over their reproductive health. The community has to take a key role to ensure availability and accessibility of condom for needy people and access to health care to all to control the spread of infection. The community can exercise control over the sale and use of injecting drugs to control infection through contaminated needles. Destigmatization of HIV infection is essential to promote community care and support for the infected people. Community can encourage the marriage between infected male and female in order to promote mutual care and support as well as to mobilize community care and support to people infected with HIV positive. For relief and rehabilitation of infected people, the community can involve in generation of funds to infected people in order to help them to establish self employment.

Sensitization of community on HIV/AIDS can be done with the support of N.G.Os, State AIDS Control Societies, Academic Institutions, local panchayats, mass media and women self help groups.

Religion

Norms, beliefs and rituals provide the cultural fabric of religion. It act as an informal means of social control agent to regulate and shape the behaviour of individual in the society. Each religion has its own structural organisation to mobilize people to impart religious values in their life. These religious organisations or missionaries can be mobilized to take part in creating AIDS free society as well as to provide care and support and relief and rehabilitation to the people infected with HIV positive. The religious missionaries can bring changes in the attitude and behaviour of people by disseminating message on morality, ethics and values of behaviour. Attitudinal change in the minds of people will help to control the spread of HIV infection by promoting gender equality and empowerment of women. Religious institutions can influence people to provide care and support to the infected people. These institutions can also establish care home and funding support to N.G.Os for the welfare of people infected with HIV positive. The religious institution can also mobilize to start employment programmes for the deprived people in general and infected people in particular. The religious missionaries can be sensitized on HIV/AIDS with the support of government and religious leaders.

Social Organisations

Social organisations, especially the Panchayat Raj Institutions are working for the welfare of the people with the principal with people's participation in all its activities. People participation is the core essence for the stability of Panchayat Raj Institutions in India. Panchayat Raj Institutions can be integrated with AIDS intervention mission along with government organisations to prevent and control the spread of infection in India. The local panchayat can be mobilized to work with N.G.Os to promote women empowerment, impart value education to public and to create awareness on safe sex practices and condom use to prevent and control HIV infection in society. It can also destigmatize the disease by involving in AIDS intervention programmes, creating information cell on HIV/AIDS and its related issues and extending funding support to infected people to take treatment. The panchayat raj institution can provide relief and rehabilitation by providing financial support to infected people for the generation of self employment for their dignified survival in the society.

The members of the Panchayat Raj Institution can be given training and motivation by the State AIDS Control Society to take part in AIDS intervention activities.

Government

Government has the power to give direction to human affairs and to mobilize people's actions towards collective goals towards realizing welfare state ideals. It also has power to bring about changes in people's attitude and behaviour. Therefore, government has to play a vital role in prevention and control of HIV/AIDS, care and support and relief and rehabilitation of people infected with HIV positive by formulating policy, reviewing law and planning and implementing programmes.

To prevent and control HIV/AIDS in India, the Government can make policy for creating AIDS free society with the support of all social institutions. It has to involve in planning, implementing, monitoring and evaluating AIDS intervention programmes in order to find the success and to frame alternative measures to reach the goal of AIDS free society. The government can frame policy to include infected people in all intervention programmes in order to enhance the effectiveness of the programmes. It has to organise regular campaigns against HIV/AIDS in all districts to create awareness on HIV/AIDS in the society. To control the spread of infection poverty alleviation programmes can be strengthened to generate employment opportunities for women to prevent their involvement in sex work. It has to create treatment facilities for STD in all public health centres to control the possibility of infection through STD.

To promote care and support, the government can influence the health care sectors to give treatment to HIV infected people along with other patients. It will help to destigmaitize the disease in the society. The Government can ensure the availability of ARV drug in all districts hospitals to promote the access of ARV drug to all infected people. Legislation can be enacted to include HIV infected people under Life Insurance Scheme. It will help not only the infected people but also their family members. To provide relief and rehabilitation to the infected people the Government can establish care home in all district headquarters. It has to rehabilitate the sex workers by creating alternative employment opportunities.

Academic Institutions

Academic institutions are considered as an important agent of socialization of individual in the society. The academic institutions - schools and colleges - not only provide formal, and systematic training to the students but it also teach more than the skills and information specified in the curriculum. Students learn values, morality, responsibility, conscientiousness, reliability, thoroughness, self-control, efficiency and emotional stability from their schools and colleges. The healthy future of the nation is vested with younger generation, especially with the students. Therefore, the students can be made aware of HIV/AIDS and their role in creating AIDS free society.

Value-based education, reproductive health education, education on gender sensitization and HIV/AIDS is important to prevent and control HIV/AIDS. This type of education can be imparted to the students through schools and college curriculum. All academic institution can have tutorial system to have close interaction with students. The tutorial system will help to understand the problems of the students in all aspects. The academic institutions can be insisted to establish counseling cell to counsel the students, especially the girl students on reproductive health and HIV/AIDS. The academic institutions can be motivated to organise meetings, workshops and seminars to create awareness on HIV/AIDS and reproductive health among students. It can also be encouraged to develop curriculum on extension activities in coordination with N.G.Os to generate awareness on HIV/AIDS and family and community care for people infected with HIV positive which leads to prevention and control of HIV infection in India. As a part of providing care and support, the academic institution can promote the involvement of parents-teacher association in its AIDS intervention activities. It will help to destigmatize the disease among the parents. Enrolment of infected children in schools and colleges is important to ensure care and support for people infected with HIV positive. It can be made possible by sensitizing parents and students through parent-teacher associations. The academic institutions can organise campaign for the promotion of relief and rehabilitation to people infected with HIV positive through their extension activities with the support of N.G.Os.

Teachers may be trained to take up AIDS intervention activities with the support of N.G.Os and State AIDS Control Society.

Hospitals

Society's well-being depends upon a healthy labor force for carrying out vital tasks. Consequently, disease and illness must be socially controlled and the people under sick can ensure holistic and non-judgemental medical care and support for proper societal functioning. Physicians, nurses and other practitioners have vital role in ensuring equal and client friendly treatment to all patients. It is the duty of the hospitals to destigmatize the diseases and to provide healthy service to care seekers to promote treatment seeking behaviour among the infected people.

The hospitals can play a vital role in prevention and control of HIV/AIDS by promoting client friendly treatment, syndromic management for STD/RTI (Reproductive Tract Infection) and counselling to sterilized couples about safe sex to prevent HIV and other sexually transmitted infection. Counselling must be made compulsory in the hospital for both the patients and parents about HIV/AIDS before and after HIV test. Destigmatization of HIV/AIDS, non-judgemental and equal treatment to HIV/AIDS patients and creating the access to ARV drugs to HIV infected people will ensure care and support in the hospitals. The health care institutions can also involve in providing relief and rehabilitation to the infected people by way of supporting infected inmates of short stay home run by the government and N.G.Os.

The health care providers can be sensitized on HIV/AIDS to treat HIV/AIDS patients like any other patients without any discrimination.

Industries

Migrant labourers are more prone to HIV infection due to their multisexual contacts with sex workers. These labourers are ignorant about HIV/AIDS and its prevention and implications. Therefore, they can be given correct information about HIV/AIDS in their workplace by the management of industries as part of Workers Education. The involvement of industries in AIDS intervention activities can help to prevent and control the spread of HIV infection among the labour community.

Involvements of industries in HIV/AIDS intervention programmes are very essential to control and prevent HIV/AIDS among migrant labourers. The management of industries can be sensitized to frame work place policy to take work place intervention programmes and influence the trade unions to take part in HIV/AIDS intervention programmes to control and prevent the infection among labourers. The industries can also involve in providing care and support to the HIV infected workers by way of retaining them in work and giving equal opportunities in recruitment for infected people. The human resource management of industries can take up advocacy role to eliminate stigma and discrimination against HIV infected people in workplace. The Employees State Insurance (ESI) hospitals can be linked with AIDS intervention mission to provide treatment to the HIV infected labourers. The industries can also involve in relief and rehabilitation of HIV infected people by opening employment opportunities for the infected people and by providing medical leave and financial assistance to infected labourers to take treatment for their HIV related illness.

The State AIDS Control Societies and N.G.Os can take responsibilities to mobilize and sensitize industries towards creating AIDS free society.

Mass Media

Media is an important agent to disseminate the message to larger society. In all societies people are very keen to know day to day events of the world through various media. Television plays a vital role in attracting all categories of people and it disseminates the information at the doorstep of the people. The print and visual media can be sensitized and mobilized to give regular coverage on HIV/AIDS news and to mobilize the public opinion towards AIDS intervention mission to control and prevent the spread of HIV infection. It can also develop networking with N.G.Os to collect case studies of infected people for their projection. The media can have social responsibility to protect the people from the dreaded diseases. Therefore, it can give correct information about HIV/AIDS to public. It will help to destigmatize the disease in the society. As a part of providing care and support and relief and rehabilitation to the infected people, the media have to cover the violation of human rights experienced by the infected people in the society and disseminating message on family and community care. The projection of HIV/AIDS related issues in media will help to mobilize community support to the people infected with HIV positive.

Non Government Organisations (N.G.Os)

N.G.Os are really interested to provide care to the uncared sections and the people at the bottom of the social stratum. Their work is people centered and hence they reach the unreached rural poor and live and work with them. They strive to promote the lives of the oppressed, deprived, marginalized, impoverished, downtrodden, hopelost, helpless, powerless, deserted and poverty stricken in the society. Therefore, the N.G.Os involvement is essential to provide care and support and relief and rehabilitation of women infected by HIV/AIDS.

There are two kinds of N.G.Os working in AIDS intervention activities. One is funding agencies which provide funds to the N.G.Os working in the field and the second is field agencies which implement the programmes for the benefit of larger society.

The funding agencies are expected to involve in :

1. Conducting research on women infected with HIV/AIDS among different cross sections.
2. Extending funds to the N.G.Os which focuses on care and support and relief and rehabilitation of women infected with HIV positive.

3. Establishment of Relief and Rehabilitation Cells in all States with partnership of Government. It can have common phone number in order to facilitate the infected and affected people to get immediate relief and rehabilitation for survival.
4. Co-ordination and networking of N.G.Os to know the success and difficulties faced in the implementation of care and support and relief and rehabilitation programmes to the infected women. It will help to find out alternative strategy for the sustainability of care and support services in the society for the people infected with HIV positive.

The N.G.Os working in the field can take up the following action for care and support and relief and rehabilitation of women infected with HIV positive :

1. Family and community sensitization to integrate the HIV infected women into the family and community.
2. Awareness building – (health and gender awareness) creation of awareness on HIV, STD, RTI, safe sex.
3. Promotion of treatment seeking behaviour among women infected with HIV positive and creation of awareness on the access to treatment.
4. Creation of positive women network to motivate the infected women to involve in positive prevention programmes.
5. Capacity building – promotion of vocational training to the infected women to generate self employment to sustain in the society.
6. Building hopes – promotion of self care and self support among the women infected with HIV to develop confidence in their life.
7. Networking with Human Right Organisations to represent the problems and humiliation experienced by the infected people.

N.G.Os can bring attitudinal change in the minds and behaviour of people related to their sexual behaviour in order to prevent and control HIV/AIDS in the society through its effective involvement in AIDS intervention activities in coordination with Government and other funding agencies.

N.G.Os are capable of mobilizing grassroot leaders and SHG members towards advocating the family and community care and support for the people infected with HIV positive. It can also conduct research on various issues of HIV/AIDS in order to help policy makers and programmes planners to prevent and control HIV/AIDS in India. The N.G.Os can influence HIV infected people to bring their co-ordination in disseminating information on HIV/AIDS to the public in general and target groups in particular. The taboo and rigidity on the usage of condom among Indian women can be removed with the support of N.G.Os working with the people.

Women Self-help Groups

Women self-help groups are emerging as a movement in Tamil Nadu in women's empowerment. The women self-help groups are more powerful in mobilizing the people towards common cause. The Integration of the women self-help group in AIDS intervention activities will help to sensitize the larger women folk within short period.

The women self-help groups can be motivated to involve in mobilizing the women to take part in AIDS intervention activities. It will help in awareness creation on safe sex as well as to sensitize the women on reproductive health and their rights. The women's awareness and their empowerment on reproductive health will prevent and control HIV infection among women of different categories. The stigma and discrimination can be removed from the society if the infected women are accepted and assisted by the members of women self-help groups. The women self help group can be motivated to provide care and support and relief and rehabilitation by accommodating sex workers and infected women in their groups and assist them through micro credit facilities in the promotion of income generation activities. Family and community care and support can be realized with the active participation of women self help groups in AIDS intervention programmes.

The N.G.Os and State AIDS Control Societies can take up the responsibility of providing training and other technical support to women self help groups in AIDS intervention activities.

Criteria to Implement Action Plan

Joint effort is an urgent need to prevent and control HIV/AIDS in the society. The institution of Government, N.G.Os,

Academic Institution and Mass Media can take a lead role to sensitize other social institutions of family, marriage, community, religion, social organisations, hospitals, industries and self help groups. Sensitization of social institutions definitely helps to sensitize the public and mobilize public commitment towards the mission of creating AIDS free society.

Scope for Further Research

The present study has been conducted with specific objectives in Chennai City, Tamil Nadu. As there are certain issues remaining unexplored in this research, the researcher presents the following suggestion for further research.

1. A similar study can be conducted throughout Tamil Nadu to obtain comprehensive view on impact of HIV/AIDS on women's social and economic life and the nature of discrimination experienced by them.
2. A study can also be conducted to find out whether the practices of reproductive health choice have a link with unsafe sexual practices in marital life.
3. A study can be conducted to find out the psychological problems of people living with HIV positive.

Integrated Approach to Provide Care and Support to Women Infected with HIV Positive

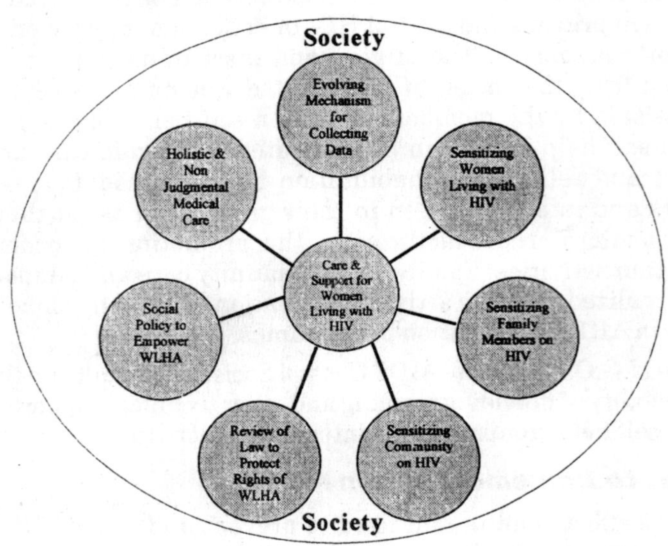

Institutionalized Approach for AIDs Free Society-Action Plan

INSTI-TUTIONS	ACTIVITIES PREVENTION AND CONTROL	CARE AND SUPPORT	RELIEF & REHABILITATION	
FAMILY	❖ Socialization of individual based on morality, values and ethic ❖ Perception, motivation and learning about sex ❖ Gender equality and women empowerment ❖ Integration of HIV infected people ❖ Sharing of information on safe sex and early treatment for STD	❖ Support to treatment for infected ❖ Caring of sick and orphaned children ❖ Moral & psychological support ❖ Property sharing	❖ Financial support to the infected to establish self employment ❖ Marriage between infected can be encouraged	A I D S
MARRIAGE	❖ Pre-marriage counseling ❖ Motivation to voluntary HIV test ❖ Awareness on sex and reproductive health ❖ Mutual trust and marital harmony ❖ Knowledge on the prevention of parent to child transmission	❖ Living together ❖ Facilitating treatment to the infected people and children ❖ Mutual care giving	❖ Marriage between infected male and female	F R E E S
COMMUNITY	❖ Community participation to create knowledgeable community ❖ Gender equality and empowerment of women ❖ Creation of awareness on safe sex ❖ Social mobilization to generate social responsibility	❖ De-stigmatization of disease ❖ Social interaction with the infected ❖ Acceptance of marriage between infected	❖ Generation of funds to self employment for sex workers and to the networks of positive people.	O C I
RELIGION	❖ Involvement of religious missionaries in AIDS prevention programmes and advocacy ❖ Networking with NGOs ❖ Imparting morality, ethics and values of individual behavior	❖ Establishing care homes with treatment ❖ Funding support to NGOs ❖ Advocating the public with regard to care and support of the infected people	❖ `Providing employment to the infected people	E T Y

(Contd.)

INSTI-TUTIONS	ACTIVITIES PREVENTION AND CONTROL	CARE AND SUPPORT	RELIEF & REHABILITATION
SOCIAL ORGANI-SATION	❖ Involving caste panchayat and local panchayat in intervention ❖ Empowerment of women ❖ Value education	❖ De-stigmatization of disease ❖ Non -discriminatory approach towards infected people ❖ Funding support to infected to take treatment	❖ Support to infected and sex workers for self employment
GOVERNMENT	❖ Legislation, funding support to NGOs, policy, planning, programme, monitoring & evaluation ❖ Formulation of policy on non-discrimination in work place ❖ Regular campaign against HIV / AIDS in all districts ❖ Generation of local self employment ❖ Treatment facilities in all PHCs	❖ Orientation to health staff ❖ Distribution of ARV through all district hospitals ❖ Insurance to HIV positive ❖ Infected people can be included in poverty alleviation programmes ❖ Allotment of fund to care and support programmes	❖ Care homes in all district headquarters ❖ Nutritious food to infected people ❖ Contact phone no. for needy for help (Help line)
ACADEMIC INSTI-TUTIONS	❖ Value based education ❖ Reproductive health education ❖ School and College intervention on HIV/AIDS ❖ Creation of guidance counseling cell ❖ Sensitization of Parents-Teachers Association	❖ De-stigmatization of disease ❖ Enrolment of infected children	❖ Design vocational training programmes
HOSPITALS	❖ Syndromic management ❖ Counseling before and after HIV test to patients and family members ❖ Client friendly treatment and ❖ Counseling to the sterilized couples about safe sex ❖ Integration of AIDS intervention with family planning ❖ Sensitization of health care personnel ❖ Breast feeding counseling		❖ Counseling cell ❖ Networking with NGOs for better treatment

A I D S F R E E S O C I E T Y

(Contd.)

INSTI-TUTIONS	ACTIVITIES PREVENTION AND CONTROL	CARE AND SUPPORT	RELIEF & REHABILITATION
INDUSTRIES	❖ Workplace intervention ❖ Creation of awareness through workers education programme ❖ Counseling cell ❖ Involvement of trade unions in intervention	❖ Employment to infected people ❖ Equal treatment ❖ Advocacy ❖ Linking ESI hospitals with AIDS intervention	❖ Employment to infected people ❖ Medical leave and financial assistance / loan for treatment
MASS MEDIA	❖ Compulsory coverage on HIV / AIDS ❖ Mobilize people participation ❖ Documentary on HIV/AIDS to educate the mass ❖ Dissemination of information and education	❖ Information for de-stigmatization of disease ❖ Projection of the violation of human rights	❖ Dissemination of message on family care ❖ Projecting the issues of abandoned
NGOs	❖ Intervention for prevention and control ❖ Mobilization of grass root leaders ❖ Advocacy to family, community ❖ Coordination with NGOs & Govt. ❖ Involving infected people in intervention	❖ ARV distribution ❖ Counseling ❖ Liaison with hospitals ❖ Advocacy to family members	❖ Care homes ❖ Capacity building through income generation activities ❖ Integration of infected in the society
WOMEN SELF HELP GROUPS (SHG)	❖ Involvement in intervention programmes ❖ Mobilization of people ❖ Creation of awareness on safe sex	❖ Integration of infected in SHGs	❖ Support to creation of income generation activities

A I D S F R E E S O C I E T Y

Bibliography

BOOKS

Abraham, Francis, 1982. *Modern Sociological Theory : An Introduction*. Oxford University Press, New Delhi.

Ahuja, Ram. 1999. *Social Problems in India*. Jaipur and New Delhi: Rawat Publications.

Benedict, B.B. Naanen. 1999. *Itinerant Gold Mines : Prostitution in the Cross River Basin of Nigeria, 1930-1950*. In Women in Prostitution by Mary A. Yeager, Cheltenham. U.K., Edward Elgar Publishing Limited.

Bongaarts.1988. *Approach to Prevention*. New York. Elsevier Science Publishing Co.

Digumarti Bhaskara Rao. 2000. *An Introduction to HIV/AIDS*. New Delhi: Discovery Publishing House.

Digumarti Bhaskara Rao. 2000. *HIV/AIDS AND NGOs*. International Encyclopedia of AIDS. New Delhi. Discovery Publishing House.

Digumarti Bhaskara Rao. 2000. *Issues and Challenges*. International Encyclopaedia of AIDS. Discovery Publishing House. New Delhi.

Doshi, S.L. 2003. *Modernity, Post modernity and Neo-Sociological Theories*. Jaipur and New Delhi. Rawat Publiations).

Dube, Siddharth. 2000. *Sex lies and AIDS*. New Delhi. HarperCollins.

Dutta, P.K. 1998. *Public Health and Social Aspects : Some Selected Essay*. Atlantic Publishers and Distributors. New Delhi.

Ellison, Bryan J. and Peter H. Duesberg. 1994. *Why we will Never Win the War on AIDS*. California. Inside Story Communication. El Cerrito.

Erving, Goffman 1963. *Stigma : Notes on the Management of Spoiled Identity*. New Jersey : Prentice-Hall.

Francois-Xavier Bagnoud Center for Health and Human Rights. 1995. *"AIDS, Health and Human Rights – An explanatory manual"*. International Federation of Red Cross and Red Crescent Societies. Harvard School of Public Health.

Harry, W. Kestler, Ronald Medley and Tim Horn. 1998. *HIV, Description of*. In Encyclopedia of AIDS : A Social, Political, Cultural and Scientific Record of HIV Epidemic, by Raymond A. Smith, Fitzroy Dearborn Publishers, Chicago, London.

Horton, Paul B. and Leslie, Gerald R.. 1970. *The Sociology and Social Problems*. (4th Ed.), Appleton Century Crofts, New York.

Hospedales, 1988. *Approach to Prevention*. New York: Elsevier Science Publishing Co.

James, W. Vander Zanden. 1990. *The Social Experience – An Introduction to Sociology*. New York: McGraw-Hill Publishing Company.

Jon, Tinker. 1988. *Extract from Ranee Sabatier's Blaming others – Prejudice, Race, and World wide AIDS*. London, Panos Institute.

Jonathan, H Turner. 2002. *The structure of Sociological Theory*. Jaipur: Rawat Publications.

Jones, Pip. 2005. *Introducing Social Theory*. Cambridge: Polity Press.

Kapadia, K.M. 1966. *Marriage and Family In India*. Calcutta: Oxford University Press.

Khorshed, M. Pavri. 1992. *Challenge of AIDS*. National Book Trust.

Khurana, Pushpa. 1998. *The Awesome Challenge AIDS*. New Delhi: Diamond Pocket Books (P) Ltd.

Kimberly, B. Sessions and Richard Loftus. 1998. *Immune System*. In Encyclopedia of AIDS : A Social, Political, Cultural and Scientific Record of HIV Epidemic, by Raymond A. Smith, Fitzroy Dearborn Publishers, Chicago, London, 1998.

Mark, Preston. 1998. *HIV, Origin of*. In: *Encyclopedia of AIDS : A Social, Political, Cultural and Scientific Record of HIV Epidemic, Raymond A. Smith,* Fitzroy Dearborn Publishers, Chicago, London.

Marx, Karl 1964. *Early Writings*. (Transulated and editated by T.B. Bottomore). New York: McGraw-Hill.

Merton and Nisbet. 1971. *Contemporary Social Problems*. Harcourt Brace. New York.

Merton, R.K. Social Structure and Anomie. *American Sociological Review*. October 1938.

Merton, R.K. *Social Theory and Social Structure*. Free Press, Glencoe, New York, 1957.

Prakasa Rao, V.V. and Nandini Rao V. 1982. *Marriage, the family and Women in India*. New Delhi: Heritage Publicity.

Ramamurthy, V. 2000. *AIDS and the Human Survival*. Authors Press, India Health Foundation.

Ramamurthy, V. 2000. *Global Patterns of HIV/AIDS Transmission*. Delhi: Authors Press.

Ramamurthy, V. 2003. *HIV/AIDS Vulnerability in South Asia*. Delhi: Authors Press.

Randy and Shills. 1987. *And the Band Played on*. New York: St. Martin's Press.

Reid., Elizabeth 2000. *Young Women and the HIV Epidemic*. In Internatioanl Encyclopaedia of AIDS – Intrduction to HIV/AIDS edited by Digumarti Bhaskara Rao. New Delhi: Discovery Publishing House.

Sabatier, Renee. 1988. *Blaming Others : Prejudice, Race and Worldwide AIDS*. London: The Panos Institute.

Sahmi, Ashok, 1993. *HIV and AIDS in India – An Update for Action*. Indian Society of Health Administrators. YES YES Prenters. Bangalore.

Sethi, Praveen. 2000. *Hand Book of Modern Tourism*. New Delhi: Anmol Publication Pvt Ltd.

Sinha, S.P. 1999. *India Sits on AIDS Bomb*. B.R. Publishing Corportation, Delhi.

Thai, Myo. 2000. *The Economic Implications of AIDS in Southeast Asia : Equity Considerations.* In: *Economic Implication of AIDS in Asia,* David E. Bloom and Joyce V. Lyons (Eds.). United Nations Development Programme Division. Regional Bureau for Asia and the Pacific. New Delhi.

Theresa, McGovern and Raymond A. Smith. 1998. *AIDS, Case Definition of*. In: *Encyclopedia of AIDS : A Social, Political, Cultural and Scientific Record of HIV Epidemic,* Raymond A. Smith (Eds.). Fitzroy Dearborn Publishers. Chicago, London.

Thomas, Gracious. N.P. Sinha, Johnson Thomas K. 1997. *AIDS, Social Work and Law*. Rawat Puplications, New Delhi.

JOURNALS

Ainsworth, Martha and Mead Over. 1994. "AIDS and African Development". *The World Bank Research Observer*. 9(2).

Alessandro, Cozzi Lepri. Patrizio Pezzotti Maria Dorrucci. 1995. "HIV Disease Progression in 854 women and men infected through injecting drug use and heterosexual sex and followed for up to nine years from seroconversion". *British Medical Journal.* Vol. 10. No. 12. February.

Amanda, Kolburn Kawal and Lynn Blinn Pike. 2004. "Role of older siblings in protectying adolescents from engaging in unsafe sexual practices". *Family Relations. Inter disciplinary Journal of Applied Family Studies.* 53(4) July.

Anastasia, J. Gage. 1998. "Sexual Activity and Contraceptive Use : The Components of the Decisionmaking Process". 29(2).

Anjum, Suresh K. 1998. "Indian women and AIDS". *Social Welfare.* 45(1).

Ann, E. Biddlecom, Beth Fredrick and Susheela Singh. 2004. "Women, Gender and HIV/AIDS – Women bear the heaviest HIV/AIDS burden, but they can't prevent its spread by themselves". *In Countdown 2015 (Special Issues)* – Sexual & Reproductive Health & Rights for all. Special Report, ICPD At Ten where are we now? Published by Population Action International, Washington D.C.

Ann, E. Biddlecom. John B. Casterline and Aurora E. Ferez. 1997. "Spouses Views of Contraception in the Pilippines". International Family *Planning Perspectives.* 23(3) September.

Ann, K. Blanc and Ann A. Way. 1998. "Sexual Behavior and Contraceptive knowledge and use among Adolescents in Developing Countractives". *Studies in Family Planning.* 29(2) June.

Any, Coen, Geeta Rao Gupta and Dina Bogecho. 2004. "Are We there yet?". *In Countdown 2015 (Special Issues)* – Sexual & Reproductive Health & Rights for all. Special Report, ICPD At Ten where are we now? *Published by Population Action International, Washington D.C.*

ARROW FOR CHANGE. 2000. "Research on Sex, Contraception and Reproduction among young Filipinas in Australia". 6(2).

Bai, Lakshmi Krishna Murthy. Bima P. Charles. 1999. "Communication Approaches to Sex workers in a Highway Project". *Health Education in South East Asia.* 13(4).

Baingana, Gladys. Kyung-Hee Choi, Donald C. Barrett Ronald Byansi and Norman Hearst. 1995 "Female partners of AIDS patients in Uganda : reported knowledge, perceptions and plans". *AIDS.*

9 (suppl 1). July.

Banatuvala, J.E. 1995. "Unlinked anonymous HIV screening Programme in England and Wales". *British Medical Journal (BMJ).* 11(12) April.

Barbara, S. Mensch, Deniel Bagah, Wesle H. Clark, and Fred Binka. 1999. "The Changing Nature of Adolescence in thssena-Nankana District of Northern Ghana". *Studies in Family Planning.* 30(2) June.

Basia, Zaba and Simon Gregson. 1998. "Measuring the impact of HIV on fertility in Africa". *AIDS.* 12(i).

Baylay, A.C. 1984. "Aggressive Kaposis' Sarcroma in Zambia, 1983". *Lancet.* 23 April.

Berkley, S. Naamara W. Okware S. 1990. "AIDS and HIV infection in Uganda : are more women infected than men? *AIDS.* No. 4.

Bhave, G. Wagle U. Desai S. 1992. "HIV surveillance and prevention". *II International Congress on AIDS in Asia and the Pacific.* New Delhi. November.

Bhave, Geeta. Christina P. Lindan. Esther S. Hudes. Seema Desai. Usha Wagle. Shrivam P. Tripathi and Feffrey S. Mandel. 1995. "Impact of an intervention of HIV, sexually transmitted diseases, and condom use among sex workers in Bombay, India". *AIDS* Vol. 9. (suppl 1).

Biggar, R.J. 1984. "Epidemiology of AIDS in Europe". *European Journal of Cancer and clinical Oncology.* 20(2).

Carael, Michel. Bernhard Schwartlander. 1998. "Demographic impact of AIDS". *AIDS.* 12. (Supp. 1)

Carovano, K. 1992. "More than mothers and whores : Redefining the AIDS prevention needs of women". *International Journal of Health Services.* Vol . 21(1).

Celentano, David C. 2000. Preventive intervention to reduce sexually transmitted infections : A field trial in the Royal Thai Army. *Achieves of Internal Medicine.* No. 160.

Chuttani, 1991. "Awareness and knowledge about AIDS among rural population in India". *CARC CALLING.* 3(4).

Dalla, Rochelle 2004. "I Fell off (The Mothering) Track : Barriers to effective Mothering among Prostituted women". *Family Relations. Inter disciplinary Journal of Applied Family Studies.* 53(2).

Deneberg, Risa. 1997. "Childhood Sexual Abuse as an HIV Risk Factor in Women". GMHC Treatment Issues. *A Publication of the Gay Men's Health Crisis.* VI(7/8).

Dev, Vasu 2005. "Ore Eravu –Highways Alahiyaha Namathu Nirubar. *Kumutham.* May 23.

Elfkord, J. Dwyer J. 1993. "HIV and AIDS in Asia and the Pacific". *AIDS Care.* Vol 5.

Evasius, K. Bauni and Ben Obonyo Jarabi. 2000. "Family Planning and Sexual Behaviour in the Era of HIV/AIDS : The Case of Nakuru District, Kenya". *International Family Planning Perspectives.* 31(1) March.

Feffrey, O'Malley. 2004. "SAHR with HIV – Can This Marriage work? Linking the response to AIDS with sexual and reproductive health and rights". In *Countdown 2015* (Special Issues) – Sexual & Reproductive Health & Rights for all. Special Report, ICPD At Ten where are we now? Published by Population Action International, Washington D.C.

Fleming, P.L. Ciesielski, C.A. Byers, R.H. Castro K.G. Berkelman R.L. 1993. "Gender Differences in reported AIDS-indicative diagnoses". *Journal of infectious Diseases*. No. 168.

Foley, M, Skurmic. 1994. "Family Support for hetrosexual partner in HIV – Serodiscordant Couples". *AIDS*. October. 8(10).

Frances, A. Althaus. 1997. "Female Circumcision : Rite of Passage or Violation of Rights". *International Family Planning Perspectivesl*. 23(3), September.

Friedlan, G.H., Saltzman, B. Vileno, J. 1991. "Survival difference in Patients with AIDS". *Journal of Acquired Immune Deficiency Syndrome*. 4.

Gangakhedkar, 1997. "Spread of HIV infection in married monogamous women in India". *Journal of the American Medical Association*. 20(2). *In International Family Planning Perspectives*. 278(23).

Gangakhedkar, R.R. 1999. " Chemoprophylaxis to Reduce Mother-to-Child Transmission of HIV-1 Infection". *AIDS Research & Review*. 2(3).

Garenne, Michel Stephen Tollman and Kathleen Kahn. 2000. "Premarital Fertility in Rural South Africa : A Challenge to Existing Population Policy. *Studies in Family Planning*. 13(1).

Golmare, 2002. 'Adopting strategic approach for reaching out to inaccessible population viz'. Abstract WePeF6707F abstract, *The XIV International AIDS Conference*.

Grosskurth, H. 2000. "Link between control of STD and HIV prevention: Mwanza and Rakai Studies". *Lancet*. No. 355. *In AIDS update*. 2000. 5(3).

Halperin, D.R. Bailey. R.C. 1999. "Male Circumcision and HIV infections : 10 years and counting. *Lancet*. 35A(192).

Hardman, K. 1997. "A Social work group for prostituted women with children". *Journal of Social Work with groups*. No. 20.

Here, GM. 1999. " AIDS and stigma". *Am Behav Scientist*.42(7) :1106-16. Available at : http :// psychology.ucdavis.edu/rainbow/html/bibabs.html.

Herek, GM, Gillis JR, Cogan J. 1999. "Psychological sequelae of hate crime victimization among lesbian, gay, and bisexual adults". *Journal of Consultation Clinical Psychology*.67(6).

Hirve.S.S. and Sathe. P.V. 1997 "AIDS awareness among Married Women in Reproductive Age group from Rural Areas of Three Coastal Districts". *AIDS Research and Review*. Vol. 2. No. 4. Oct-Dec.

Inn Mackinnon and Adam Piore .2001. "The Quiet AIDS crisis". *SPAN*. Vol. XLII. Number. 5. September/October.

Isabelle de Zoysa. Michael D. Sweat and Julie A. Denison. 1996. "Faithful but fearful : reducing HIV transmission in stable relationships". *AIDS*. Vol 10, (Suppl A)

Jacob K. John. 2000. "Do most individual with HIV/AIDS consider suicide?". *Abstract in First International Conference of AIDS*. India.

Jacob K.S. Eapen V. 1987. "AIDS Phobia". *British Journal of Psychiatry*. No.150.

Jagatheeswary. P.A.T. Shameem Banu and Rosy Vennila. 2000. "HIV/AIDS and STD – A Five year study at Chennai Medical College". *First International Conference of AIDS*. India.

Jeanette J. Rodrigues. Snjay M. Mehendala. Mary E. Shepherd. Anand D. Divekar. Raman R. Gangakhedkar. 1995. "Risk factors for HIV infection in people attending clinics for sexually transmitted diseases in India". *British Medical Journal*. Vo. 11. No. 8. Oct.

Jeff Goodwin. 1978. "The Libidinal Constitution of a High Risk Social Movement : Affected ties and solidarity in the Huk Rebellion 1946-1954. In *American Sociological Review*. Vol. 62. No. 1. 1997.

John C. Caldwell, Pat Caldwell, Bruce K. Cald ell, and Indrani. 1998. "The Construction of Adolescence in Changing World : Implications for Sexuality, Reproduction, and Marriage". *Studies in Family Planning*.Vol. 29. No. 2. June.

John Stover and Peter Way. 1998. "Projecting the impact of AIDS on mortality". *AIDS*. Vol. 12. Supplement. 1

John T. Babu P. Jayakumari H. Simoes E. 1987. "Prevalence of HIV infection in risk groups in Tamilnadu, India". *Lancet*.

Jones, Heidi. Nafissatau Diop. Ian Askew and Inoussa Kabore. 1999. "Female Genetal Cutting practices in Burkina Fasa and Mali and Their Negative Health Outcomes". *Studies in Family Planning*. 30(3).

Karen Hardee, Kokila Agarwal, Nancy Luke, Ellen Wilson, Margaret Pendzich, Marguerite Farrell and Harry Cross. 1999. "Reproductive Health Policies and Programs in Eight Countries : Progress Since Cairo". *International Family Planning Perspectives*. Vol. 25. Supplement. January.

Kelly. R.J. and Gray. R.H. 2003. "Age Differences in Sexual Partners and Risk of HIV-1 Infection in Rural Uganda". *Journal of Acquired Immune Deficiency Syndrome*. No. 32.

Kim, Best. 2001. " Removing Specialized Cells may Explain Protection Effect. *Net Work. Family Health International*. 20(4).

Kim, Best. 2001. "HIV Infected women less fertile". *Net Work*. Vol. 20. No. 4.

Kim, Best. 2001. "HIV Positive Women have Different Needs". *Net Work.* Vol.10. No. 9.

Kim, Best. 2001. Does Circumcision Reduce HIV Risks?. *Net Work. Family Health International*. 20(4).

Korber, Bette. Muldoon. M. Theiler J. Gao F. Gupta R. Lapedes A. Hahn B.H. Wolinsky S and Bhattacharya T. 2000. "Timing the ancestor of the HIV-1 pandemic strains". *Science*. No. 288. 9 June.

Krishnamurthy, Vijaya Srinivasan. Charles B. Lakshmim Bai. 1999 "HIV/AIDS and safe sex practices among female sex workers in India – Risk perception". *Health Education in South East Asia.* 13(4).

Lamey, B and Malemeka. N. 1982. "Aspects cliniques at pidemiologiques de la cryptococcose a Kinshasa" *Medecine Tropicale*. Sep-Oct. 42(5).

Limsuwan, Y., Kanapa S., Siristonapun Y. 1986. "Acquired immune deficiency syndrome in Thailand, a report of two cases". *Journal of Medical Association Thai*. 69

Lobo, Francis. 1999. "HIV/AIDS and the meaning of life : Lessons for community services". *Leisure Issues*. 2(4).

Maclure, Malcolm. 1998. "Inventing the AIDS virus hypothesis : An example of scientific versus unscientific induction". *Epidemiology*. No. 9.

Martin, S.L. 1999. "Domestic Violence in northern India", *Amercian Journal of Epidemiology*, 150 (4).

Martin, S.L. 1999. "Sexual Behaviour and Reproductive Health Out comes : associations with wife abuse in India". *Journal of the American Medical Associations*. 282(20).

McEwan, R.T. 1992. "Sex and the risk of HIV infection : the role of alcohol". *British Journal of Addict*. 87(4).

McGrath, J.W. Ankrah M. Schumann D.A. Nkumbi S. Lubega M. 1993. "AIDS and the Urban family : its impact in Kampala, Uganda". *AIDS Care*. No.5.

Melkote, Srinivas R. Sundeep R. Muppidi and Goswami, D. 2000. "Social and economic factors in an integrated behavioral and societal approach to communications in HIV/AIDS". *Journal of Health Communication.* No. 5.

Michal, C., Latham and Elizabeth A Preble. 2000. "Appropriate feeding methods for infants of HIV infected mothers in sub-Saharan Africa". *British Medical Journal.* 16.

Morbidity. and Mortality Weekly Report. 1982. *"Opportunistic Infection and Kaposis' Sarcoma among Haitians in the United States"*. 13(2).

Moses, Stephen, Francis A. Plummer, Elizabeth N. Nagugi. Nico J.D. Nagelkerke, Aggrey O. Anzala and Jackonaiah O. Ndinya-Achola. 1991. "Controlling HIV in Africa : Effectiveness and cot of an intervention in a high-frequency STD transmitter core group". *AIDS*. No. 5.

Nair, B.K.K. Viswan. M.P. Venugopal. B.S. Nair. P.S. 1973. "An Epidemiological study of Veneral Diseases". Vol. 6.

Nancy, L. Sloan, Beverly Winikoff, Nicole Haberland, Christa Coggins, and Christopher Elias. 2000. "Screening and Syndromic Approaches to Identity Gonorrhea and Chlamydial Infection among Women". *Studies in Family Planning*. 31(1).

Nataraj, Hyamala, 2002. "Women in Prostitution – Need for Informed Intervention" *Manushi.* No. 124.

Naveed, Syed V. 1998. "Interpersonal Relationships of Relatives and Friends of HIV/AIDS Patients". *Layola Journal of Social Science.* 12(2).

Offenstadt, G. 1983. "Multiple Opportunistic Infection Due to AIDS in a Previously Healthy Black Woman from Zaire". *New Englnd Journal of Medicine*. 308.

Osinubi., Tokunbo Simbowale 2003. "Perception Change is Crucial". *Health Action*. January.

Panda, S. 2000. " Transmission of HIV from injecting drug users to their wives in India". *International Journal of STD and AIDS.* 11(7).

Panda, S. 2000. "Indian Council of Medical Research Project on HIV/AIDS and Substance Abuse, Calcutta". *Indian Journals of STD and AIDS.* 11(7).

Pape, J.W. 1983. "Characteristics of the Acquired Immuno Deficiency Syndrome (AIDS) in Haiti". *New Englnd Journal of Medicine.* 309(16).

Phanuphak, P, Locharernkul C, Panmuong W., Wilde H. 1985. "A report of three cases of AIDS in Thailand". *Asian Pacific Journal Allergy Immunol*. No. 3

Potterat, J.J. Phillips. L. Rothenberg. R.B. and Drrow w.w.w. 1985. "On becoming a Prostitute : An exploratory case-comparison study". *Journal of Sex Researh*. No.20/21.

Pottert, J.J. Rothenberg R.B. Muth. S.Q. Darrow W.W.W and Phillips Plummer L. 1998. "Pathways to prostitution : The Chronology of sexual and drug abuse milestones". *The Journal of Sex Research*. No. 35.

Punia, Deepa, Punia, P.K. and Kaur, S.1996. "Sexual Victimization of female Children in Haryanvi Folk Songs". *Social Defence*. 38(125). July.

Rajkumar, R. Chellam Balasundaram and Ravi Chandran M. 1996. "AIDS Control-Awareness and Action Needed". *Social Welfare*. 42(12).

Ramasamy, P, Sabhesan S. 1988. "Promiscuity and family pathology". *Indian Journal of Social Work*. 44(2).

Richard, W Goodgame. 1990. "AIDS in Uganda". *The New England Journal of Medicine*. 323(6).

Rutenberg, Naomi Carol E. Kaufman. Kate Macintyre. Lisanne Brown. AliKarim. 2002. "Pregnant or Positive : Adolescent Child bearing and HIV risk in South Africa". *Working-Policy Research Division. Population Council*. No. 162.

Ryder, R. 1989. "Deprivations caused by Poverty increases AIDS among women". *New England Journal of Medicine*. 320(25).

Sandala, Luciano, Peter Lurie. M. Rosemary Sunkutu. Edgar M. Chani. Esther S. Hudes and Norman Hearst. 1995. "Dry Sex and HIV infection among women attending a sexually transmitted diseases clinic in Lusaka, Zambia". *AIDS*. 9 (suppl 1).

Singh, Richa. 2001. "Masculine Identity Workers and HIV/AIDS". *Economic and Political Weekly*. 36(2).

Singh, Susheela, Deirdre Wulf, Renee Samara and Yvette P. Cuca. 2000. "Gender Differences in the Timing of First Intercourse : Data from 14 Countries". *International Family Planning Perspectives*. 26(1).

Srinivasan, Vijaya Prasanthi R. and Yayanthi. V. 1999. "Evolving an Innovative Strategy for Control of Sexuallyn Transmitted Diseases in a Developing Country". *The Gandhigram Institute of Rural Health & Family Welfare Trust Bulletin*. 34(1).

Szabo, Robert Roger V Short. 2000. "Does male circumcision protect against HIV infection?". British Medical Journal. No. 320. In *AIDS update*. 2000. 5(3).

The United Nations Documents. 1998. "On the Impact of HIV/AIDS on Adult Mortality in sub-Saharan Africa". *Population and Development Review*. 24(3).

Thomas, William A, Christoper, A.J. and Saravanan. 1996. "Awareness is shield Education is the Sword". *Social Welfare*. 43(9).

Ties Boerma J. Andrew J. Nunn and James A.G. Whiteworth. 1998. "Mortality impact of the AIDS epidemic : evidence from community studies in less developed countries'. *AIDS*. 12 (supp. 1).

Tobia, Nahid Amany Abouzied and Eimn Sharief. 2004. "Health Risk Vs Defending Rights". *In Countdown 2015 (Special Issues) – Sexual & Reproductive Health & Rights for all*. Special Report, ICPD At Ten where are we now? Published by Population Action International, Washington D.C.

Usha, M.S. 2001. "Women and AIDS in India". *Women'Link*. 7(2).

Vandepitte, J. 1983. "AIDS and Cryptococosis Zaire 1997. *Lancet*. 23 April.

Weiss, Helen A. Maria A. Quigley and Richard J. Hayes. 2000. "Male circumcision and risk of HIV infection in Sub-Saharan Africa : A systematic review and meta-analysis". *AIDS*. No. 14.

Weniger, B.G. 1991. 'The epidemiology of HIV infection and AIDS in Thailand'. *AIDS*. No. 5 (suppl 2)

William, R. Finger, 2001. "Reaching Youth, Men May Improve Services". *Net work*. Vol. 20. No. 4.

WISE Words. 2000. "Power and Prevention". *Am Publication of Project Information*. No. 6. October.

Young, Ellie Wright. 1991. "The effects of Family structure on sexual behaviour of adolescents". *Adolescence*. 26(104).

Zabin, Laurie Schwab and Karungari Kiragu. 1998. "The Health Consequences of Adolescent Sexual and Fertility Behavior in Sub-Saharan Africa". *Studies in Family Planning*. 29(2).

Zhu, Twofu. Bette T. Korber. Andre J. Nabmias. Edward Hooper. Paul M. Sharp. and David D. Ho. 1998. "An African HIV-1 sequences from 1959 and implications for the origin of the epidemic". *Nature*. No. 391. Supplement. 5 February.

REPORTS

AIDS Update, 2000

Ainsworth, Martha, Chris Beyrer and Agnes Soucat. 2000. *"Thailand's response to AIDS : Building on success, confronting the future"*. Bangkok. World Bank.

APAC. *"HIV Risk Behavior Surveillance Survey in Tamil Nadu and Pondichery". Report on Sixth Wave.* AIDS Prevention and Control Project. Voluntary Health Services. Chennai.

APAC. *"HIV Risk Behavior Surveillance Survey in Tamil Nadu" Report on Fourth Wav"*. AIDS Prevention and Control Project. Voluntary Health Services. Chennai.

APAC. *"HIV Risk Behavior Surveillance Survey in Tamil Nadu". Report on Fifth Wave.* AIDS Prevention and Control Project. Voluntary Health Services. Chennai.

APAC. 1998. *"Community Prevalence of Sexually Transmitted Diseases in Tamil Nadu. A Report on Third Wave"*. AIDS Prevention and Control Project. Voluntary Health Services. Chennai.

APAC. 1998. *"HIV Risk Behaviour Surveillance Survey in Tamil Nadu". AIDS Prevention and Control Project.* Voluntary Health Services. Chennai.

Asian Red Cross and Red Crescent Regional AIDS Task Force. 1997. *"Regional workshop on Home and Community Care for People living with HIV/AIDS (PLWHA)"*. Chiang Mai, Thailand, 3-7 June.

Bharat, Shalini 2000. *"India : HIV and AIDS-related Discrimination, Stigmatization and Denial"*. Geneva : UNAIDS

Ekstrand M. 2003. *"HIV/AIDS in India"*. AIDS Policy Research Centre. University of California. August.

Joyce, V. Lyons. 2000. *"Economic Implication of AIDS in Asia"*. United Nations Development Programme Division. Regional Bureau for Asia and the Pacific. New Delhi.

Karuppaih. 2000. *"A Study of Socio-cultural and Economic correlates of HIV/AIDS in Madras City"*. Report of the Research Project Sponsored by University Grant Commission. University of Madras. Chennai.

Mennonite Central Committee. 2005. *"Report on HIV/AIDS in Nepal"*. June. 18. http ://www.mec.org/getinv.html

NACO. 1998. *Country Scenario 1997-1998*. National AIDS Control Organization, Ministry of Health and Family Welfare, Government of India.

NACO. 2003. *Facts & Figures – HIV Estimate (2003) : A note on HIV estimate*

NACO. 2004. *Annual Report 2002-2003 and 2003-2004*

NACO. 2004. *Facts and Figure*

National Family Health Survey. 1993. *"Tripura Summary Report"*. International Institute for population Science. Bombay.

Parliamentary Forum on HIV/AIDS (PFA). 2004. *"Young Ambassadors' Fight against HIV / AIDS – National Students & Youth Parliament Special Session on HIV / AIDS". New Delhi. November 6-7.* Supported by UNAIDS, NACO, Delhi Govt., NYKS, AIU & Students Organization.

Peter, Piot. 2000. *"Gender Is Crucial Issue In Fight Against Aids, Says Head of UNAIDS"*. Press Release. UNAIDS. 5 June.

Reid, G. and Costigan G. 2002. *"Revising the Hidden Epidemic : a situation assessment of drug use in Asia in the context of HIV / IDS"*. The Centre for Harm reduction, The Burnet Institute, Australia January.)

Sathiamoorthy and Suniti Solomon. 1997. *"Socio-economic Realities of Living with HIV"*. In Socio-economic Implications of the Epidemic, ed. Peter Godwin .New Delhi : United Nations Development Program. Asia-Pacific Office. May.

Status of Women in India. 1975. *"A Synopsis of the Report, National Committee on the Status of Women, (1971-74)"*. New Delhi: The ICSSR. Allied Publications.

Tamil Nadu State AIDS Control Society. 1998. *"Meeting the challenge – Annual Report 1997-98"*. Tamil Nadu AIDS Control Society, Chennai.

Thomas, Cox and Bal K. Suvedi. 1994. *Sexual Networking in Five Urban Areas in the Nepal Terai - An Assessment* AIDS and STD Prevention Network, Valley Research Group, Kathmandu, Nepal, March.

UNAIDS. 1997. *Briefing paper.*

UNAIDS. 1998. *Report on gender related vulnerability and obstacles to prevention and coping.*

UNAIDS. 1999. *Report on the global HIV/AIDS epidemic.*

UNAIDS. 2000. Report on the Global HIV/AIDS epidemic.

UNAIDS. 2001. *Children and young people in a world of AID"S.* August.

UNAIDS. 2002. *Mother to Child Transmission.*

UNAIDS. 2002. *Report on the global HIV/AIDS epidemic.*

UNAIDS. 2002. *Report on the global HIV/AIDS epidemic.*

UNAIDS. 2002. *Report on the global HIV/AIDS epidemic*. July

UNAIDS. 2003. *A Joint Response to HIV/AIDS*

UNAIDS. 2004. *Questions & Answers : Basic facts about the HIV epidemic and its impact.* 1/10, July.

UNAIDS. 2004. *Report on the Global Epidemic.*

UNAIDS/WHO. 2004. *AIDS epidemic update. December*

UNDP (undated). *AIDS in South and Southwest Asia : A development Challenge*. New Delhi.

UNDP. 1999. *AIDS in South and Southwest Asia – A Development Challenge*. HIV and Development Project. South and Southwest Asia.

UNDP. 2004. *Migration and HIV in South Asia.* New Delhi.

United Nations Development Fund for Women (UNIFEM). 2002. *Reducing Vulnerabilities of Young Women to STI / HIV / AIDS*. New York.

United Nations/Commission on the Status of Women. *Effects of the Acquired Immunodeficiency Syndrome (AIDS) on the advancement of women*. E/CN.6/1989/6/Add.1. in Expert Group Meeting on Women and HIV/AIDS and the Role of National Machinery for the Advancement of Women. Vienna. 24-28 September 1990. In Interrelationships between the status of women and HIV-Epidemic : a Review of published Literature. EGM/AIDS/1990/ bp 2. 21 July.

US. Centre for Disease Control. 1981. "Pneumocystic pneumonia – Los Angeles". *Morbidity and Mortality Weekly Report*. 30(21).

WHO. 1988. *Social Aspects of AIDS, Prevention and Control.* AIDS ACTION, Issue 2 March.

WHO. 2001. *HIV/AIDS in Asia and the Pacific Region.*

WHO. 2003. *AIDS Epidemic Update.*

WHO. 2003. *HIV/AIDS in Asia and the Pacific Region. Western Pacific-South-East Asia.*

World Bank (2000) *'Thailand's Response to AIDS : Building on Success, Confronting the Future* Thailand Social Monitor.

ABSTRACT

Reid, Jeanette Brown. 1998. *"HIV/AIDS : The Emotional Impact on Two Young Women Whose Mothers are HIV-infected (Immune Deficiency*). DAI—A 59/03, University of South Florida.

Riedel, Marion C. 1998. "Women Living with AIDS : How do family role tasks affect the custody plans and mental health of their adolescent children? (Immune Deficiency). DAI—58/12. Columbia University.

Rwabukwali, Charles Barwogeza. 1998. *"Gender, Poverty, and AIDS in Kabarole, Western Uganda : The socio-cultural context of risk and prevention behaviors (Immune Deficiency).* DAI—A 58/10. Case Western Reserve University.

Schneider. 1989 *"AIDS in women in the Federal on Federal Republic of Germany"* by Bunikowski, J. Estermann, M.A. Koch, abstract presented at International Conference on the Implications of AIDS on Mothers and Children, Paris. November.)

Schoultz, Kristasn Kay. 1998. *"Understanding Social Vulnerability : Gender and sexually Transmitted Infection in Niamey, Niger (Hausa, Prevention).* DAI—A 59/04, Brown University.)

Shankaran. S.S. 2002. *"Intervention for women and children in the red light area"*. Abstract WePeF6910. The XIV International AIDS Conference.)

Singh and Malavia. 1990. *"HIV prevention interventions among prostitutes in India : Delhi experience"*. Abstract published in VI international Conference on AIDS. San Francisco. Vol. 3.)

Sivaramamurthy. V. 2000. *"Sexuality, Sexual behaviour and Awareness about HIV/AIDS among rural men near Salem"*. Abstrct in First International Conference of AIDS. India.

NEWS LETTER

AIDS IN INDIA. 1995. *"Women and AIDS : Issues and Concern"*. Newsletter of the National AIDS Control Organization. March.

Lawyers Collective HIV/AIDS Unit Positive Dialogue. 2000. "Criminalisation of Livies". *Newsletter*. 7. November.

Machika TANNO. 1997. "The Agony of a family of AIDS patients : A case study about 42 year old single man died of AIDS". Proceedings of the 11th Congress of the Japanese Society for AIDS Research. *AIDS Research Newsletter*. Dec. 4-5. Kumadmoto.

Meena Gopal. 2000. "Gender and Disease : A Research Note". *Social Sciences and Health News Letter*. 1(1)

National Institute of Social Defence 2004. "Tackling the Challenge of HIV/AIDS". A Newsletter of National Institute of Social Defence. 5(11).

National Institute of Social Defence. 2004. "*Condom use declines drastically in urban India : Survey*". *A Newsletter of National Institute of Social Defence.* 5(11)

National Institute of Social Defence. 2004. "*HIV among married Indian women likely to increase : report*". *A Newsletter of National Institute of Social Defence.* 5(11).

NEWS PAPERS

Aarthi Dhar. 2005. "AIDS vaccine may be available in eight years". *The Hindu.* 8 February.

Aarti Dhar. 2005. "Sharp fall in number of new HIV cases – India continues to have most number of cases after South Africa". *The Hindu.* 26 May.

Anandhi Subramanian. 2004. "Pushing at the barriers". *The Hindu.* Magazine. 12 December.

Biswas, Ranjita. 2005. "Of human bondage". *The Hindu.* 3 April.

Break Through Organization. 2005." Married women are increasingly affected by HIV". *Thinamalar (Tamil Daily).* 23 April.

Deenabandu. K. 2003. "Policy shift in Battle against AIDS – Health department to offer district specific, micro-solutions". *The Hindu.* 27 August.

Dinesh Varma. 2004. "AIDS awareness high, but access to information inadequate". The Hindu. 3 May. http :// www.thehindu.in

Gayathiri Devi, R. 2004. "Measures sought to stop violence against women". *The Hindu.* 30 November.

Kannan, Ramaya. 2005. "They live under the shadow of HIV/AIDS – Over 10 per cent of street children had STD". *The Hindu.* 25 August.

Kannan, Ramya. 2003. *The Hindu.* 1 November.

Kannan, Ramya. 2004. "Treatment in Government Hospitals/ Discrimination – HIV-affected women will be on advisory panels". *The Hindu.* 5 March.

Krishnamurthy. 2005. "Need to check sexually transmitted infections – Study among two high-risk groups". *The Hindu.* 6 May.

Ledger, Wendy. 1997. "It's a delicate issue for business sector-Special issue". *East African Standard.* 21 July.

Menon, Meena. 2005. "Suicides by HIV positive patients in Mumbai – People feel there is a feeling of neglect". *The Hindu*. 3 May.

News Today. 2002. "Police, prostitutes nexus cannot be denied – Southern belles in brothels up North". 10 February.

Olson, Elizabeth. 2000. "Red Cross say three diseases kill many more than disasters". *The New York Times*. 29 June.

Paul, George. 2005. "HIV/AIDS patients and doctors". *The Hindu*. 4 September

Prasad. R. 2005. "HIV : trial shows male circumcision cuts risk". *The Hindu*. 25 August.

Quraishi. 2005. "India seized of AIDS problem". *The Hindu*. 21 April.

Samgaeswaran K.T. 2004. "Is it yet another crime against women?". *The Hindu*. 22 September.

Sharma, K. 2005. " Blaming women". *The Hindu*. 12 June.

Sharma, Kalpana. 2005. "Is this what we call progress? – What is happening to women in U.P. makes for a relentless horror story". *The Hindu*. Magazine. 17 April.

The Hindu 2004. "AIDS Study/Violation of Rights – Women face stigma, discrimination". 6 December.

The Hindu. 1991. "To Err Is Human, But At What Cost?". 5 January.

The Hindu. 1996. "Dissemination of information to combat AIDS mooted". 13 December

The Hindu. 2002. "Open Page – Crime in Chennai". 19 March.

The Hindu. 2003. "AIDS patients in 6 States to get free drugs". 1 December.

The Hindu. 2003. "Slum women show the way to fight HIV stigma". 1 December.

The Hindu. 2004. "$9 billion needed to fight HIV/AIDS". 22 April.

The Hindu. 2004. "A ticking time bomb", 5 December.

The Hindu. 2004. "AIDS Meet/Asia Facing Grave Threat - Leaders not doing enough : Annan". 12 July.

The Hindu. 2004. "AIDS spreading fast in areas near highways". 30 November.

The Hindu. 2004. "Hospitals lacking in positive attitude to HIV patients" 21 April.

The Hindu. 2004. "ILO'S ominous estimates". 11 July.

The Hindu. 2004. "India reaffirmed political commitment to the spread of AIDS" 12 July.

The Hindu. 2004. "Innocent Victims". 30 November.

The Hindu. 2004. "Make HIV test before marriage mandatory : victims". 30 November.

The Hindu. 2004. "Partner in the anti—AIDS battle". 2 December.

The Hindu. 2004. "Project for home-based care for AIDS patients". 1 December.

The Hindu. 2004. "Women at Risk". 1 December.

The Hindu. 2004. "Women near mines suffer untold misery". 26 April.

The Hindu. 2005. "AIDS vaccine may be available in eight years". 8 February.

The Hindu. 2005. "Caring for children orphaned by HIV/AIDS". 29 March.

The Hindu. 2005. "Editorial- Death in a booming economy". 17 April.

The Hindu. 2005. "HIV Cardinal supports condom use". 10 February.

The Hindu. 2005. "India rebuts U.N. Claim on HIV prevalence – Number of infections less than 1 per cent". 26 May.

The Hindu. 2005. "India seized of AIDS problem". 21 April.

The Hindu. 2005. "Life insurance for the HIV positive". 10 March.

The Hindu. 2005. "Supporting HIV/AIDS – affected children". 31 March.

The Indian Express. 1990. "The Plight of AIDS Patients". 8 July.

The Indian Express. 1999. "Homosexuals educated on safe sex". 14 October.

The Indian Express. 2001. "HIV patients can do all the work that others are doing as long as they feel physically comfortable". 29 May.

The New Indian Express. 2004. "The Positive side of life". 1 December

The New Indian Express. 2004. "World AIDS Day 2004- "Care, support, treatment" 1 December.

The Week. 2001. "What you must know about AIDS". 19 August

Thinamalar. 2005. "AIDS infected husband, wife approached District Collector along with three female children for care and support. 29 June.

Thinamalar. 2005. "AIDS Noie pathippil Manilathil muthalidathai nokki Theni Mavattam". 15 February.

Thinamalar. 2005. "Paathikkapadum Appavi Pengal". 1 January.

Thinamalar. 2005. "Salaththai kalakkum teem sex : Padukuliel vilum manaviyar". 14 June.

Thinathanthi. 2003. "Kanavan-Manaiveyaga Enaintha AIDS Jodi" 17 January.

Venkatarangam, Lily. 2002. *The Hindu*. 24 November.

WEB SITES

Amnesty International. http ://web.amnesty.org/library/index/ENGACT770012004

and sexually transmitted Inductions, 2004 Update, India.

Avert Organization. 2004. *HIV/AIDS in Eastern Europe and Central Asia*. http ://www.avert.org/ecstatea.htm.

Avert Organization. *People living with HIV*. www.avert.org. Last updated December 10, 2004.

Avert Organization. www.avert.org. Last updated Jan.5, 2005

http ://www.avert.org/indiaaids.htm.

http ://www.eurasianet.org/htm

http ://www.unaids.org/bangkok 2004/report.html

http ://www.walnet.org/csis/groups/nswp/

Jawahar, K.R. 2004. *Central Asian Republic – A Demographic Profile*. http ://www.asthabharathi.org/oia Aproz/Central/20 asian.htm.

Jo Bindman, Jo Doezema. 1997. *Net work of sex work Project*.

Monthly updates on AIDS, NACO, 31 March 2005. http :// www.avert.org/indiaaids.htm

NACO. 2003. *Facts and Figures*. http ://www.nacoonline.org/facts.hitestimates.htm.

NACO. 2003. *State wise HIV Prevalence (1998-2003)*. http :// www.avert.org/indiaaids.htm

NACO. 2004. *Monthly update on AIDS. 31 August*. http :// www.avert.org/indiaaids.htm.

NACO. 2004. State wise HIV Prevalence (1998-2003). http :// www.nacoonline.org/facts.hitestimates.htm

Naz Naza. 2004. *Central Asia : What is being done about AIDS?*

Noble, Rob. 2004. *Caribbean Statistics Summery*. Avert Org. September 2004. www.avert.orgn/aidstarget/htm

Noble, Rob. 2004. *South and Central American Statistics Summery*. Avert Org. September 2004. www.avert.orgn/aidstarget/htm

Population Reference Bureau. 2005. *Without My Consent—Women and HIV related Stigma in India*. www.prb.org

Ramya Kannan. 2003. *Study to address gender bias against AIDS victims*. The Hindu. March 7, 2003. http ://www. Thehindu.com/ 2003/03/07/stories/20030307055290500.htm

Tamil Nadu State AIDS Control Society. 2005 – *Home page*. http :// tnsaacs.tn.nic.in

The Hindu. Debate, dithering and deadly AIDS – Opinion News Analysis. November 17. www.thehindu.in

The World Bank Group. 2005. *World Bank Assist Central Asia in Combating AIDS*. www.worldbank.org/eca/aids.

UNAIDS. 2004.*HIV/AIDS statistics on Myanmar*.

UNAIDS/WHO. 2004. *Epidemiological facts sheets on HIV/AIDS*

WHO HIV/AIDS programme : http ://www.who.int/hiv/en/

NEWS

Sun News. 2005. 1.30 pm on 17 March.